From Sin to Salvation

From Sin to Salvation

STORIES OF
WOMEN'S CONVERSIONS, 1800
TO THE PRESENT

Virginia Lieson Brereton

*Indiana
University
Press*

BLOOMINGTON & INDIANAPOLIS

The paper used in this publication meets the minimum requirements of American National Standard for Information Sciences—Permanence of Paper for Printed Library Materials, ANSI Z39.48-1984.
⊗™

Manufactured in the United States of America

Library of Congress Cataloging-in-Publication Data

Brereton, Virginia Lieson.
From sin to salvation : stories of women's conversions,
1800 to the present / Virginia Lieson Brereton.
p.   cm.
Includes bibliographical references and index.
ISBN 0-253-31213-2 (cloth). — ISBN 0-253-20636-7 (paper)
1. Conversion. 2. Autobiography—Women authors. 3. American prose literature—Women authors. 4. Women in Christianity—United States. 5. United States—Church history—19th century. 6. United States—Church history—20th century.   I. Title.
BR110.B44   1991   90-46091
248.2′4′082—dc20

1 2 3 4 5 95 94 93 92 91

To Jack

Contents

Acknowledgments

I wish to thank the School of Education at the University of Michigan and the Murray Institute at Radcliffe for giving me the time, place, and funding to pursue the subject of conversion narratives. At Michigan I benefited especially from the help and encouragement of David Angus, Ruth Bordin, John King, and Jeffrey Mirel. Jeff has continued to follow the progress of the manuscript over the years and has remained a good friend. At Radcliffe I came to know Jane Hunter and over lunch or a snack enjoyed many a discussion with her about the rites of passage of young American women in the past couple of centuries. For many years I've belonged to the New World Colloquium at Harvard Divinity School and am deeply grateful both for the intellectual companionship there and for the critiques of parts of my work by Mark Chavez, Elizabeth Clark, Phyllis Cole, Maria Erling, David Hall, William R. Hutchison, Steve Marini, Mark Massa, Mark Peterson, Richard Seager, David Watt, and many others. Carolyn DeSwarte Gifford gave a penultimate draft of the manuscript her characteristically careful and shrewd reading. (She must be absolved of the errors and omissions that remain.) I also profited from the support of another good friend, Kirby Farrell.

Without the libraries with their treasure troves of conversion narratives, this project would have been impossible; I'd like especially to thank the librarians at the Clements Library at the University of Michigan, the Schlesinger Library at Radcliffe, Harvard's Widener Library and the Andover-Harvard Library at the Divinity School, and the Winn Library at Gordon College.

Above all, I'm grateful to my husband, Jack, whose familiarity with English literary studies (and many other areas) has helped me fill some of the gaps in my own knowledge. Mostly I am thankful for the fascination we share for the English language in all its rich and varied forms.

Introduction

This book sets out to describe nineteenth- and twentieth-century Protestant women's accounts of their conversion experiences. Historians and literary scholars have long studied spiritual narratives from the seventeenth and eighteenth centuries and earlier but, for the most part, have overlooked or ignored more recent examples, though they appear in far greater numbers.[1] My purpose here is to extend our knowledge of conversion narratives by exploring the successors of the Puritan versions down to the present, tracing their slow evolution from a genre describing a nearly universal Protestant experience in the nineteenth century to their less central position in the twentieth, as they became largely confined to conservative evangelicals.

Female conversion narratives fit into the growing category of nontraditional literature (of course, from another viewpoint, they could hardly be more traditional). They are nontraditional only in the sense that they exist outside the literary canon, in fact, outside the purview of most historians and others to whom canonicity is a less compelling claim. Feminist scholars have frequently argued the need for more serious attention to what they call "women's vernacular literature," of which conversion narratives are rich examples. Feminists have also pointed out the necessity for women to explore and develop ways of talking about themselves and their lives. Women, they contend, have traditionally been discouraged from writing about themselves. Most autobiography and certainly the much-celebrated bildungsroman have remained mostly male preserves. This book is in part a response to the summons of feminist scholars: in the conversion narratives ordinary women have for centuries possessed a rare and sanctioned way to tell their stories. It seems high time to collect and study these stories.

I also argue in my final chapter that classical Protestant conversion narratives have helped shape the ways women have told "out of church," or secular, stories in the past few decades—tales of radical personal transformation to feminism, lesbianism, women's studies, and health and happiness.

Like so many other ventures in women's studies, this one is cross-disciplinary. I approach this study with several interests: in rhetoric, in women's lives, and in American religious history. For this reason my book looks in several directions and may appeal to different (though not contradictory) audiences. As a study of the pattern and language of conversion, its interest is in the nature of narrative and of religious rhetoric in general. But as an examination of the ways in which Protestant women told a particular kind of story—how they recognized their sinfulness and yielded their hearts to God—the book fits into the growing concern with women's autobiography and women's writing.

At times it may seem as if these two goals—the first to define the conversion narrative as a general literary type, the second to describe women's particular uses of that genre—may get in each other's way. In an ideal world the narrative would already have been delineated as a genre, and I could concentrate on the female examples. In effect, I am building both the foundation and the tower at the same time, with the resulting periods of awkwardness.

Another goal of this study is a better understanding of religion and culture in nineteenth- and twentieth-century America. We have begun to examine the roles that women played in those two centuries and in doing so have come to recognize that one of the primary theaters for women's activity has in fact been religion. Therefore, what women have had to say about their religious pilgrimages—how they came to the realizations and actions they did and what happened as a result—can tell us much about Protestantism in America and about women's role in Protestantism.

Here I should note that I am working with an emerging historiography: in deciding to deal with both nineteenth- and twentieth-century narratives, I am doing violence to the traditional version of religious history, which tends to regard Protestant evangelicalism of the two centuries as very different creatures. In this old historiography—to parody it somewhat—nineteenth-century evangelicalism is coterminous with mainline Protestantism, and the experience of conversion is normative for the majority of Protestants; in contrast, twentieth-century evangelicalism—including fundamentalism—is a marginal aberration, a holdout after mainline Protestantism has taken other directions. By the twentieth century, conversion has become exotic, no longer typical of Protestantism as a whole. Of course, this historiography is already dated. Because of the work of scholars such as Ernest Sandeen, George Marsden, and Joel Carpenter, increasing numbers of historians no longer regard fundamentalism as a wild aberration; they are also readier to see the continuities between the evangelicalisms of, say, 1850 and 1950. But habits of thought persist, and admittedly it still appears odd to juxtapose the narratives of Ann Judson in the early nineteenth century and Anita Bryant or Shirley Boone in the twentieth. I hope this study will not only render this juxtaposition less startling, but also make it seem desirable for a better comprehension of both centuries and all narrators.

As readers will readily see, the conversion narratives—whether of Judson or Boone—are highly formulaic, composed according to the requirements of a strictly defined convention. There is good reason, in fact, to suppose that narrators—consciously or unconsciously—perceived and shaped their experiences so that they were conformable to the formula. The form of the conversion narrative has tended to discourage originality of plot or expression, and though the nineteenth-century examples employ what I call a "language of the heart," it is a very stylized language indeed. And unlike many other forms (e.g., the diary), the nineteenth century versions do not easily document what women's studies scholars have discovered elsewhere, an "emergence of self." Even the longer twentieth century examples, which tend to reveal the narrator as an individual and a developing personality, do not emphasize the coming into being of an original voice, a unique viewpoint. (Those who range too far from the sheep, to use a scriptural analogy, may lose sight of both the flock and the

Shepherd.) Nevertheless, as I argue in chapters three and seven, within the confines of a very tightly defined—and male originated—narrative convention, women found surprising scope for the expression of their feelings and aspirations.

In view of what I have said about the formulaic quality of these narratives, readers will not be surprised when I assert that the narratives bear a complex relationship to the reality of women's lives. I have resisted thinking of the narratives as direct accounts, as straightforward, accurate historical testimony. Throughout I try to maintain a distinction between my subject—the conversion experience as it is represented in a form of popular literature—and conversion itself. That is, I do not attempt a thorough examination of the phenomenon of conversion, only its literary expression in the narratives. (Conversion narratives themselves can hardly provide a full picture of the experience since ipso facto they all end happily—they are invariably success stories.) A full exploration of the larger issue, conversion, would require additional evidence, including counter examples by failed converts and resistant Christians, statistics (e.g., on church membership, on Dwight Moody's attempts to follow up on his converts), exploration of the psychology of conversion and of changing theological views of conversion. At the same time as I underline the distinction between the life as "really lived" and the narrative, I am constrained to add that I *do* assume a connection of some sort between the two. In many lives, the narratives testify that *something important happened*, something of a distinctly religious character, something that brought lasting changes to the narrator's life. Whether it happened exactly as the narrator relates, we can never know.

Judging literary merit is not my concern here; it is an increasingly problematic ascription at any rate. But I would like to emphasize my conviction that to describe the conversion narratives studied here as highly formulaic is not in the least to denigrate them. As students of narrative have pointed out, all texts are in some sense formulaic; they all follow some convention; even realistic fiction honors the convention of realism.

I have relied on my reading of hundreds of narratives and parts of narratives, some very short, some book length, some first person, some third. I have drawn mostly upon *published* narratives rather than upon ones in private diaries and journals, because I am interested in the ways the narratives were used to communicate, to inspire, and to educate. In choosing composed and published narratives I have confined my attention to productions of *middle-class*, educated women—mostly from the Northeast. When I have analyzed black women's narratives, I have looked mainly at those of literate and relatively well-off black women.[2] I have limited myself to Protestant traditions; I have not attempted to look at women's conversion narratives in other traditions such as Roman Catholic or Jewish.[3]

I have divided the book into two parts, one on the nineteenth century and the other on the twentieth. This is an arbitrary decision on my part, and one made mostly for convenience. The arbitrariness of the decision is explained by the fact that a more exacting periodization eludes me. Certainly the traditional periodizations of American history—early Republic, Civil War, Reconstruction, Progressivism, World War I, and so on—seem inadequate, as does any attempt to coordinate closely the history of conversion narratives with that of better-known aspects of American literature. The typical periodizations of Protestant American religious history might seem more promising. One familiar way of conceptualizing religious history—following the lead of William McLoughlin—has been to divide it into an alternating series of revivals and religiously quiescent periods. One would expect to find more and richer conversion narratives during periods of religious awakening, fewer during periods of declension. One problem with this expectation is that we're beginning to question the accuracy of this scheme of religious awakenings; has it been unduly influenced by our preoccupation with Reformed Protestant groups to the exclusion of Wesleyan, Pentecostal, and other movements? Have we failed to see some of the awakenings in the latter groups? Another problem is that in tallying numbers of conversion narratives at any given point, it makes a difference where we look. At first glance it would seem that the number of readily accessible published narratives diminishes as we get to the late nineteenth and early twentieth centuries. Established publishing houses and periodicals seem to have become temporarily less interested in the narratives during that period. "Ah ha," we are tempted to exclaim, other interests must have loomed larger; women occupied themselves with different concerns—the vote, social reform, economic survival, careers. But if we survey relatively out-of-the-way periodicals and presses—for instance, *The Christian and Missionary Alliance, Triumphs of Faith, Christian Workers Magazine*—we find innumerable testimonies to faith. In the 1880s, 1890s, and for the first two or three decades of the twentieth century, in fact, we discover intense excitement about a whole array of new experiences; we encounter women who claimed to have been healed at God's touch of tuberculosis or crippled limbs, or who rhapsodized about an intense "inflowing" of the Holy Spirit that caused them to shout and sing and speak in unknown tongues. The springs of religious narrative never *do* seem to dry up, or even to diminish, even though at times they flow far from the sight of the academy or the literary journals of the land.

Relating *numbers* of conversion narratives to particular periods of time is one troubling issue; it is even more difficult to chart changes in content over the decades. There are several reasons why this is so. To begin with, narratives were often published many years after the events they describe. Thus, we are forced to ask whether a given narrative uses the same language and concepts the narrator chose at the actual time of conversion, or whether the telling has altered over the decades. In other words, has the conversion story been related repeatedly in much the same way, or, as is more probable, has it been accommodated to later language and religious ideas? Further, there were undoubtedly regional differences among narrators in their choice of conversion language. We must wonder whether new aspects of conversion language cropped up in some regions of the United States first and then spread from there to other regions, and if so how fast? Was the direction of influence always the same? We don't know. To make matters more complex, there were definite denominational distinctions among narrators, but at the same time much crossover in language. Perhaps the most important saboteur of our efforts at categorizing changes was the existence of models of the "old" rhetoric side by side with newer narrative models. Some expressions were kept alive by narrators long after they had died out of the speech of most other Americans. And various conversion narrators have retained traditional usages at different rates, depending on factors such as temperament, audience, geography, and educational background.

Thus, if by some miracle we were able to gather all the narratives published in any given year we would find many commonalities, but also a confusing range of styles and vocabularies and religious interests. It is this sort of phenomenon that makes it difficult to claim that between 1850 and 1900, say, the narratives all changed in certain identifiable ways to reflect particular shifts in religion and in the culture. In the end a 1800s–1900s split seems as reasonable—or unreasonable—as any. There *are*, to be sure, broad changes—"macro" shifts—discernible over the two centuries, and in fact a major part of my interest in attempting to cover such a wide swathe of time was the chance to discover some of those changes.

A final word about another question of geography: I have already acknowledged the regional differences among narrators in the United States. I should also introduce the issue of narrators from Great Britain. In a sense it's another arbitrary act for me to limit my purview to the United States, since American and British narrators shared so much in common. It's even possible that at times there were more similarities between speakers on the eastern seaboard of the United States and those from England on the one hand than between eastern and western U.S. narrators on the other hand. At any rate, it is important to note that many of the models popular both in the nineteenth and twentieth centuries have been British, as have the frequent visitors here at American religious conferences and conventions. There has been much borrowing back and forth between British and American narratives.

When I get to the twentieth century, much of my attention focuses on the period after 1950. This is not a matter of choice but rather is due to a couple of factors. First, early in this century the religious establishment dismissed fundamentalists as historically marginal, while conservative evangelicals themselves undervalued both their own histories and their historical documents. Therefore relatively few materials from that era have been preserved—and, when preserved, they tend to be inaccessible. Second, many of the most valuable descriptions and interpretations of conservative evangelical experience—the studies of skilled and empathetic sociologists, ethnologists, and folklorists—hail from the present or recent past. We have few comparable field studies from earlier decades.

Covering so much time—some of it with enormous informational and interpretive gaps—and also attempting to bring to bear a number of academic disciplines makes for messy history at best. But I hope that I have made a successful start at charting the territory, so that others interested in this subject may get their bearings and add the necessary correctives and do justice to the many areas I have left untouched or inadequately examined.

Part One

Nineteenth-Century Conversion Narratives

The metaphor of salvation—giving in to Christ, submitting to His will, accepting Him as Master—came naturally to women. Salvation was and is a poetic transformation of a relationship that women learn from early childhood. They trust and obey their fathers, look to their brothers for protection, and then become wives. Becoming the bride of Christ is not part of a man's training. Washed in that fount of blood, he will never be purely masculine afterward. Out in the wilderness in the nineteenth century, women surely realized that to get a man to kneel down to Christ was the first step in domesticating him and taming him.

Shirley Abbott, Womenfolks:
Growing Up Down South

ONE

The Pattern and Tradition

In 1799, just before the new century, a "young lady" from Bowdoinham, Maine, confessed,

> The 6th day of last Feb., I was taken as it were out of the belly of hell, and my feet set upon a rock, and a new song was put in my mouth, even praise to the most high. The heavens, which I before thought wore a gloomy aspect, now seemed to glitter with the glory of God. And the animal creation seemed jointly to whisper praises to their Creator. This new scene reminded me of man in his first happy state. In this frame [of mind] I had a view of the justice of God, and of Christ's sufferings, which I can describe to none but those who have drank of the same fountain. February 9th, I was enabled to follow my blessed Saviour into the water; but I have since been brought to feel that I am nothing, and to abhor myself.[1]

Nineteenth-century evangelical Protestants told and wrote conversion stories like this constantly. Not only did the narration help to confirm and strengthen the convert's own faith, it also pointed others to the same beliefs and experiences. For one of the primary purposes of the conversion story was to teach, edify, persuade, and exhort. By spreading the reports of the great event in their lives, evangelicals hoped that the unconverted would be inspired to go and do likewise.

In using conversion narratives as teaching and inspirational devices, nineteenth-century Protestants were following a well-established tradition. Decades before, Jonathan Edwards had remarked, "There is no one thing that I know of which God has made such a means of promoting his work among us, as the news of others' conversions."[2] This belief continued to hold sway; in 1809 a Connecticut clergyman admonished his listeners: "Go, study to promote the worship and honour of the true God in your own family, in your own country, among your own kindred. *Go, testify how great the things the Lord hath done for you*; that others may learn to fear, trust, and obey the God of Israel" (my emphasis).[3]

The nineteenth-century conversion narratives followed remarkably uniform patterns. They typically opened with the convert's early life, went on to describe a period of increasing sense of sinfulness, climaxed with conversion proper, and concluded with an account of the "fruits" of the experience—usually zealous conduct of evangelical activity. Often they were told in the first person, but they also appeared in biographical form, with a third person making liberal use of quotations from the convert's letters, diaries, or journals.

Though both men and women wrote and recited narratives, the form was particularly congenial to women. There are many possible explanations for this, some of which will emerge in later chapters. But at the most obvious level, nineteenth-century women simply had more narrative material to draw upon; widely considered to be more religious and moral than men, they converted more frequently and probably with more fervor. The records show that they attended church in greater numbers.[4] Men who got "new hearts" typically attributed them to the ministrations of converted wives, mothers, or sisters. In addition to having more conversion experiences to relate, women had more use for the instructional element in the narratives. They had become virtually identified with religious instruction—indeed, with teaching of many kinds. Between about 1830 and 1860 they came to dominate common school teaching; during this same time they staffed most of the Sunday school classes, and conducted much of the educational work on foreign mission fields. The conversion narrative served women as an effective teaching device at the very time when they had assumed much of the responsibility for educating the citizens of the new nation.

Although the old and the middle aged experienced conversion, the phenomenon was usually associated with youth. Few converts had gone beyond their twenties before "giving their hearts to God"; it was even fairly common for boys and girls (particularly girls) between about seven and twelve to profess conversion. At times conversion penetrated class boundaries, but it was largely a middle-class luxury—or necessity.

Though the conversion narrative dealt with the experience of an individual Christian in his or her relation to God, its narration was often a public exercise. Surprisingly, this statement holds true for women as well as men, despite cultural norms that otherwise confined female activity largely to the private sphere. Conversion and its attendant events and circumstances might take place in solitude, but frequently the first thing a convert did was to tell a friend or relative (or a crowd), or to undertake some decisive action that let others know what had transpired. Those who experienced a change of heart in public assemblies would often signify this fact in a public manner, perhaps by accepting the altar call. Those converts who hung back from telling their unconverted acquaintances, sometimes in fear that they would be ridiculed, automatically cast doubt upon the authenticity of their experience. In short, conversion carried with it the obligation to declare, to proclaim, and to invite emulation.

What distinguished conversion narratives from a myriad of other teaching vehicles was that they were supposed to help initiate others into an experience that traditionally was difficult to transmit widely because it was in some sense mystical, ineffable, paradoxical. Most evangelical Protestants, for instance, agreed that would-be converts must reject all reliance on their own abilities, all "self-dependence," as they put it; they had to renounce any belief in their own merit, yielding their wills utterly to God's. For it was he who brought about their conversion, not they themselves. But at the same time, these Protestants believed that prospective converts must labor constantly to prepare their hearts to receive the "operations of the spirit." In short, conversion required of the convert both enormous effort and also the cessation of all struggle.

Yet, despite the difficulties inherent in communicating paradoxical religious realities such as this, the experience of conversion had to be accessible. Protestants interested in evangelism on a massive scale could ill tolerate obscure answers to the frequent question, "What must I do to be saved?" They demanded—or at least professed to demand—plain unadorned language. The conversion narrative needed to be capable of the widest possible dissemination if conversion was not to be an exclusive possession of the fortunate few. As befitted a democracy, the ranks of "saints" should potentially include everyone. Even the dwindling number of Calvinists who continued to profess adherence to the doctrine of election often proceeded as if they assumed the possibility of universal salvation.

Furthermore, evangelicals, well aware that they were helping to build a new republic, regarded conversion as a moral and civic as well as a spiritual necessity. True morality, they believed, was impossible without a "new heart." And democracy, to fulfill its millennial promise of prosperity and justice for all, demanded no less than that all its citizens be "new creatures in Christ." The success of political and moral reforms depended upon the creation of an army of the converted, female no less than male.

If conversion actually stopped short of becoming a universal American experience, it nevertheless made great inroads among the populace, especially the female sector, to judge from accounts of revivals and from the profusion of testimonies to the experience. Conversion was the norm among nineteenth-century Congregationalists, Presbyterians, all Reformed groups, Baptists, and Methodists; it also became common in the evangelical wings of the Episcopalian and Lutheran churches. To understand how an essentially ineffable experience became available—at some level at least—to so many, we will need to examine the language and experience of conversion. As one reads many of these narratives, it becomes clear that all converts, men and women, used much the same rhetoric to describe what had happened to them; they employed common images and identical repeated phrases, quoted many of the same scriptural verses, and built their narrations upon similar structural patterns.

But the language and pattern seem to have reverberated differently for men and women, as we shall see. By the time girls or women approached the time for conversion they had already undergone social, cultural, and psychological experiences that caused them to hear and interpret the recurrent phrases in their own ways. Before we can explore these ways, however, we need a more intimate acquaintance with the standard conversion narratives of the nineteenth century.

The "classic" narrative of the nineteenth century followed a predictable outline. Usually narratives treated five stages of the conversion experience: (1) life before the conversion process began, when narrators more or less ignored the question of salvation; (2) a period when narrators became acutely aware of their sinfulness and of the possibility they would be damned forever; (3) the surrender to God's will in conversion proper, during which converts felt the oppressive sense of sinfulness lifted and gained confidence or at least hope that they were saved; (4) a description of the narrator's changed behavior and attitudes, resulting from conversion; and (5) an account of periods of discouragement and low spiritual energy followed by renewals of dedication. (This account of five stages is my own; narrators themselves did not normally speak of stages.)

Most conversion narratives of the early nineteenth century began with the narrator's early life. Rarely did converts emerge from the ranks of the unchurched; almost without exception they recalled a devout relative, most often a mother; frequently they had attended church regularly, had been taught to pray, and had studied their Bibles. But despite an "outward" piety, most narrators recalled their early lives as "spiritually dead," and condemned "sins" they had largely failed to recognize or regret at the time. In this respect male and female narratives usually diverged. Women rued transgressions such as novel reading, dancing, and theater going, or they criticized personality traits such as a quick temper, willfulness, flightiness, or impetuousness. Men usually had more obvious misdeeds to regret. As boys they had consorted with bad companions, blasphemed, cursed, and reveled in drunkenness; they were more likely than their female counterparts to have gloried in their contempt for religion. They had been wilder, less subject to parental restraint. (In this usually stylized accounting of sins, neither men nor women mentioned sexual encounters or fantasies.)

Seldom did such a nominally "Christian" childhood pass without some misgivings, however. Often narrators remembered a period in which they had become uneasy about the state of their souls. But typically such compunctions passed after a brief time, to yield to renewed frivolity and forgetfulness.

At length, however, a time arrived when the feeling of sinfulness and the fear about one's future state could not be shrugged off or ignored in pleasant diversions. Death, illness, or a minister's or friend's remarks might touch off this new period of uneasiness; the difference this time was that instead of eventually diminishing, the anxiety increased. In a typical response to this sense of sinfulness, narrators would attempt to reform their behavior. They might forgo dancing or swearing or turn their backs upon former friends. They would likely become punctilious in performing public and private devotions and would study the Bible assiduously. Initially, as a consequence of improving their behavior, narrators reported satisfaction and peace. But relief from the sense of sin proved to be shortlived, for true reform proved impossible. They soon realized how difficult it was to keep resolutions, and even when they managed to do so, they still had to battle unworthy thoughts. At the very least, they would realize that they were filled with pride over their new comportment, not at all a mark of true reformation.

As the futility of any attempt at real reform sunk in, the respite from anxiety ended, and narrators would wrestle in earnest with their sense of sinfulness. Thus would begin the second stage, the period of "conviction of sin." Prospective converts wrote that they could recall all their sins in agonizing detail. But more than just separate misdeeds rankled; what truly overwhelmed them, they wrote, was the generalized sense of deep, ineradicable sinfulness, of sin that was imbedded in their very natures because they were sons and daughters of Adam. They would realize that their very wills were corrupt, that they carried internally a *disposition* to sin about which they could do nothing. One "convicted" young woman described her state of mind:

> I then thought I was cursed in very deed, which flung me immediately almost into despair; and in the greatest agony I fell to the earth. Viewing myself undone forever, and eternally lost, I was in the most deplorable situation conceivable, and despaired of ever going to that place [heaven]. I thought that the earth was just about to swallow me up alive, into everlasting destruction of both soul and body, and really expected to fall into the bottomless pit, where there was no recovery . . . my distress was of such a nature that medical assistance was entirely baffled: I fainted and fell to the ground.[5]

Would-be converts were usually well aware that in order to be saved they had only to submit their wills entirely to God's. "Jesus knocks," it was often said, in an allusion to Revelation 3:20; "you have only to let him come in." Yet for some reason they found they could not admit him. Something in them—pride, it was often said—kept resisting the offer of free grace. Some could not shake the idea that they must try harder to make themselves acceptable to God and therefore more deserving of salvation. Others underwent recurrent periods of rebellion; why, they demanded, should *they* have to share Adam's sin? Surely God was tyrannical and unfair.

The period of conviction could be traumatic; according to reports, a few of the "convicted" committed suicide or succumbed to madness. Even when they were not driven to one of these extremes, some certainly wondered whether death or insanity might not be preferable to their present condition. (Since this period of spiritual wrestling happened at an early age, it invites comparison with what may be a present-day version, the traumas of modern adolescence.)

For nineteenth-century youths in the accounts we have (and of course they are by their very nature accounts of *success*), the period of struggle usually issued in conversion. For some it was difficult to explain why conversion happened at one time and not another. Sometimes no particular event or circumstance seemed to account for the timing of the event. Often, to be sure, there was a precipitating factor. The prospective convert might happen upon a particular scriptural passage, usually one promising God's mercy for the sinner, for example, "Come unto me, all ye that labor and are heavy laden, and I will give you rest" (Matt. 11:28), or "him that cometh to me I will in no wise cast out" (John 6:37). Rarely was such a verse unfamiliar to the convert, but this time the well-known words would suddenly strike him or her in a new, surprising, and forceful way. For others it was a sermon containing reassurance and solace that initiated conversion proper. For yet others, a chance remark made by a friend or stranger made the difference.[6]

Conversion could take a number of forms. Sometimes ecstasy accompanied it, sometimes a wonderful vision of Christ or his angels, sometimes simply profound peace and confidence. In some cases narrators could pinpoint their conversion to a certain day or hour; the popular notion was that it took place in an identifiable instant. In other cases, however, conversion happened more slowly, over a period of days or weeks or months, during which the anxiety associated with conviction gradually abated. For some converts it was not possible positively to assign the time or occasion of conversion until after it had passed and its lasting results had become apparent; only in retrospect, then, would such converts recognize the authenticity of their conversion.

Narrators claimed that conversion—if it was genuine—brought permanent changes in character and behavior. Most converts became patient, quiet, even-tempered, gentle, cheerful, self-denying, and uncomplaining. At the same time, they revealed more self-confidence, courage, and inner strength. For, however completely converts had recognized their own nothingness in relation to God's power, they also had gained a new authority of their own by virtue of their conversion. Endowed with God's grace and transformed into his "instrumentalities," they now were delegated to go out and tell others what the Lord had done for them. One female convert declared,

> I had the strength of God to talk to them; my tongue seemed to be let loose and my heart was enlarged; it seemed that my mouth was filled with arguments; the scriptures flowed into my mind, text after text, as though the whole Bible was committed to my memory. It being in the city, two hundred had collected before I had done speaking.[7]

Thus converts felt called to be zealous, to labor energetically, to declare, to teach, to win souls. Of course, the notion of outwardly directed activity in the world would seem common enough in connection with men; the surprising fact is that *women* found it quite natural to enter into strenuous public activity as well. Though in the early nineteenth century they were usually expected to stay close to home, cultivate domestic virtues, and remain silent in public assemblies, they nevertheless shared the strong sense of being summoned as the Lord's emissaries as a consequence of their conversions. The meekest and shyest among them might well take it upon herself to visit strangers in her community—often the poor or immigrant—to proselytize. Groups of converted women organized local missionary societies to collect money and dispense missions information; after the Civil War women became bolder: they formed missionary societies of national scope in almost every denomination. And women who would not otherwise have thought about writing down their experiences, let alone publishing accounts of them, nevertheless felt the obligation of putting their conversion stories into print and advertising their new hearts in public forums.

Rarely did conversion signal the end of the convert's struggles. Most narrators would go on to tell about a period when delight and assurance yielded to doubt, as converts discovered that some of the old "corruption" persisted in their hearts. In fact, the sense of spiritual coldness and the evidence of "backsliding" might grow so strong as to make converts wonder whether they had actually been converted in the first place. After varying amounts of time, however, the spiritual deadness usually gave way to a period of renewed consecration, accompanied by a return of peace and joy. (Wesleyan groups—and later Calvinists too—began to institutionalize an occasion of rededication as "entering into" "holiness" or "sanctification.") Often this alternating pattern of spiritual light and darkness persisted, usually with less drastic swings, throughout the convert's life. Only in death did these Christians expect to belong wholly to their Lord, utterly dead to sin and temptation.

Death usually played a prominent role in the conversion story, for the manner of one's passing was considered the sign and seal of a genuine conversion and a holy life. Of course, when the narrative was in the first person, the convert's actual death could not be recorded by the narrator; however, an account of the death was often appended to such first-person narratives by a witness. In the narratives, the truly converted faced their "approaching dissolution" as they had lived. Ideally they remained "sensible" to the end; they endured all manner of physical suffering cheerfully; they remained serene, their glance fixed on the "heavenly crown" awaiting them; and they declared themselves wholly resigned to God's will, neither praying to recover if that was not his plan, nor beseeching him to shorten their travails. The demise of women seemed to occasion particularly "affecting" deathbed scenes. Dying women, whether young or old, became more beautiful the closer they approached the end. In older women the lines of age softened; the younger women—often consumptive—displayed fever-bright cheeks and pale foreheads.

This, then, was the basic "formula" for the conversion narrative, and it remained constant throughout the nineteenth century. There was room for variation, of course. The narratives differed in length, from the brevity of the account quoted at the start of this essay, to book length. They appeared in any number of forms: diaries, journals, collections of letters, autobiographies and biographies, memorials, "literary remains," memoirs, or some combination of these.

The order of events outlined above was most typical, but could be altered. Sometimes, as in the opening narrative, the time of the greatest sense of sinfulness occurred not before the conversion but after. Occasionally, the period of conviction would not take place at all, though the narrator, conscious of readers' expectations, would note its absence and offer evidence for the genuineness of the conversion despite the omission. Letters and diaries sometimes contained only part of a narrative, although the practiced eye will be able to tell *which* part is present. It was not unusual for the time period covered by the narrative to be telescoped: a narrator might undergo conviction of sin, conversion, and a call to Christian activity all in one day. This rapid progression was especially frequent in conversions that took place during revivals, when social pressures and emotional prods worked most relentlessly.

Other variations in narratives stemmed from differences in denominational emphases. For Baptist converts like the young woman quoted at the beginning of the chapter, the rite of baptism played a prominent part in the conversion account. Baptist and Methodist narrators, especially on the frontier, might describe physical manifestations connected with their spiritual awakening, such as "barking" or "jerking." Furthermore, frontier narratives written by members of these denominations might be more colloquial, idiomatic, humorous, and less "literary."[8] Though theological concerns had waned among most nineteenth-century Protestants, those converts from Calvinist backgrounds might be more inclined than others to speak about their acquiescence to certain theological doctrines as part of the conversion process, for instance, recognizing the absolute sovereignty of God (they typically professed the willingness to be damned if that was the will of God). But, allowing for these variations, the essential outline of the nineteenth-century conversion narrative is unmistakable, and those who departed very far from the form often felt the need to justify their divergence.

THE TRADITION

Early nineteenth-century Protestants who undertook to tell or write the stories of their conversions could and did look to any number of guides and models from the preceding centuries. Almost everyone took note of the conversion of St. Paul, though his experience, so sudden and without warning, gave American preparationists (those who believed the heart must be "prepared" for conversion) some trouble. With Paul's account in mind, they always had to admit that, after all, conversion could happen totally unpredictably and without the slightest effort on the convert's part. A number of short conversion passages in the Bible could also be consulted to define and describe the process of conversion.[9]

But nineteenth-century American evangelicals owed their greatest debts to seventeenth- and eighteenth-century English Puritans. Among these the best known was John Bunyan, whose *Pilgrim's Progress* and *Grace Abounding to the Chief of Sinners* were widely available in any number of new editions, both English and American, during the nineteenth century. Probably just as influential as Bunyan were a series of guides for would-be converts written by English clergymen: Richard Baxter, *Call to the Unconverted* (1657); Matthew Mead, *The Almost Christian Discovered* (1662); Joseph Alleine, *Alarm for Unconverted Sinners* (1672); William Law, *Serious Call to a Devout and Holy Life* (1728), which Samuel Johnson testified had brought about his own conversion; and especially Philip Doddridge, *On the Rise and Progress of Religion in the Soul* (1745).[10] All of these books had active publishing histories during the early nineteenth century, both in the United States and Great Britain. Alleine's *Alarm*, Baxter's *Call*, and Doddridge's *Rise* were all republished by the American Tract Society, as well as by other United States publishers. Doddridge was a particular favorite in a very popular crowd; until late in the nineteenth century, seldom did two years pass in a row without a new *Rise and Progress* issuing off some press in Boston, Philadelphia, New York, or elsewhere.

Nineteenth-century narratives are full of references to Doddridge; his book helped prospective converts to acknowledge their sinfulness and to recognize the "evidences" of conversion, and to put words to these experiences. The very titles of his chapters outlined the stages of the spiritual pilgrimage nineteenth-century Protestants expected to travel. His guide began by attempting to "awaken" sinners out of their spiritual lethargy; approximately one third of the book was devoted to impressing upon readers their utter sinfulness and depravity—and the consequent certainty of their "eternal ruin" unless they availed themselves of God's grace. Next Doddridge explained what conversion entailed—abandonment of "self-dependence" for dependence upon God; then he went on to characterize what he referred to as the "Christian temper"—the attitude and behavior of the truly converted Christian. He sought to help the convert keep up "continual communion with God," and described periods of backsliding and how to cope with them; finally he closed with a "serious view of death." Each chapter contained appropriate prayers and meditations written from the sinner's point of view and in words a repentant sinner might use; these helped give form and phrasing to the prayers and meditations of nineteenth-century Protestants; and it was Doddridge's example of a "covenant with God," entered into by a new convert, that served as the basis for hundreds of nineteenth-century covenants.

It was not unusual for a nineteenth-century wife to give an unconverted husband a copy of Doddridge. And if a sister could ascertain that a sailor brother had died in the South Seas with a copy of Doddridge in his possession, it was a hopeful sign that he had "witnessed a good confession" at the end and might now be enjoying heavenly "bliss." But the other manuals were also close runners up. Converted Christians might take a few copies of Alleine's *Alarm* with them on a walk, just in case they encountered some poor lost souls in need of it. (In 1844, for instance, one could purchase eight *Alarms* from the American Tract Society for only a dollar, for precisely this evangelistic purpose.)[11]

Nineteenth-century writers of conversion narratives also looked for guidance to the American Puritans.[12] Foremost among a number of seventeenth- and eighteenth-century narratives that circulated in the nineteenth century was Jonathan Edwards's account of his own spiritual experiences, *Personal Narrative*, which seems to have been widely distributed throughout the 1800s; bearing the title, "The Conversion of President Edwards," it appeared under the imprint of the American Tract Society and of the Congregational Board of Publication, among others. Moreover, excerpts from Edwards's conversion showed up in newspapers of the period.[13] His influence on the nineteenth-century narrative was also exercised through his *Faithful Narrative of the Sur-*

prising Work of God (Boston, 1738), which was republished many times in the early 1800s. This work contained Edwards's reports of the conversions of Abigail Hutchinson and Phebe Bartlett and also offered what amounted to a morphology of the conversion experience, which could be treated by hopeful converts of the nineteenth century as guides and as sources for language with which to describe their own conversions.

Though other Puritan conversion accounts, buried away in diaries and journals, were not readily available to early nineteenth-century readers, some of these could be known second hand through Cotton Mather's biographies in his *Magnalia Christi Americana* (1702). (Mather had access to some of the journals and quoted from them.) Elizabeth White's conversion narrative, *Experiences of God's Gracious Dealings*, written around 1660, was first published in 1741 during the Great Awakening for the explicit purpose of inspiring others; presumably copies of it still circulated in the early 1800s. The autobiography of Thomas Shepard (1605–1649) appears to have been published for the first time in 1826, in Boston, to raise funds for Shepard's old church.

Besides drawing upon two clear and related Puritan traditions of narrative, American and British, nineteenth-century evangelicals also consulted a variety of other examples from earlier centuries. Any account of conversion held intense interest for nineteenth-century Protestants, if it seemed analogous to their own situations. William Cowper (1731–1800), for example, appealed to nineteenth-century Protestants not only as a devotional poet and hymnist but also as a conversion writer; his narrative, though not widely available today, was apparently well known to the nineteenth century. Methodists and others read John Wesley's account of his "Aldersgate experience." Great favorites among women particularly were the spiritual narratives of Hester Ann Rogers and Jeanne Marie ("Madame") Guyon (1648–1717). Rogers, who underwent a classical Protestant conversion, was an associate of John Wesley. Guyon was a French Catholic pietist, a friend of Fénélon. The choice of Guyon as a source of inspiration for American evangelicals is not as unlikely as it sounds at first; she came from the wing of the Catholic church that had "Protestant" leanings and was repeatedly persecuted by church authorities; furthermore, by their selection of language, evangelical translators managed to make her sound even more Protestant.[14]

In addition to the confessions of New England Puritans, another genre developed by them probably influenced nineteenth-century narratives. Captivity narratives, in which Puritan men and women recounted the stories of their capture and detention by Indians, together with their "deliverance" from captivity, contained many of the same elements—and much of the same language—as conversion narratives. In captivity Puritans experienced a little foretaste of the hell they knew they so richly deserved; their faith received testing and their wills humbling. Like prospective converts they searched their Bibles or their memories of Scripture for texts that shed light on the meaning of their tribulations; they interpreted everything that happened to them—all "mercies" and "afflictions"—as coming through God's agency. Their redemption from captivity (ransom was usually paid) became for them an analogue of the soul's salvation from sin and damnation. And captivity narrators had much the same reason for writing down their experiences and publishing them, that as one female narrator put it, "thereby the merciful kindness and goodness of God may be manifested, and the reader . . . provoked with more fear and care to serve Him in righteousness and humility."[15] Captivity narratives remained popular throughout the eighteenth century in America; somewhat altered, the form continued to flourish during the nineteenth century, with both earlier and later examples available to nineteenth-century converts.[16]

It hardly needs saying that conversion narratives changed between the seventeenth and nineteenth centuries, as did the sensibility that gave rise to them; no reader would be likely to confuse a seventeenth- and a nineteenth-century narrative. Seventeenth-century usage slowly dropped out, especially in passages of ordinary description. Muted was the reference to the "howling wilderness" that had so impressed itself on the seventeenth-century consciousness.[17] The devil and external "temptations" introduced by him, though still present, were blamed less for sinners' resistance to salvation than their own stubborn wills. Moreover, nineteenth-century Protestants abandoned some of the intense Puritan interest in theology, and for this reason the later narratives were less likely to contain doctrinal formulations and allusions to theological tenets.

Still, a striking number of identical phrases and images persisted in conversion narratives throughout the seventeenth, eighteenth, and nineteenth centuries, and conversion events followed essentially the same pattern. Nineteenth-century familiarity with—and reverence for—earlier narratives and manuals helps explain this otherwise surprising degree of continuity. An additional source of linguistic connection was the use of the same English translation of the Bible in all three centuries—the King James Version, whose seventeenth-century prose strongly affected Protestant utterances in those centuries.[18] At any time in American history, then—1650, 1750, 1850 (or 1950, for that matter)—it is possible to locate a common form of narrative, and the narrative of each period bears more than a passing or accidental resemblance to its counterparts in other centuries.

TWO

The Language of the Convert

In the summer of 1827, when Anzonetta Peters was fourteen, an eighteen-year-old acquaintance "was arrested in the morning of her days, and consigned to the mansions of the dead." Anzonetta was affected by this death and also by the demise not long after of a servant named Jane ("Jane's spirit left its tenement of clay"). According to Anzonetta's mother, it was about this time that her daughter showed the first signs of being "serious": "she was seen with her Bible often in her hand," and "she retired to her room to commune there in secret."[1]

Anzonetta's earlier life, as she herself recalled it, had been "careless":

> I have been distressed at times on account of sin for several years, but I always strove to get rid of these painful feelings. Whenever my mind has been thus awakened, I have been led to think seriously of God and eternity for a little while, to read my Bible and try to pray; but soon my impressions would wear off, and I again relapse into a state of indifference and carelessness.

But not during the time following the two deaths. She tried to read a novel and "there darted into my mind these solemn words, *The day of the Lord is at hand. . . .* it was the first and last novel that I ever attempted to read." The dread phrase about "the day of the Lord" haunted her, as she recalled at the time:

> Then I asked myself, "What is my state? Were I summoned to the bar of a pure and holy God, how could I stand up and render my account!" I looked back upon my past life, and could not find a single act which I thought would please God.— I had done nothing but sin. I was overwhelmed with fear, and filled with alarm, lest he should cut me down in the midst of my disobedience and guilt. . . . I am afraid to go to sleep, lest I shall awake in eternity. This passage of Scripture, also, I hear sounding in my ear a thousand times a day: "*It is appointed unto men once to die, but after this the judgment.*"

She described a minister's sermon that she heard during this period, recalling "his searching, solemn appeals, and earnest entreaties to the impenitent, to turn from chasing the phantoms of pleasure, and to make God their everlasting portion." Her agony of mind was severe:

> I still had so much pride in my unsubdued heart. . . . Fears were at this time aroused within me that were never removed, till the precious blood of sprinkling [a reference to Jesus' blood] was applied to my soul, by believing on the Lord Jesus Christ. . . . I believe few brought up as I was, under the very shadow of the cross, were ever so long in going to Christ, or passed through such fiery conflicts.[2]

She described her troubles at the time, apparently in conversation with her mother:

> I wish to give my heart to God: I know I ought to, but I find so much opposition within, that I cannot submit. I am afraid some dreadful affliction will have to be laid upon me, before the obduracy of my heart can be subdued, and I made willing to surrender all into the hands of God. It seems as though just then some malign spirit had stepped between me and my Maker to cloud my mind, and prevent my prayers from going up to God. Sometimes I am filled with fear and dread, in attempting to draw near the Most High. He appeared to me too holy a Being for so polluted a creature as I am to speak to. And when I try to think of the Saviour's blood, as that which expiates sin, and opens a new and living way to the Eternal's throne, I am tempted to think that that blood was shed for every one else except me. My great, my constant fear, is, that God will call me from this world, while I am still in this rebellious, impenitent, unpardoned state.[3]

Her mother gave her *Advice to a Young Christian*, and upon occasion she received comfort from her minister's preaching. But the struggle was protracted. Finally one day she took communion, though she still doubted her readiness to do so. Afterward, she recalled,

> I had retired for prayer; but my heart was so hard that I could not say a word. I tried to lift my thoughts to God; and presently a ray of light broke in upon my dark mind, for these words of the Saviour were brought to my recollection with wonderful vividness:—*If any man love me, he will keep my commandments, and my Father will love him, and we will come unto him and make our abode with him.* These words seemed to banish all my fears. I felt that I did love the Saviour, and was determined to try to keep his commandments, and was therefore enabled to lay hold of the promise. It was the first promise I ever had so directly brought to my mind; and I then felt the sweet assurance of my acceptance with God. I had many seasons of delightful communion with the Saviour after this.

Her mother described this evening in ecstatic terms:

> When she left her room her countenance was like that of Moses, when he came down from the mount, radiant with heavenly light and peace and love. *The peace of God, which passeth all understanding,* had come down upon her soul like the

gentle summer shower upon the mown grass. Now a new song was put into her mouth—even praise unto our God.[4]

The struggle was not over, however; not long after the memorable evening, "I again walked with a cloud upon my soul." She was still capable of bursting out, "*I am vile—I am vile.*" But her mother saw her spiritual victory as complete:

> she was enabled to take hold of the promises of God in Christ, with a hope which was an anchor in her soul, both sure and steadfast. The cross of Christ, now became all her theme. The blood of Jesus Christ, which cleanseth from all sin, was the ground of her pleading before her Father's throne. And now she took increasing delight in reading the Scriptures, and pouring out her soul in private prayer. Fear first drove her to the mercy-seat, but love . . . bound her with a golden chain to that hallowed spot.[5]

Today's readers may be inclined to dismiss these passages as impossibly burdened with stock religious language. Stock it indeed is, and yet precisely in that feature lay much of its interest and its appeal for the nineteenth century. Indeed, even for the modern reader or hearer there is sometimes a magnetic, memorable quality about some of the narratives that comes of reading a number of them and that has little or nothing to do with commonly accepted notions of literary merit—or with assent to their religious message, for that matter.

The stock quality is readily understandable. Most prospective converts were drenched in the language of conversion from birth. They heard narratives recited in worship services, prayer meetings, revivals, and in their own family circles. They read the narratives in books, newspapers, magazines, and in personal letters from friends and relatives. They heard the steps of conversion outlined in sermons and read descriptions of the process in manuals from the nineteenth century and earlier. They sang hymns that alluded again and again to the experience, and devoured pages of devotional verse like that of Lydia Sigourney, one of the nineteenth century's favorite religious poets.

Several ingredients explain the "stock" quality of nineteenth-century conversion narratives. First, of course, is the similarity of "plot"; no matter what the particular details, the narrative is essentially a success story, since it moves inevitably from failure to fulfillment, from sin to salvation. Second, the language of the narratives was strongly influenced by the King James Bible, particularly in passages meant to inspire. Narrators constantly quoted from Scripture, with and without quotation marks; frequently the quotations were so imbedded in a narrator's own prose that it is difficult to tell exactly where one begins and the other leaves off. In the passages above, for instance, Anzonetta and her mother explicitly quoted the Bible (the underlined portions), but without any punctuation or other indication the mother also used phrases from Psalm 40:3 ("a new song was put into her mouth, . . . "; cf. chapter 1, note 1); I John 1:7 ("the blood of Jesus Christ which cleanseth from all sin");

and several sources—Matt. 19:8, and Mark 3:5 and 10:5—for "hardness of heart." The idea of God as one's "portion" comes from the Psalms, among other places (see, e.g., Psalms 16:5; 73:26; 119:57).

Narrators such as Peters and her mother often alluded to biblical events, places, and characters, comparing their own circumstances to those of scriptural persons. Even when they were not quoting or alluding, they tended to echo biblical usage anyway. For instance, they used words and phrases that had by the nineteenth century become archaic and therefore were identified by the ear as "biblical" (e.g., the use of words such as "tarry," "vile," or "season" [in a sense other than one of the four divisions of the year—a "season of refreshment"]). Furthermore, narrators commonly chose biblical versions of the pronoun ("thou," "thy"), King James forms of verbs ("shalt," "builded," "availeth"), inversions in the positions of verbs and adverbs ("it withstands not the arrests of death"), and biblical prepositions such as "unto," "believed on," and "accepted of."

Third, even when narrators were neither quoting Scripture nor sounding "biblical," they still often chose from a common pool of nonbiblical words and phrases to describe their experiences and perceptions. For instance, persons "under conviction" (or "convictions") were repeatedly and as a matter of course described as "engaged," "anxiously inquiring," "under serious impressions," "awakened," "alarmed," "wrought upon by the Spirit of God," and "under great concern."

A fourth source of the stock quality of the nineteenth-century narratives was the propensity of many narrators to use eighteenth-century poetic diction. As suggested earlier, nineteenth-century Protestants admired the eighteenth-century poet, William Cowper; his name came up much more often than that of the more contemporary William Wordsworth, who was advocating the abandonment of eighteenth-century poetic practices. In the manner of the eighteenth century, many nineteenth-century narrators used "circumlocutions." Converts talked, for instance, of "sublunary bliss," or the "splendid orb which rules by day"; for them the human body became a "tenement" or "tabernacle" or "house" of "clay." The deceased were "consigned to the mansions of the dead." Sometimes narrators favored phrases straight out of eighteenth-century pastoral poetry: "plenty smiled around his habitation," recalled one convert of his father. The world was likely to be a "vale of tears," and God's wrath would come over the sinful in "billows."[6]

In short, because narrators drew upon a common stock of words and phrases, some biblical and some not, and dealt with basically the same themes and sequence of events, their narratives usually sounded formulaic. (The briefer and more condensed they were the more this was likely to be true.) What Daniel Shea says of spiritual autobiographies in the Puritan period—often they were "not so much composed as recited"—applies to the nineteenth century as well.[7] In fact, many nineteenth-century conversion narratives—or parts of narratives—had doubtless been delivered orally in public, sometimes more than once, before they were finally committed to writing.

Partly because they were formulaic, narratives generally did not betray a strong sense of particular person, of an individual voice, as, for instance, Augustine's *Confessions* decidedly did. Most nineteenth-century writers showed little disposition to play with language or to use it in original and startling ways. One advantage of the absence of individual voice or of interest in personal circumstances was that converts could speak or write publicly of their deepest, most shattering moments without really giving up their privacy. This was particularly useful for women, who sometimes accused themselves of temerity for any public utterance at all. For such narrators the degree of anonymity afforded by formula was a decided virtue.

The formulaic aspect offered advantages when the narrative was used as a popular teaching and inspirational device. Though the form foreclosed much originality, it did aid in the rapid composition and extensive dissemination of narratives. "Inquirers" and converts could easily grasp the essentials of the narrative and proceed to tell *their* stories in terms their hearers could understand and recognize immediately. Narrators in fact experienced and recalled conversion in ways that were conformable to the formula.[8] Furthermore, the repeated phrases and constant echoing of biblical constructions must have had a hypnotic effect on hearer or reader, like an incantation, thus increasing the utility of the narrative. As students of epic, children's literature, and popular song well know, repeated phrases and refrains often increase a song's or story's effectiveness and the ease with which it is learned and transmitted.[9]

The fact that the prose of nineteenth-century conversion narratives was often rhythmic further increased the ease of its dissemination and the probability of its retention by hearers or readers. (See for example, the narrative that begins chapter 1; reading it aloud increases the impression of rhythm; my guess is that "as it were" was added as much for the sound as for the meaning.) The influence of biblical rhythms encouraged this tendency; so did the repetition of formulaic phrases that had often been repeated partly because they *were* rhythmic.

THE LANGUAGE OF SIN

Narrators devoted some of their greatest narrative energy to describing the period of conviction of sin. As if refusing to grant their earliest years much importance, they dealt briefly with that period, moving quickly to the onset of the time of anxiety and despair. They dismissed their childhoods with such repeated adjectives as "thoughtless" and "careless." It was common for them to speak in a kind of shorthand of consorting with "thoughtless companions," or to recall having once been part of the "thoughtless crowd." Hymns echoed this usage, with their addresses to the "careless sinner" and exhortations such as "sinner, why so thoughtless grown." Narrators might specify some of their early "sins," but seldom in detail and rarely with the retrospective gusto of Bunyan in *Grace Abounding*. The "thoughtless companions" almost always remained faceless and nameless. Keeping to generalities, narrators might mention their early attachment to the "pleasures" or "vanities" "of this world."

In contrast, the intensity with which narrators described their experience of their sinfulness reflected its impact upon them (in addition to their desire to impress its importance on others).[10] A large vocabulary had evolved to describe the state of conviction. Some narrators, following the Bible, called it the "gall of bitterness"; for others, recalling Bunyan, it became the "slough of despond." Persons "under conviction" were described as "mourning" their sinful state.[11]

Several common phrases described what went on during the period of conviction. At the outset, sinners' hearts were "pricked" or "pierced"; they felt as if an arrow had been shot into their hearts; their consciences were "wounded." Sinners under conviction became aware of the "strivings of the Holy Spirit" with them; and they feared that should they resist the Spirit too long he would cease forever to "strive" with them.[12] Persuaded that nothing could save them from the "just wrath" of an angry God, they would lament that they were "undone utterly"; sometimes they would dream of being consigned to hell at the Last Judgment, as Jesus uttered the dread words from Matthew 25:41: "Depart from me, ye cursed, into everlasting fire." They often characterized themselves during this time as "humbled in the dust." Borrowing the cry of the publican in Luke 18:13 they pleaded, "God be merciful to me a sinner."

But the greatest verbal vehemence of all was reserved for characterizations of sinners as they began to see themselves with the ever greater clarity that conviction gave. "Vile" and "wretch" were favored terms, often used together: "myself so vile a wretch"; "such a vile wretch as I am." Again and again the convicted spoke of themselves as "rebels" against God; they described their "enmity" toward him.[13] They lamented their inner "pollution" and "corruption." Sometimes it seemed they vied with each other in comparing themselves to animals, reptiles, and worms. One sinner likened herself to lepers and pharisees, "fit only," she added, "to claim kinship to dragons and owls."[14]

In energetic attempts to plumb the depths of their guilt and alienation, sinners commonly resorted to superlatives. They were the "chief of sinners"; they feared they had committed the "unpardonable sin." This practice, like so many others, followed well-worn paths. Bunyan, of course, had used the biblical phrase "chief of sinners" in the title for his narrative *Grace Abounding* and had written, "I thought none but the Devil could equalize me for inward wickedness and pollution of minde." And Edwards had insisted, "It has often appeared to me, that if God should mark iniquity against me, I should appear the very worst of all mankind; of all that have been since the beginning of the world, to this time: and that I should have by far the lowest place in hell."[15]

One wonders whether nineteenth-century superlatives, in addition to their conformity with narrative tradition, were valued because, ironically, they elevated sinners to the very center of the cosmic drama. The greatest sinner in the world obviously elicited the greatest mercy to be had. Drama and a starring role of sorts may have been particularly attractive to women, who usually led protected and sometimes dull and restricted existences within the domestic confines. Probably the superlatives also enhanced the pedagogical purpose: in effect the narrators said to readers or hearers: "No matter how bad you think *you* are, believe me, I was much worse. In fact, I was the very *worst*. But God saved me nevertheless, and doubtless he will do the same for you."

Thoughts of hell haunted sinners under conviction; indeed, such ideas were deemed necessary in awakening the thoughtless to a sense of their peril. Most statements about hell were stylized: sinners were "hastening" to their "eternal ruin"; they were "sinking into" "unending woe"; they stood on the brink of "the horrible pit," or the "pit of destruction"; they faced "everlasting burnings"; they could envision the "lake of fire and brimstone," and imagine themselves "writhing in the torments of the damned"; they trod the "broad way" to destruction (Matt. 7:13); they must "fly from the wrath to come."[16]

Though the nineteenth-century references to hell and God's wrath lay well within the tradition, some phrases seem more characteristically tied to that later century: "heedless ruin," "eternal woe," and "eternal sorrow." For some narrators of the later period, one can speculate, hell had lost a little of its physicality; it had grown softer and sadder, as much a state of mind as a place of physical torture. The condemned person was now a "wanderer far from God." To a sentimental age, the worst fate was not physical pain or dread sights, but mental anguish stemming from remorse, alienation from God, and separation from loved ones.

THE LANGUAGE
OF THE CONVERTED

Sarah Hamilton's conversion was made possible, she said, when "I remembered that the man of God [a Baptist minister] told me that Christ came to save even the worst of sinners and I thought I could not be worse than the vilest." A thrilling moment followed this realization:

> surprising astonishment filled my soul: I beheld the Son of God expiring in agonies unknown, to gratify the malicious rage of wicked men. I thought he died to save my life, and arose again for my justification. . . . I then saw that God could be just and justify him that believeth in Jesus, even such a wretch as I was. In this view, no tongue can tell the extacy of joy that I was the subject of; my distress left me, and I could give glory to God with all my heart. I longed to praise him with every breath; my prayer was, Lord, what wilt thou have me to do? Lord, speak; for thy servant heareth.[17]

Similarly, Harriet Livermore described her conversion:

> I retired to my chamber and locked my door. No eye but those flames of fire which fill all Heaven with light, was upon me. I sat in the corner of the room, trying to meditate upon my situation, when a sudden impulse moved me to give myself away

to Jesus. I dropped quick upon the floor, crying, "Jesus, thou Son of David, have mercy on me." I can recollect no more, till I stood upon my feet and walked around the room, where all about me seemed wrapt in mystery. And as poor as was the offering I presented, even my sinful self, Jesus took me up in his arms of mercy. I was a volunteer in the act of giving myself up to God. . . . Feeling a solemn stillness in my mind, as I walked the room, I could not account for the alteration, as it had so recently resembled the surging waves in a violent gale. The noise of an accusing conscience was suddenly hushed . . . The first thought that I recollect passing through my mind, breathed perfect purity; it was like this—O, I hope I shall never sin again . . . I believe when a soul is given to Christ, he . . . separates the weeping sinner from old crimes; and heals every wound, making perfectly whole. The new-born soul is white as snow.[18]

Despite the centrality of the moment (or moments) of conversion, most nineteenth-century writers expended fewer words and images in describing their actual conversions than upon the experience of conviction. Narrators' relative reticence about the apparent climax of the narrative may stem from a couple of circumstances. Traditionally writers who have attempted to describe the intense time of contact with God or Christ had resorted to sense images— taste and touch as well as sight and sound. Furthermore, those who wrote of communion with the divine had often turned to sexual imagery. But as good Victorians, most nineteenth century narrators—and women in particular— shied away both from sensuous imagery and any conscious use of sexual metaphor.

If nineteenth-century narrators did not particularly dwell upon the point of mystical communion with God or Christ, they never tired of phrases and images to characterize their new relationship to God and Christ once conversion had taken place. Many phrases expressed their dependence upon God; they were enabled to "cast their all upon him," or, alternatively, to "cast all their cares upon him." (1 Pet. 5:7) They spoke often of the "sufficiency" of his grace to save (2 Cor. 12:9), in the same breath with which they referred to their own "nothingness" and "humility." Quoting Luke 10:42, they labeled divine grace as "the one thing needful." "Not my will, but thine be done," they were likely to say, echoing Luke 22:42 (the passage's particular usefulness to women is obvious). Often they referred to themselves as "children of God" and "returned prodigals." In good spiritual times they were conscious of God's constant presence in their lives, and were inclined to describe all their actions as guided by him. They spoke of the "Lord's leading," and might report, for instance, "The Lord led me to speak to her."

Yet, if converts used the language of humility and dependence, they also experienced unexpected reserves of energy, strength, authority, courage, and confidence as a result of their new relationship with God, and these too were reflected in their language. They were proud to be called "disciples," who enjoyed a "closer walk with God," and were conscious of a gradual "growth in grace." God had given them a commission to evangelize the world, with his help, and instructed them to "pluck sinners as brands from the burning"; they were his "watchmen on the wall," the "laborers" in his "vineyard."[19] Even within the scope of the narrative, converts began to use the language of instruction and exhortation, often punctuating their accounts with direct addresses to the reader, in which the hortatory voice, the sense of urgency, and the attempt to inspire by means of appeal to biblical allusion played prominent parts. Hamilton, writing in 1803, said,

> I think, . . . that however unworthy I may be of such honour, I wish to invite and exhort all who know not these things by happy experience, that they will try the experiment for themselves. . . . O, my friends, I long for your happiness; I long to see you rejoice in hope of the glory of God; yea, I long to see the saints on earth join their rejoicing songs of praise to God, with the seraphic angels in heaven, at the news of the return of one more prodigal. Come then, O sinner! come and be happy: for why will ye die? That God in whom you live, move, and have your being, tells you plainly that he delighteth not in the death of him that dieth; but that he turn and live, say, Turn ye, turn ye, for why will ye die?[20]

Julia A. J. Foote directed her "Christian sisters,"

> you will not let what man may say or do, keep you from doing the will of the Lord or using the gifts you have for the good of others. How much easier to bear the reproach of men than to live at a distance from God. Be not kept in bondage by those who say, "We suffer not a woman to teach," thus quoting Paul's words, but not rightly applying them."[21]

Repeatedly, converts characterized their closer relationship with God in such terms as "striving for a heavenly crown," standing before the "throne of grace," or "gathering" at the "mercy-seat." In contrast to their former hopeless efforts to establish their own righteousness, they were now "clothed in his righteousness." They possessed "peace" which "flows like a river," and "passeth understanding."[22] Whereas before they were "blind," now they could see; with their new sight they were accustomed to say that Christ "appeared to me to be the chief among ten thousand, and altogether lovely" (Song of Solomon 5:10, 16). In the words of Philippians 3:8 they professed to "count all things but loss for the excellency of the knowledge of Christ Jesus"; echoing 1 Peter 2:9, they called themselves "a peculiar people to show forth his praise."

Just as most of the "convicted" had stylized pictures of hell, the converted had stock visions of heaven. To these nineteenth-century Protestants, heaven was a region of endless summer, filled with light, singing angels, and flowers perennially blooming. God presided over this blessed land from his great white throne; the saved ones, arrayed in white robes (as in Revelation), stood in contentment before the throne. In the shorthand heaven often became "glory" or "bliss" or "eternal felicity"; sometimes it was the place of "many mansions."[23] (It was also the "abode of bliss" that James Joyce was later to parody in *Ulysses*.) Biblical place names came into play: heaven was "the promised land yea the peaceful Canaan"; one "crossed one's Jordan" in order to get there.

It was almost obligatory for converts to contrast the anticipated joys of heaven with the now-meaningless pleasures of this life. Christians became "dead to self and world." They were particularly hard on "the world," drawing on a long tradition, both Christian and poetic. "Vain," "empty," "carnal," "ensnaring" became favorite incantations with which to banish the things of this life. One writer inveighed against "the vanity of all temporal enjoyments," another against "all the empty honours worldlings can bestow," another against "this vale of tears." Women, particularly, renounced the world of fashion and ornament—"babylonish dress," in the phrase of one.

Converts often spoke victoriously of being "assured" of their own salvation; on the whole they sounded more confident and more triumphant than their Puritan antecedents. Nevertheless, absolute certainty about one's "future state" was often considered bad form; rather, it was regarded as suitably humble (and perhaps demure, in the case of women) for converts to express tentativeness when describing their soteriological status. Thus, a seeker expressed a "trembling hope that she had become a disciple of Christ," and it was common for converts to say that they "indulged a hope," or had "obtained a hope in Christ," or harbored a "secret hope that I shall live beyond the grave." As the nineteenth century went on, the language of hope tended to drop out and confidence replaced it, as more and more Christians subscribed to the assumption that salvation was a simple and straightforward matter: all one had to do was sincerely to desire it and to trust that Christ's sacrifice on the cross had made it possible.[24]

THE FEELING HEART

In an 1844 narrative a convert discovered the preeminence of the heart. He had reached old age as a notorious infidel, with the reputation for refuting every rational argument in defense of Christianity. Inevitably, of course, as in all narratives, he finally succumbed, but he made it clear that assent to doctrine had nothing to do with his change of heart. Rather, it was a church elder, so distraught about the man's soul that he approached him with "eyes bedimmed with tears" and his "breast heaving with emotion," who was finally able to move the hardened old sinner. In his meeting with the infidel, the elder found himself too overwhelmed to do more than repeat helplessly, "I am greatly concerned for your salvation." Nevertheless, he succeeded in initiating the process that issued in the old man's conversion. In a prayer meeting soon after his spiritual crisis, the one-time scoffer stood up, like the other participants, to tell his story. As "his bosom heaved with suppressed emotion," he explained how the tears of the elder had made the decisive difference: "Had the elder reasoned with me, I could have confounded him; but here is no threadbare argument for the truth of religion. Religion must be true, or this man would not *feel* as he does" (my emphasis). Finally he reached the climax of his account: "I have often been requested to look at the evidence of the truth of religion, but, blessed be God, I have evidence for its truth *here*," and he laid his hand upon his heart.[25]

The centrality of feeling was also the theme of a pamphlet from the same decade entitled "Pastor and Inquirer." The "inquirer" was a woman named Sarah, whose dilemma was that though she *knew* she was sinful, she did not *feel* it.

> *Pastor:* You have never . . . felt or been convinced that you were a sinner, a great sinner, in the sight of God?
>
> *Inquirer:* I cannot say that I have. I know it, and know that I ought to feel it, but I must confess it has never yet come home to me as I suppose it should do.[26]

Under the pastor's tutelage, Sarah in due course was able to *feel* her sinfulness, was converted, and died an exemplary Christian death.

Of all the familiar phrases and images that appeared and reappeared in narratives, none were so pervasive or so important as those having to do with the feeling heart. This organ had always played a large role in the imagery of Puritan devotional literature; as Norman Pettit points out, it served as the Puritan "metonym" for the whole person.[27] And Joseph Alleine, in *Alarm to Unconverted Sinners*, warned his readers, "If I have not your hearts, I have nothing."[28]

Certain images of the heart recurred constantly in spiritual narrative from the seventeenth through the nineteenth century: initially it was described as "hard," "stony", "obdurate," and "wounded." Hardly a narrator or conversion-manual writer can be found who did not ascribe one or all of these hearts to sinners under conviction. Likewise, few writers from the seventeenth through the nineteenth centuries neglected to speak of the truly converted as having "broken," "melted," "new," or "subdued" hearts. Furthermore, many narrators quoted certain scriptural formulations having to do with the heart: "The heart is deceitful and desperately wicked" (Jer. 17:9); "a broken and a contrite heart, O God, thou wilt not despise" (Psalm 51:17); "I will take the stony heart out of their flesh and give them a heart of flesh" (Ezek. 11:19); and "Therefore hath he mercy on whom he will have mercy, and whom he will he hardeneth" (Rom. 9:18—assumed to refer to the heart).

Thus, the heart had long figured in spiritual narrative; in the nineteenth-century conversion narrative, however, it moved into particular prominence and was especially closely connected with emotion and tears; one could say, in fact, that the heart sometimes seemed to have become the chief protagonist in the narrative. Nineteenth-century narrators constantly condemned their unconverted hearts for being "sinful," "wicked," "corrupt," "trifling," "foolish," "unsubdued," "wandering," "rebellious," "dreadful," "weak," "ignorant," "cold," and "flinty." Anzonetta Peters exclaimed,

I want to serve God; but I feel *something* within me rising up in opposition to his authority, and prompting me to rebellion. What a strange heart I have! Did ever any one have such a heart before?[29]

As in the infidel story earlier, the events of conversion often gave rise to "overflowing" and "bursting" hearts, floods of tears, and "affecting scenes." Once sinners' hearts had been "pierced," they often wept for their transgressions. ("I love in solitude to shed / The penitential tear," went one hymn.)[30] After experiencing a change of heart, converts typically wept from joy and relief. Indeed, tears became a standard sign of the sincerity of the heart, even in male converts.

Nineteenth-century narrators had particular reason to focus on the feeling heart. American Protestant evangelicalism of that century has commonly—and I think justly—been characterized as a "religion of the heart" more than a theological system. Another way of saying much the same thing is to describe the nineteenth century as an era of religious *feeling*, an age of particularly intense religious sensibility—sensibility and feeling, it must be added, that could be easily observed by others or unequivocally described to them. The more intense the emotions one could demonstrate the truer the conversion and the more powerful its potential impact upon others.[31]

A crucial ingredient of the "religion of the heart" was of course the prominence of Protestant women in nineteenth-century American religious life. Women of this period were especially identified with the ability to feel. It is not unusual that the "inquirer" who came to *feel* her sinfulness was a woman. Men, it was assumed, dominated instead in the realm of reason. Still, in the area of religion the heart was not exclusively a female domain; as the story of the infidel-turned-saint attests, men could also demonstrate considerable reserves of feeling, often, to be sure, under the influence of women and at some cost to their manliness (the elder in the story is somewhat unmanned).[32]

The cultivation of female sensibility was advocated in an essay widely known among American evangelicals, "Strictures on the Modern System of Female Education," written by Hannah More (1745–1833), an English Anglican. In her description of a proper pious upbringing for girls, More discussed the function of religious feeling. At its best, she said, sensibility implied "honest warmth," "lovely susceptibility of heart," "genuine feeling," all of which tended to foster "a warm, tender, disinterestd, and enthusiastic spirit." Sensibility had its dangers, she warned; if not properly governed it could lead to "unnatural irritability" and an "excess of uncontrolled feelings." Allowed to run wild, sensibility could even lead to crimes of passion and suicide. When carefully guided by the "Divine Spirit," however, a woman of sensibility could become more deeply devout than her less feeling sisters. She would "become more enamored of the beauty of holiness," would gain "a keener taste for the spirit of religion," and would serve as "the lively agent of Providence in diminishing the misery that is in the world, into which misery this temper will give her a quicker intuition than colder characters."[33]

It is this sensibility described by More and so clearly reflected in the conversion narratives that links them in language and subject to the "sentimental novels" read eagerly by early nineteenth-century Protestants, especially women.[34] Strictly speaking, evangelicals were not supposed to read novels. Fiction was suspect because, like other "innocent" pleasures, it took its readers' minds off eternity. At best it was a waste of precious time; at worst a corrupter of morals.

But despite the widespread opinion—not limited to evangelical Protestants—that novel reading was a questionable activity, nineteenth-century women persisted in consuming novels with gusto. It was not unusual for them to recall sitting up late into the night with a book they found impossible to put down, weeping over a heroine's misfortunes. Though, as the narratives testify, converts often gave up this kind of reading as a mark of moral reformation, many were of course well acquainted with the genre and its language by the time they forswore the activity. In fact, evangelicals frequently debated over which novels might be edifying enough to justify reading. (Hannah More herself had written a novel, *A Wife for Coelebs*.) Many of those read in the nineteenth century in fact had religious themes and thus might be sanctioned. Love stories could be instructive; it was quite common for fictional romances to take place between converted women and unconverted men; usually such love stories ended upon an edifying note, as the man experienced a change of heart under the woman's gentle but persevering influence.[35]

Certain of the better known English novelists—Henry Fielding, for example—had long been regarded by American evangelicals as definitely off-limits. On the other hand, Samuel Richardson's pious and virtuous heroes and heroines often received a high evaluation from the devout. Even Mary, the "little Puritan" of Harriet Beecher Stowe's *The Minister's Wooing* (1859), had relished *Sir Charles Grandison*, if with a few twinges of conscience.[36] And Richardson's Clarissa was frequently regarded by many nineteenth-century evangelicals as an appropriate model for Christian women.

In the sentimental novels, as in the evangelical conversion narratives, the feeling heart was absolutely central. Richardson's Clarissa said of Lovelace, the sometimes "vile" hero, "he wants a heart: and if he does he wants everything." Furthermore, the hearts of fictional protagonists, like those of the conversion narrators, were "bursting," "overflowing," "wayward," "obdurate," and "hard," though their objects might be different. Like sinners under conviction, novel heroines bathed their pillows in nocturnal weeping; and tears could be discerned upon occasion to "glisten" on their eyelids. Fictional heroes and heroines were subject to bouts of melancholy, just like Christians meditating upon the depth of their sinfulness. Heroines in novels were "ruined" or "undone"; the same words were used of unrepentant sinners facing damnation. Death scenes and a preoccupation with the subject of death played prominent parts in both novels and narratives. For both genres death was relished as an appropriate occasion for the maximum display of sensibility. (One novel boasted fifty-seven death scenes!)[37] In short, such were the links between the novel and narratives that it was no coincidence for at least one book-length conversion narrative to be written in the epistolary style, in the manner of Richardson and his imitators.[38] Nor does it seem surprising that the greatest evangelist of the early nineteenth century was named Charles Grandison Finney, after Richardson's most prominent Christian hero.

The power of the nineteenth-century conversion narratives, then, resided less in an appeal to intellect than in an appeal to feeling. The narratives relied upon their readers' or hearers' assent to the language, their willing participation in the events of the narrative, and their readiness to share the emotions these events aroused. For their effectiveness the narratives depended upon the existence of a largely female audience that would consent to be moved, visibly and sometimes extravagantly, an audience that in fact *wanted* to identify with a narrator's uneasiness, fear, anguish, despair, debasement, amazement, ecstasy and triumph—albeit in a thoroughly predictable and familiar sequence. The assumption behind the narrative was that readers or hearers, deeply stirred by the conversion account, would go from vicarious participation to experiences of their own. In short, in attempting to encourage desirable attitudes and behavior in their audiences, the narrators resorted to the same use of sensibility that made sentimental novels irresistible.

THREE

The Nineteenth-Century Narrative and the Lives of Women

There is an obvious, literal reading of the nineteenth-century narrative: whatever else it did besides, the narrative described an intense spiritual experience. At issue in the narrative was nothing less than the destiny of the soul. When narrators turned to God they believed they were being saved from an actual eternal hell of physical and emotional suffering. Once converted, they enjoyed a sense of acceptance by a gracious and loving savior and of union with him. A sometimes overwhelming sense of guilt fell away. They could now take their places in a community of other converted Christians. These salvation events were not sentimental daydreams of a vapid piety; they were momentous, dramatic, and shattering.

But of course conversion took place in a wider social and cultural setting, and therefore its narration had great significance for women as social and cultural actors. Like other forms of nineteenth-century female writing, conversion narratives both affirmed women's role in a patriarchal society and subverted some of the assumptions of that society. Feminist literary critics sometimes apply the notion of surface and submerged plots to women's fiction; these categories are useful in looking at conversion narratives as well.[1]

The surface plot, in which a woman moved from a state of sinfulness and rebellion to one of complete acquiescence to God's will, often corresponded to the process of her adaptation to the expectations of the culture. The central event of the narrative—the absolute surrender to God, the renunciation of her own will—stands as an analogue of her obedience and submission to a father, brother, or husband. The convert's "Christlike" qualities—meekness, mildness, gentleness, humility, and reluctance to complain or condemn—were the very ones customarily demanded of nineteenth-century women. Furthermore, the convert was expected to downplay the concerns of this world—turn her back on "this vale of tears"—making it unlikely that she would question her husband's hegemony in financial and other important family matters, let alone care to meddle in political and economic affairs in the wider sphere. Through conversion she was taught to renounce the pleasures of this world, including those of her own body; theoretically, therefore, the converted woman preferred to stay retired and protected at home, all her attention devoted to domestic tasks and the Christian upbringing of her children.

All this is true: and yet conversion narratives seem to contain a submerged plot as well. Probably most women converts were unaware of it; certainly they ignored its subversive aspects. The most important part of this second plot was the outcome of conversion; converts felt obligated by the very fact of this momentous experience to tell their stories and persuade others to repeat the pattern. But to do this women had to act anything but submissive and retiring; they had to overcome their shyness and timidity enough to exhort relatives, enter strange homes, address groups of strangers, inspire and organize other women, and, of course, publish their stories. The energy released by conversion made all these activities possible; in fact, the experience of conversion often resulted in exuberance and a loss of inhibiting self-consciousness. Maggie Van Cott, experiencing holiness at a Methodist class meeting, found herself in the church aisle, "both hands uplifted, and, with strong clear voice, shouting aloud the victories of the cross."[2] Jarena Lee, also a Methodist, and a black woman, reported of her conversion, "That moment, though hundreds were present, I did leap to my feet and declare that God, for Christ's sake, had pardoned the sins of my soul."[3]

At least, this is what the narratives reported. They unfailingly made a connection between the experience of conversion and its rather astonishing consequences. Rather than becoming retiring flowers, women went on to dedicated, bold, and often courageous activity. After she was converted, Anzonetta Peters (see chapter 2), painfully shy and retiring, took to visiting the homes of the poor and immigrants of her town. She was "led by the love of souls," her biographer said, "to enter the tenements of want. . . . to read a tract—to entreat the wretched inmates to think of their never-dying souls, or to lift up her voice in the midst of them in prayer to her heavenly Father."[4] Caroline Hyde, born in 1794 and converted during her twenties, asked, "Lord what wilt thou have me to do?" and went on to organize a Sabbath School and later an infant school in Philadelphia.[5] Taking leave of family and friends, the converted Ann Judson embarked with her missionary husband, Adoniram, for Burma, where she suffered a martyr's death.

To be sure, much of the activity that involved converts in nursing, succoring, and proselytizing the poor, ignorant, and helpless lay within the traditional bounds of Christian benevolence prescribed for nineteenth-century women, even if the performance of these tasks often belied the usual prescriptions of female submissiveness and passivity. But conversion led to other endeavors that were at best questionable. For instance, publication by a decent Christian woman was considered a doubtful activity, especially early in the century. Harriet Livermore, publishing her long autobiography in 1826, anticipated the criticism that her venture into print was too "exposed," too "publick," and attempted to deflect social censure by appealing to her high purpose: "Grace says, 'Let God be praised, poor sinners saved.' Nature says, 'O shame on such publicity in a female.' "[6] Even later in the century, women who published their narratives usually felt obliged to deny any desire for publicity, protesting that publication would never have occurred to them except for the importunities of friends who urged them to write their stories for the benefit of other "poor sinners." Harriet Cooke, for instance, prefaced her 1861 autobiography:

> Often, as I have reviewed the dealings of God with me, I have desired to leave my testimony to His mercy and faithfulness; but the thought of sending it forth in the form of a *printed book* never entered my mind till it was suggested by a few pupils and afterwards urged by several Christian friends, who felt that the record of such an experience might tend to strengthen many weary, sinking pilgrims.[7]

Julia A. J. Foote, a black Methodist, explained her authorship of an 1886 "autobiographical sketch": "I have written this little book after many prayers to ascertain the will of God having long had an impression to do it. I have a consciousness of obedience to the will of my dear Lord and Master. . . . My earnest desire is that many—especially of my own race—may be led to believe and enter into rest."[8]

At least female authorship of conversion narratives could be said to have its precedents and justifications, even in the eyes of cultural conservatives. But a few converted women entered the public arena in ways not at all permitted by the prevailing cult of domesticity. Maggie Van Cott became a Methodist minister. Harriet Livermore traveled thousands of miles alone as an evangelist. Sarah Hamilton found herself addressing two hundred people. They were the exceptions among converted women, of course, but one could argue that they were only taking the behest to tell the good news to its logical limits.

Even within their homes, women seem to have been emboldened by the experiences of conversion to address themselves to the souls of their menfolk, sometimes quite aggressively. Phebe Slocum addressed letters to her seamen brothers soon after her 1869 conversion, telling them of her experience and urging them to follow suit. She included suitable protestations of her humility, but betrayed no lack of authority or confidence in her grasp of the truth:

> Now, my dear brothers, I have told you of my experience, . . . I have told you of it as willingly as He revealed it to me, and I now ask you not to cast it aside unheeded, because it comes from your unworthy sister, but be assured the subject is one worthy of your closest attention. Do not condemn it because you have not had an experimental knowledge of it, but strive for it by humble, earnest prayer. It is reality; there is no delusion about it.[9]

Even when the men were willing "inquirers," their women usually took the lead. There are relatively few instances in the literature of nineteenth-century conversion in which a husband was converted before his wife and exhorted her to follow suit.

Another result of a woman convert's complete surrender to God's will was also far-reaching: she could now claim to obey a higher authority than those which had claimed her allegiance in the past. God's will of course became sovereign in her life. But how was his will to be determined? In part through traditional Protestant teachings—as interpreted by men—but also through women's own study and reading of Scripture and through God's voice in their own hearts. If the divine will as determined by a convert's studies or meditations ran counter to the dictates of the culture or of the principal male in her life, the will of God was paramount. To be sure, it often happened, not accidentally, that God and culture spoke with the same voice. But the underlying reality in a converted woman's life was the possibility of appeal to a higher authority.

Some women did indeed oppose the divine will to the human. Hester Rogers aroused her family's opposition because she became associated with the then-not-respectable Methodists—but "the Lord gave me a mouth and wisdom to plead my own cause with arguments from his word, so that they were in some measure all put to silence."[10] In converting and becoming a Methodist, Sarah Hamilton rejected the Roman Catholicism of her family. Since she was widowed it was particularly difficult—and inconvenient—for her to bring down her family's hostility. Her father disowned her; her brother pursued her with a mob; penniless and homeless, she became dispirited: "Satan tempted me to give up my determination to live devoted to God; I was almost tempted to go to my father and feign a repentance of my dissenting from the Romish Church." But she read her Bible and was strengthened in her resolve: "He that will not forsake father and mother for my sake is not worthy of me."[11] Julia A. J. Foote, ejected from the African Methodist Episcopal Church for preaching the gospel, said, "The only safe way was to fall on Christ, even though censure fell upon me for obeying his voice. Man's opinion weighed nothing with me, for my commission was from heaven, and my reward was with the Most High."[12]

Sometimes an unconverted husband's reluctance to allow his wife go to church or a revival meeting became the occasion for a clash of wills. Epstein quotes one such incident, when a husband requested of his wife,

> If she had any affection for him, and as she valued the peace of the family, not to go forward [to church]. . . . "No," said she, "I love you most tenderly, but I love Christ more. I have waited for you for more than twenty years, and now I shall go forward, and as to the consequences, I will leave them with Him in whom I have put my trust."[13]

Nor was opposition to a male relation's will confined to adult women. The accounts of nineteenth-century revivals are rife with narratives of "pious little girls" who braved the ire of "sin-hardened" fathers to bring them to salvation. One such daughter was driven from home by her father and then beaten when she returned to offer him a tract. Another small girl was forbidden by her father to attend a revival meeting. At first she obeyed, but stole out to the meeting before it was over. He went after her in a fury, and grabbed her, whereupon "she looked up with a heavenly smile, and said, 'It's too late now, pa; I have given my heart to the Saviour.' "[14] Fortunately the recalcitrant father, brother, or husband almost always came around in the end (or suddenly died), at least in the narrative version, eliminating the necessity for continued conflict and, incidentally, demonstrating the power of female persuasion bolstered by divine providence.

Thus, the first part of the conversion narrative's submerged plot concerns the "fruits" of conversion: the empowerment of women to leave their homes, to write and publish books, to address groups of other women, to exhort the unsaved, and, if need be, boldly to flout the wills of their fathers and husbands.

Another part of the submerged plot was the emphasis on the period of rebellion and anger preceding a woman's conversion. (The same emotions might reappear after the conversion as well, as a convert realized that her surrender to God was something less than total. Rebelliousness did, in fact, prove to be a perennial problem for spirited women.) To be sure, the expression of rebellious, resistant feelings was an accepted feature of the surface plot; the feelings were sanctioned, even approved, as long as ultimately they were a prelude to the tale of capitulation and surrender. In fact, a woman who did not admit to feelings of "enmity toward God" was suspected of hiding the true depths of her wickedness from herself and others.

In one narrative the support for a woman who disrupted an inquiry meeting in a decidedly unladylike manner is striking: "Miranda N." was known for her beauty and "uncommon sweetness of disposition." On the day of the meeting, however, she created a "disturbance" unlike herself by sobbing very loudly and obtrusively over her sins. When the minister asked, "what have *you* done which makes either your heart or your life so heinously sinful?" she replied, "in a voice that reached the extreme parts of the room and thrilled every heart, for she was known and loved by every person there,—'I HATE GOD, AND I KNOW IT. I HATE CHRISTIANS, AND I KNOW IT. I HATE MY OWN BEING. OH THAT I HAD NEVER BEEN BORN!' " Miranda N's outburst was approved by her audience, startling as it may seem; her behavior was allowed by the narrative convention, though perhaps her exuberance and choice of a public platform was unusual.[15] In strength of feeling if not in volume of sound she was matched by the memorable example of a woman whose "enmity rose to such a height, that she could have consented herself to go to Hell could she but carry God with her."[16]

One does not have to venture very far into psychology to speculate on the benefit that women must have derived from the chance to express their anger and rebellion, both at the time of the experience and later in the recollection and the telling of it. In fact, a sense of covert pleasure emerges from these accounts of rebellion, and this is where the surface plot verges into a submerged one. Women in the nineteenth century obviously did not receive many legitimate opportunities to vent anger, particularly toward the men in their lives: but directing resistance and hostility at a powerful male deity through the conversion narrative was a protected and sanctioned way to do so. Not only did the formula of the conversion narrative promise resolution of these emotions; in addition, the anger and misbehavior could be dissociated from oneself by ascribing them to the agency of Satan. (And of course the anger was deflected away from family members who may sometimes have been the closer objects of women's ire.)

Rebellious feelings could also be enjoyed at secondhand by the narrator's hearers or readers. Vicarious participation in wickedness appears to have been at least one of the reasons for the enormous popularity of the heroine Katy in the fictitious conversion narrative, *Stepping Heavenward* (1869). Katy began with all the usual prospective convert's faults: she loved reading novels and having "a good time"; she easily got distracted when she was praying; she insisted heaven sounded "dreary." She was passionate, quick tempered, impulsive, and sharp tongued. When her mother criticized her she refused angrily to kiss her ("I really believed Satan himself hindered me"). The usual objects of female benevolence—sick and poor people—repulsed her. Most seriously, she could not seem to yield her will to God; she had a "wicked reluctance" to give him her "all." She compared herself to a child who misbehaves and is therefore sent away from the table screaming. "But when her mother offered to take her back if she would be good, she screamed yet more. *She wanted to come and wouldn't let herself come.*"[17]

At about age nineteen, Katy finally experienced a sort of qualified conversion. (Her course would remain up and down, albeit in a generally "heavenward" direction.) Fortunately for the interest of the narrative, Katy did not achieve moral perfection very quickly. She managed to reject her husband-to-be the first time around, not recognizing his sterling qualities; once safely married, she proceeded to quarrel regularly with a difficult sister-in-law, despite her earnest attempts to see her as a God-sent "mortification" to which she ought submit gracefully. Nor did she turn into an enthusiastic homemaker: she complained,

> Does the whole duty of woman consist in keeping her house distressingly clean and prim; in making and baking and preserving and pickling; in climbing to the top shelves of closets lest a little dust should lodge there, and getting down on her hands and knees to inspect the carpet?

When the vexatious sister-in-law suggested that Katy get up and offer her own chair to her tired husband, she snapped, "a silly subservience on my part is degrading to him and to myself."[18]

Apparently, to judge from the book's publication history, readers found the well-intentioned but often naughty and recalcitrant Katy utterly engaging. One young admirer wrote in her diary,

I am reading *Stepping Heavenward* by Mrs. Prentiss & I like it ever & ever so much as I think that Katherine in the book before she gets good is exactly like me—I feel the same in ways. I love her & I love the book this is my third time reading it. On my birthday I am going to try to turn over a new leaf & be a better girl & try to please Mama more to conquer my ungovernable temper & be better in all ways.[19]

The conversion narrative, then, gave women—both tellers and readers—a measure of free play, a vehicle for the expression of their feelings, and a testimony to their abilities. The narrative also helped them to make sense of cataclysmic events in their lives about which they could do very little. Nineteenth-century women had to deal more frequently than their twentieth-century counterparts with the death of a child, for instance. In the conventions of the narrative, the loss of a son or daughter was understood as yet another way—one might say the ultimate way—in which the convert had to yield to God: if he wanted to take her child she must be obedient to him in this too. The loss of a child was also interpreted as a timely reminder that one's home was in heaven, not in this world. Perhaps one had loved the child more than God, and needed to be chastened. On a more comforting note, the narrative also rehearsed the assurance that mother and child would be reunited in heaven.

In addition, the narrative helped women to adjust to less wrenching circumstances that were nevertheless vexing: a difficult husband, poverty or sickness, troublesome in-laws or acquaintances with whom one must deal, or simply the boredom and humdrum of everyday domestic life. All these made sense because in the narrative they were seen as "trials" of one's virtue; they were "tribulations" sent by God to refine and purify one's piety. The exercise of patience and good will in dealing with those who had claims on one's time and attention resulted not in subservience and defeat for a narrator but rather in a demonstration of her true strength and moral superiority.

WOMEN AND CONTROL OF THE NARRATIVE

Whatever meaning and significance women derived from the conversion narratives, they accomplished it under what were at first glance unpromising circumstances. To a great extent men, particularly ministers, defined the shape of women's narratives in the nineteenth century. Ministers often counseled women who "sought an interest in Christ"; their sermons typically set off a period of conviction or brought on conversion proper; ministers authored most of the guides to the experience; they wrote many of the third-person versions; usually they gave the sermons at women's funerals, thus interpreting the meaning of the deceased's life. And women converts often used male narratives as models and inspirations. In these respects the conversion narrative was a male form or genre; it remained for women to assert control over it and use it for their own ends.

The fact that ministers took a large hand in interpreting women's conversion experiences may not have been as restrictive as it might at first seem, however. Of all men, ministers had the greatest interest in making religious activists and allies of women, in encouraging them to participate in church affairs. Unconverted husbands, on the other hand, sometimes had occasion to rue their wives' religious zeal. But—except on the relatively rare occasions when women threatened his authority as a consequence of their conversions—a minister had every reason to welcome their help in exhorting their menfolk, proselytizing their unsaved neighbors, mobilizing other women, teaching Sunday school, organizing missionary efforts, and performing the other tasks of the church.[20]

Influential as ministers may have been, women themselves were also involved in important ways in determining what form their narratives would take. First, of course, women often wrote their own accounts. However subject to convention and outside influence narrators were, nevertheless they had a chance to put their own stamp upon them. Despite the uniformity, individual styles showed up: one woman chose an ornate "literary" style; another quoted Scripture almost continuously, but in such a way as to make it sound like *her* language; another kept her distance from events, using the third person. Even when a minister penned a woman's account, he generally testified that he accurately quoted her own words, garnered from letters, a diary, or a journal.

Second, women used female as well as male models. There were any number of collections of biographies of converted women. Harriet Livermore, for example, described reading the "memoirs of pious women," "abridged from Gibbons by Dr. Dana." In addition to Rogers and Guyon, mentioned in chapter two, women read the lives and letters of such exemplars as Caroline Fry (1787–1846), Countess Huntington, Susanna Wesley, Isabella Graham, Ann Bacon, Frances Havergal (the well known English hymn writer), and Sister Dora (an early deaconess). The English moralist Hannah More exerted a powerful influence on many young women; in an 1834 diary Harriet Catherine Grew reported reading "Mrs. H. More's pious reflections and confessions. I trust I see a faint likeness to her ardent aspirings and humble confessions, in my slow advancing soul. Oh! blissful thought, I hope one day to see her, and all my dear brethren and sisters in my Father's mansion."[21] Women were particularly drawn to the stories of the pioneer missionary women of the nineteenth century, such as Ann Judson and Sarah Boardman Judson. Not only were these women of eminent piety; many were leaders of great influence and courage.

There are hints to suggest that women used female writings to formulate and bolster their own notions of conversion. In *Stepping Heavenward*, the heroine Katy frequently engaged in theological discussion with her father-in-law. He represented an earlier generation, closer to the Puritans, that emphasized God's wrath and the uncertainty of salvation; he chided Katy for her light-heartedness (her "levity"), and habitually intoned, "The heart is deceitful above all things and desperately wicked." He argued that his young grandson should early be taught he was "in a state of condemnation," and could not understand how Katy was able to face the prospect of death with equanimity. Why, he demanded, did she not have "some dread of the King of Terrors," why "such absolute *certainty* of having found favor with God as to make the hour of departure entirely free from such doubt and such humility as becomes a guilty sinner about to face his judge''? Katy, a little taken aback at first by this verbal assault, managed a strong recovery: "I had given myself to Christ, and He had received me, and why should I be afraid to take His hand and go where He led me?" To support her position she read him the letters of Caroline Fry, moving him to tears and, in effect, besting him in theological debate. Katy was a woman with her own ideas—somewhat advanced in that they emphasized the love and mercy of God rather than his wrath—and she was willing to appeal to the writings of other women in support of her views.[22]

Not only was the experience of women influenced by the writings of other women; throughout the conversion process a woman received advice, comfort, and inspiration from her spiritual sisters as well as from ministers. Among female influences, most obvious was that of a mother, who customarily appeared in the narratives as a paragon of piety and Christian benevolence. In addition to providing a model, she often tendered advice, admonition, and encouragement.[23]

Sometimes a mother had died too early to aid her daughter's conversion, or the daughter was too reserved to appeal to her. In this case, a woman's world abounded with surrogate Christian mothers who could be models and guides. Sometimes the would-be convert had a helpful conversation with the minister's wife, sometimes a mother-in-law, or some other older woman. The increasing number of young women who attended female academies in the nineteenth century often regarded their teachers as their chief spiritual counselors. Harriet Cooke, who became head of a girls' school in Middlebury, Vermont, regarded it as her duty to see as many of her pupils converted as possible, as did Anna P. Sills, the first principal of Rockford Female Academy, and Mary Lyon of Mt. Holyoke. Cooke's *Autobiography* (1861) contains not only her own narrative but her account of the conversions of many of her students, in which she took an active role as exhorter, comforter, and counselor. Mary Mortimer, who grew up an atheist, was brought around by a moral philosophy course at the Geneva (New York) Female Academy and by the pointed questions of one of her teachers there: "Mary, have you yet resolved to be a Christian?"[24]

Often prospective converts confided in their female peers. Harriet Cooke went to her first Sunday evening prayer meeting in the company of female companions, and a friend was ultimately instrumental in her conversion. Cooke had entered the period of conviction, but did not know how to move beyond it: "the arrow entered into my soul, and I knew not what it was that had barbed the point." Nor did she seek advice at first: "pride kept me from appealing to any one for direction, in this time of need." At length, however, when her misery had reached a "crisis," the crucial information came from her friend Catherine, who, she reported, was "the only one who urged upon us [Cooke's sister was in a similar state] the duty of submission." Not long after, following Catherine's counsel, Cooke was able to "throw myself upon the mercy of a crucified and divine Redeemer" and "find peace in believing."[25]

Much counsel and comfort was exchanged by contemporaries through letters. Harriet Catherine Grew described the satisfactions of corresponding with Christian friends:

> It is delightful to me to know of the spiritual health of my dear friends. May we not be helpers of each other's joy, by imparting our knowledge and experience to those who are journeying with us to heaven? I have few intimate acquaintances to whom I can communicate my feelings, but I find it pleasant to do so, and to receive the sympathy of those who love Him who, above all things, engages my soul's affections. How holy is the christian tie![26]

Sometimes Grew asked friends to pray for her; at other times she dispensed advice. To a female friend who had suffered some "affliction," she wrote, "You must now feel the inability of earthly things to support you, and I trust that in God you have found an everlasting Father and friend, who will never forsake you. He afflicts, not willingly, but for our own profit." She admonished the same friend on another occasion:

> Do, my beloved M., strive above all things to keep your thoughts and affection above this vain world. We must not be conformed to the fashions and customs of the world, if they are injurious to our spiritual health. Let us show to all, with whom we associate, that we are not of the world.[27]

Martha Day, converted in 1831, had the comfort beforehand of being able to unburden her self-doubts to a friend who, she assumed, was experiencing similar feelings:

> One great trouble of mine is, that I cannot read the Bible, in such a way as to feel the force of it. . . . I ought to ascribe this, in part, to my indolence, but it seems to me that there is more in it than this—a moral blindness, a coldness and hardness of heart. We read that "the word of God is quick, and powerful, and sharper than any two-edged sword," but I feel none of this power. . . . I cannot but think this is also your case. My dear friend, when shall we escape from this dreadful darkness?[28]

In fact, the female influence was pervasive: ministers were usually the only males who *did* counsel women. (And often they did this unbeknownst to themselves, through their sermons.) In their day-to-day religious lives, women were surrounded by women. Even pious fathers—not as numerous as pious mothers anyhow—were seldom pictured in the narratives as involved in their daughters' spiritual lives. Godly fathers, it seems, were people to be admired from afar.

What kind of advice did women converts most frequently need? First, they sometimes needed clarification about what the steps of conversion entailed; this was true particularly if they had grown up outside the orthodox evangelical tradition and therefore were not as familiar with the pattern as others (Cooke, for instance, a self-described "Arminian," did not know that submission was the key to advancing beyond the period of conviction). Second, even those who had known the pattern all their lives often needed assistance through the period of conviction. Would-be converts wondered whether they felt their sinfulness deeply enough; those who had fallen into despair and could not seem to move beyond self-condemnation needed to be reminded that God's grace was available even to them. Converts walked a tightrope; they were expected truly to suffer from a sense of sinfulness, but they were not supposed to overdo it.[29] Women particularly got mired in contemplating their sins; they engaged in a sort of orgy of repentance; they *wallowed* in grief over their sins, paralyzed, unable to embark upon the active dimension of the Christian life. Often a female informant was able to point out that repentance had been carried far enough, that in fact its prolongation was functioning as an excuse not to make the final and complete surrender to God.

Finally, when it came to conversion proper, those who were unable to pinpoint a day or a moment had to be reassured that conversion was no less authentic because it happened gradually and almost imperceptibly. (This reassurance is pervasive in the literature; clearly many converts assumed that sudden conversion was a sine qua non.)[30]

MALE AND FEMALE NARRATIVES

It is risky to make generalizations in comparing female narratives with male ones. The formula was quite uniform for all evangelical Christians of either sex, and within the gender groupings there was enough variation to present the exception to any rule. On the whole, however, women's narratives reveal more struggle, more painful self-examination, more intensity, more agonizing about "sins" that a later age would consider harmless. (On the contrary, the twentieth century would regard a certain amount of rebelliousness, for instance, as downright healthy.) Men's conversions appear to have been more matter-of-fact; some even seem pro forma. It is possible some men professed Christ without a lot of thought or feeling (it was easy enough, since the language was readily available to them), at least in part to satisfy an importunate wife or mother or sister and thereby restore domestic peace. Often male conversion entailed moral reform first and foremost; it seemed to center on a resolve to live and speak differently, to give up drinking or gambling or swearing or womanizing. Whereas with women the issue was often a rebellious heart, an unwillingness to surrender, with men—if there was substantial resistance at all—it was more often resistance to the whole idea of religion, to the social and cultural pressure to convert. Or men who had led generally "upright" lives had a difficult time admitting they were sinful.[31] Women were usually willing, even eager, to convert, but once embarked on the process they ran into obstructions in themselves; they found they could not go all the way. Men were often reluctant even to begin the process, but once on their way they often seemed to accomplish it with less fuss.

It is interesting to compare the experiences of brothers and sisters. Harriet Cooke in her *Autobiography* described the conversion of her daughter and son. As was typical in most families, the daughter's conversion was accomplished first, even though she appears to have been younger; the brother was the family holdout. The daughter's period of conviction, initiated by a remark of her mother, was traumatic; she studied her Bible constantly and "for weeks no smile of peace beamed from a face usually radiant with joyousness." She could not sleep; she begged others to pray for her: "at times she seemed almost in despair." Finally a pastor's remarks "encouraged her to hope that her heavenly Father might extend mercy to her, and . . . she gave herself to God, . . . trusting only to the merits of her Saviour for acceptance." The brother proved more resistant to the demands of the gospel; he had already passed through a college revival and a critical illness without serious concern about the condition of his soul. Five years after leaving college he was teaching at an unidentified school where "much religious influence had manifested itself among the pupils." He had gone to New York during the vacation to escape this atmosphere, then to Middlebury, Vermont, to visit his mother. (He almost changed his mind about visiting when he learned there were revivals in progress at Middlebury too.) At his mother's school he did consent to attend the daily religious meetings, but she recalled "as yet I perceived no deep anxiety on account of sin, though he was serious and attentive." At length her son's pastor reported to her a conversation with him and concluded: "have you *faith* to hope that the last unconverted member of your family is now one of God's dear children? I believe it is even so. . . . I trust he has made an entire surrender of himself to God's service." The son experienced no deep soul searching, at least none the mother could discern, and she had to accept the minister's somewhat spare and equivocal description of her son's spiritual condition rather than witnessing the outward evidences of its progress (e.g., tears, radiant smiles) that were so plentiful in her daughter's case.[32]

Cooke's son is an example of the resistant male who seems to have converted in spite of himself or for extra-religious reasons (we do not know the precise reasons in his case). There are also examples of males who were religious by temperament (*they* usually became ministers or missionaries). Katy of *Stepping Heavenward* had a brother, James, who accepted Christ because it seemed to come naturally to him to do so. While his sister was struggling through her spiritual ups and downs, he lived on easy terms with evangelical teaching. Upon receiving her brother's letter announcing his decision to become a missionary, Katy wrote in her diary:

> Such expressions of personal love to Christ, and delight in the thought of serving Him, I never read. I could only marvel at what God had wrought in his soul. For me to live to Christ seems natural enough, for I have been driven to Him not only by sorrow but by sin. Every outbreak of my hasty temper sends me weeping to the foot of the cross, and I love much because I have been forgiven much. But James as far as I know, has never had a sorrow, except my father's death, and that had no apparent religious effect. And his natural character is perfectly beautiful. He is warm-hearted and loving and simple and guileless as a child, and has nothing of my intemperance, hastiness, and quick temper. . . . Life has done little but smile upon him; he is handsome and talented and attractive; everybody is fascinated by him, everybody caresses him; and yet he has turned his back on the world that has dealt so kindly with him, and given himself, as Edwards says, "clean away to Christ!"[33]

James as described by his sister had some typically feminine characteristics; he was not exactly a man's man. Toward the end of the nineteenth century the converted male, unless he was endowed with James's temperament and goals, had become more and more of a rarity. Conversion had turned increasingly into a female mode. By 1905, when Robert Speer wrote a series of biographical sketches of devout young men, most of them born in the 1870s, he took pains to stress the *manliness* of his subjects, explaining, "I have ventured to use them as a challenge and contradiction to those who think Christianity a weak and unmanly thing, or as a fine but impractical thing." Speer emphasized the athletic interests of his Christian young men and quoted one of them who equated conversion with "being manly enough" to "make a stand."[34] Speer's young men did not surrender or yield; they took a stand; for the time being the language of surrender had become largely the province of women.

The narrative may not have been congenial to many men, but it seems to have served some nineteenth-century evangelical women in a number of unexpected ways. In fact, it served in a sense as their veiled and mostly unconscious critique of women's place in American society. One familiar persona of the female narrative was the woman who appeared to have all the ingredients of earthly female happiness—godly parents, good health, material comfort, a decent education for the time, and, if she was old enough, a thoughtful husband and well-behaved children—but who nevertheless lacked something critical. Middle-class American women of the nineteenth century seemed to have everything women could desire: they were petted, admired as moral influences, put on pedestals; they had most of the things money could buy, and they had leisure. And yet they were often bored and unhappy, sometimes even miserable, and they suffered from psychosomatic illnesses. Of course, according to the surface plot the crucial fulfillment unconverted women lacked—"the one thing needful," in the frequently quoted words of Scripture—was the assurance they were saved. When through conversion a reasonable hope of salvation and a meaningful relationship with God were obtained, contentment and peace followed. But the submerged plot reads slightly differently: through the process of conversion, women found not only life eternal but worthy occupation in this world for their time and energy; they no longer had to think of themselves as creatures of idleness and fashion, mere adornments in their father's or husband's homes; they had been enabled to see themselves as protagonists with God in a cosmic drama, their souls the objects of his solicitude. Moreover, they had found meaningful (and steady) work: they had tapped the power to influence life and death outcomes at the individual level, and, at the cultural level, to help change the course of Christian civilization. In this sense, women's conversion narratives are not just about finding God; they are also about finding a worthy role in the world as well.

Part Two

Twentieth-Century Conversion Narratives

*Disbelief is a conscious refusal to accept
a particular version of reality, and believing involves the conscious acceptance
of "doctrine," of particular claims about
reality and one's relationship to it. But
disbelief is also, in the case of evangelical Christianity at least, an unconscious
refusal to participate in a particular narrative mode of knowing reality. Likewise, belief also involves an unconscious
willingness to join a narrative tradition,
a way of knowing and being through
storytelling, through giving and taking
stories. You cannot give born-again stories, you cannot fashion them, without
acknowledging belief, but you can take
them, you can absorb them, and that's
how you "believe" when you are under
conviction. You get caught up in the stories, no matter what your conscious beliefs and disbeliefs are.*

Susan F. Harding, "Convicted
by the Holy Spirit:
The Rhetoric of Fundamental
Baptist Conversion"

FOUR

Change and Continuity
in Twentieth-Century
Narratives

Far from declining as a genre, conversion narratives have enjoyed a robust life in the twentieth century. In fact, given the boom in the print media and in electronic communications, they have undoubtedly received much wider dissemination than any earlier ones. Consider these two narratives, one from the Billy Graham campaign and the other from a book-length autobiography. A young woman wrote in a letter to Billy Graham:

> Until last January I was a stranger to Jesus. I was a rebel, thief, a drunkard, a hard drug taker, an adultress, a hippie, a self-centered, confused young woman. Thinking I was going to stump everyone with my cynical questions, I went to a Bible study about a year ago out of curiosity. That night I became seriously interested in the Bible. Finally after searching and studying the Scriptures for months, John 3:16 spoke to my heart and I gave my life to Christ. I never knew this kind of happiness could exist. God shows you how to love and what it feels like to be loved. He was what I had been looking for since my early teens. He was "the bag" I hadn't found. It seemed to me that drugs, liquor, free love, and bumming around the country would make me free, but they were all traps. Sin was the trap that led me to confusion, unhappiness, guilt, and near-suicide. Christ has made me free. Being a Christian is exciting because there is always a new challenge, so much to learn. Now I wake up glad to see the day. He has made me new.[1]

This woman's narrative nicely illustrates the continuity between twentieth-century narratives and those of the past. Her story follows an old recipe, complete with the stock character who goes to a religious meeting to scoff and ends up persuaded.[2] Except for the particularly twentieth-century words (hippie, bag) and its greater simplicity of diction, it could have been written a century ago. This sort of capsulized narrative, done according to an old formula, is legion in the literature of conservative Protestantism of this century.

But while conversion narratives have retained numerous earlier elements, they have also changed substantially. Book-length narratives are more abundant than earlier, the best known probably being Charles Colson's *Born Again*. These are of necessity more detailed, individualistic, and "original" than the brief ones and often contain material of interest to the reader (especially if the teller is famous) but sometimes only loosely connected to the core of the conversion story itself. They show more interest in the psychology of the convert, and they take place in a distinctly more secular environment. Let *The Late Liz* (1957), by Elizabeth Burns, represent a conversion narrative of this longer, more complex kind. Burns by her own testimony was born just before the beginning of this century, to a wealthy family. She attended Smith College. Her mother, apparently a passive figure who was at some point divorced from her father, does not figure much in her recollections. As a small child she was cared for by a woman who read the Bible and taught the little girl to pray. Burns associated whatever security she had enjoyed as a child with this mother substitute.[3]

Burns's father, as she recalls him, was a domineering personality with whom she was continually in conflict. In rebellion she married a man he disapproved of. The marriage, beset among other things with sexual problems, was a disaster. She was haunted, she recalls, by "a natural hunger for approval." Men fell in love with her only to find their affection unreturned. She could not believe in her attractiveness but rather felt herself "a congenital wallflower." To judge from her account, she had some insight into the nature of her problems. "She spends a lifetime running from" her father, she remarked of herself, "yet the same lifetime is spent comparing every man she meets to him." What she found when she looked within her troubled self was a "deep subsoil of hurt and fear and guilt, middle layer of self-pitying rebellion, top layer of frustration mixed with some new and unimagined and unbelievable elixir of power."[4]

Not surprisingly, this pain and conflict resulted in alcoholism, abuse of sleeping pills, and an estranged son (who died in World War II). Finally, as a third marriage began to come apart, she made a serious suicide attempt. This crisis brought a turning point; mysteriously, when she woke up in the hospital, she experienced a hitherto unknown sense of inner quiet whose source she did not understand:

> Lying utterly still, I waited. Unable to accept, I was now accepting, letting myself be claimed, letting this something mount and permeate and cover the self I'd been as the tide rises to cover what was formerly dry and bare. What it was or where it came from I did not know nor was there a need to know. . . . The air was radiant with a gladness to burst the heart. An outpouring, drenching and cradling and upholding the person who was I, yet not I. The scant, leftover shred of me, as yet unspoiled, was going back. Back to the One Who had always been waiting, only now the barrier between had disappeared.

This exquisite sense of being a "washed page," of having "all eternity" in which her "tiny soul" could "grow" was of course difficult to sustain at this level of intensity. Upon leaving the hospital she had after all to deal with the same old anxieties; she tried too hard to progress spiritually; her third husband left her despite (or because of) her transformation; she was sorely tempted at times to take a drink; a willful person, she found herself "dreadfully resistant" to placing herself in God's hands. She did find support; she turned to a church community and came upon a particularly understanding minister. Another son had previously found "the Big One" and acted as spiritual counselor to his mother.[5]

But even with such support, life as a new Christian was not easy, and one of her difficulties was, interestingly, rhetorical. Burns, seldom at a loss for words, described herself as initially tongue-tied in the face of her experience. She had not at first known how to name what had happened to her, or the agent that had brought it about (she had settled for "Glory"). Nor did she know how to pray: "It's a foreign language; I've tried and tried and all that comes out is conversation. From me to Him. Or thoughts, just thoughts. All those names confuse me, God, Lord, Jesus, Christ. For my money, He's the *Father*." (The psychological significance of this choice did not escape her!) Burns did not easily adopt the formulations of other Christian narrators either. She complained to her minister, "I don't like the word *conversion*. It's halleluiah, sawdust trail, blood of the Lamb; that junk. It smacks of people with JESUS SAVES on the back of their cars." Her pastor defended this language. "The halleluiah approach doesn't appeal to me either; on the other hand, this is God's affair, not ours. He must reach people wherever they can be reached."[6]

Apparently by the time she came to tell her story, Burns was able to make her peace with some of the standard conversion rhetoric, though she obviously leavened it with her own original images. She described her postconversion struggles as "a hammock, swinging jerkily between two ways of life, the way of self and the way of self-surrender. . . . I, Elizabeth, born Burns, was being cleansed; brought down, emptied, scrubbed raw, in order that one day I could be of service." She even came to quote approvingly a current favorite evangelical slogan, "Let go, let God." Finally, addressing herself, she summarized her experiences in one of the oldest of conversion formulas: "Indeed you have been lost! And have been found."[7]

As the foregoing narratives tend to suggest, any attempt to distinguish simply between "nineteenth-" and "twentieth-" century narratives is arbitrary. Obviously converts did not suddenly change their language as they stepped over the temporal boundary into 1900. Rather, they have made shifts in their narratives only slowly, irregularly, and largely unconsciously. Though they have gradually "modernized" their language, they have also continued to take their linguistic cues from narratives, hymns, and manuals written decades and even centuries earlier. The fundamentalists among them have inclined to deliberate rhetorical conservatism.[8] The result is that twentieth-century narratives represent a complex blending of rhetorical patterns from many different time periods.

One way to approach the complex matter of rhetorical changes in twentieth-century conversion narratives is to proceed "backward"—that is, to examine what changes in the culture as a whole may have affected the narratives. First, conversion in its classical Christian sense became a less normative experience for American Protestants; the traditional Protestant conversion narrative had to compete increasingly with numerous other narratives of personal transformation. This development has made the language of the narrative problematic in ways it had not been before. Thus, we see Liz Burns above groping for words in a manner her nineteenth-century counterparts would have found unnecessary. She was obviously ripe for a conversion, but not necessarily a Christian or even religious one. Prospective converts like Burns were less likely to know the language of Christian conversion in advance or to find it acceptable when they did know it (see Burns's objections to the "sawdust trail" language). To appeal to them, the narrative increasingly needed to adopt the language ordinary people knew and used. Or, alternatively, its purveyors had to teach and disseminate its special, unique language with greater skill, intensity, and self-consciousness than had been necessary in the past. Often once people were converted they required ways to acquire the conversion language they were only partially familiar with; they had to learn to recast their experiences according to already existing formulas taught them through books or dialogue with more experienced Christians. Chapter 6 deals in some detail with the wealth of instruction available to twentieth-century converts and would-be converts.

Second, the emergence of the fundamentalist movement in the 1920s undoubtedly brought changes in the narratives. The ability to testify to conversion became one of the badges of faith that distinguished conservative evangelicals from other Protestants. (Other such "badges" were belief in the inerrancy of Scripture, the physical resurrection of Jesus Christ, and his imminent return to earth.) To be "soundly converted," as a writer put it in the 1930s, helped identify one as a member of a definite religious camp. In the context of the fundamentalist-modernist struggle, it became more important than ever for converts to get the narrative "right." Thus, the emergence of fundamentalism pushed the conversion narrative to become even more formulaic, more standardized, and more "correct" than before. Sometimes conservatives acknowledged the existence of a separate rhetoric; as sociologist Nancy Ammerman's "Bible believer" subjects said in the late eighties, "When Christians get together, it's almost like we speak another language."

Another significant cultural factor has been the change in the speech of Americans. In this century standard American English has become more informal, simpler, and colloquial. It has felt the impact of Madison Avenue: the repeatable quotes and the preoccupation with persuasion—less by reasoned argument than by subliminal appeal through appealing music, short memorable slogans, and striking images. It has also responded to the emergence of the electronic media, with their preference for the arresting phrase and the thirty-second spot. Movies came on the scene at the beginning of the century; radio appeared in the 1920s, and television in the 1950s. Narratives reflect these and other linguistic influences. The flowery poetic diction reminiscent of the eighteenth and nineteenth centuries has all but disappeared, and even when narrators turn to poetic language, they are much more likely to have twentieth-century models in mind than Cowper or Wordsworth. The accent of narratives has become more Southern, as evangelicalism in the twentieth century has become increasingly influenced by Southern speakers. Convert Susan Atkins, who had never set foot in the South, observed that she had become "so addicted" to a certain Christian TV station

> that it had begun to affect my speech patterns when praying or speaking about the Lord. Several of my Christian friends had asked me why I seemed to slip into a Southern accent when praying or praising the Lord. . . . It dawned on me one night that I had been learning about prayer and ministry from several television ministers—Pat Robertson, Jim Bakker, Paul Crouch. . . . [9]

Another change has come from altered attitudes toward human emotions, though it is difficult to trace the exact shifts in those attitudes. In the nineteenth century an authentic conversion meant *feeling* the right way—that is, the way a convert was supposed to feel. Her heart melted, she wept copiously, she felt joy and exhilaration. Emotions had to stay within accepted bounds, of course, but their absence suggested a deficiency in the testimony. As time went on— and on the question of time I'm purposely vague—more and more commentators on conversion—narrators and observers—expressed skepticism about the role of the emotions in religious experience. Even as early as the 1880s, Hannah Whitall Smith, whose *Christian's Secret of a Happy Life* has served as a vade mecum for many twentieth-century converts, denied that lack of the "proper" feeling ought to stand in the way of entering the holiness experience, the so-called second conversion. Achievement of holiness is mostly a matter of will, she insisted; the feelings will follow along in due time if the will is right:

> The one chief temptation that meets the soul at this juncture is the same that assaults it all along the pathway, at every step of its progress; namely, the question as to *feelings*. We cannot believe we are consecrated until we *feel* that we are: and because we do not feel that God has taken us in hand, we cannot believe that He has. . . . Begin to believe, and hold on to it steadfastly, that He has taken that which you have surrendered to Him. You positively must not wait to feel either that you have given yourself, or that God has taken you. You must simply believe it, and reckon it to be the case. And if you are steadfast in this reckoning, sooner or later the feeling will come. [10]

Not everyone took seriously the warning against treating emotion as a reliable indicator of supernatural experience; for instance, early–twentieth-century pentecostals shouted and sang and laughed and wept with wild abandon (it looked especially wild to their numerous critics), but prescriptions about moderation in feeling have come to affect even them. Recent pentecostal writers advised, "you do not have to become emotional in order to speak in tongues," and again, "our emotions are undependable, and if we try to guide our lives by them it will lead to confusion." [11]

Several factors probably help explain evangelical reluctance to put too much stock in the emotions. First, they noticed a high incidence of backsliding among converts who had been brought to Christ during exciting revivals. Clearly intense emotion did not guarantee a sound conversion or a permanent "decision for Christ." This gap between declaration and long-term behavior had been particularly striking in the late nineteenth and early twentieth centuries, perhaps because methods of investigating and following purported converts had improved. Second, twentieth-century culture increasingly rejected the Victorian sentimentality of the previous century. Emotional demonstrativeness was automatically suspect unless its cause was understandable to all. Even women began to apologize for their tears. Third, as American society slowly absorbed the teaching of modern psychiatry—with its emphases on the subconscious and sublimated sexuality—it learned to regard feelings with a certain amount of distrust. If one felt impulsive love for the Lord one moment what was to guarantee one wouldn't feel hostility the next? Were unremitting guilt feelings always true indicators of real guilt? It began to seem extremely doubtful that emotions were the deepest, most dependable part of a human personality.

Of course, psychiatry did not much appeal to conservative evangelicals in the twentieth century. Even in the past couple of decades the aid of psychiatrists has continued to be compared unfavorably to the healing wrought by religious conversion and nurture. Yet more and more of the ideas of psychiatry and psychology have filtered through to conservative evangelicals. In fact, the most far-reaching twentieth-century cultural influence has been evangelicalism's growing awareness and appropriation of psychology, of the therapeutic. Though the beginnings of psychology as a discipline lay in the late nineteenth century, evangelicals had largely resisted its impact until after World War II. When at length they turned to psychology, however, they embraced it with an enthusiasm to make up for lost time, as a glance at the titles in any contemporary "Christian" bookstore will testify. They popularized psychological concepts, "Christianizing" them and making them readily accessible to ordinary Americans.[12]

Evangelical acceptance of popular psychology during the 1950s—a development that has not perceptibly slowed—had an enormous effect on how narrators understood and talked about conversion. Whatever else it entailed, conversion came to mean an occasion of psychological healing, when a divided, unhappy personality could be integrated. A proper conversion was now understood to foster the growth of self-confidence, peace of mind, and happiness.

This altered understanding of the consequences of conversion affected how the story was told. Narrators talked less about the future status of their souls and more about the current condition of their psyches. Earthly contentment rather than heavenly bliss became the primary "fruit" of conversion. Evangelical writer Marjorie Holmes made the distinction when she prayed to God, "I know you must be out there—somewhere. And if I can only find you, . . . perhaps I can be saved. Not in the sense of an afterlife, but saved from the choking futility of this life now."[13] The language of twentieth-century angst, alienation, existential anxiety, panic, and boredom—so abundant in our culture—was as likely to provide a rhetorical resource to describe the initial miseries in the conversion process as the more traditional language of sin and rebellion against God. Another evangelical writer summed up the plight of unconverted humanity in pure twentieth-century talk show terms: "all of us— the panic-ridden, drug-addicted, booze-addicted, television-addicted, bored, lonely, cancer-fearing mortals of our time."[14] By the late twentieth century God as stern judge had virtually disappeared from the story. On occasion he could be a strict teacher, but only because he was so full of love and concern. God would no sooner really threaten, punish, and reject than would the wise therapist. The overriding theme in the twentieth century has been the abundance of divine forgiveness, acceptance, and grace. These win over the recalcitrant, the rebellious, the angry, and the stubborn, rather than the threat of eternal punishment.

Given the enormous cultural and social changes in the last century, it would be strange indeed if narratives had not changed in significant ways. Yet, for all the divergences, the essential steps are the same: as a young woman the narrator goes through a period of misery which may become excruciating. Then, often in the nick of time, when the sufferer is on the brink of self-destruction and annihilation, something happens to end or ease the pain. The something that happens may be sudden and final, or it may work only gradually, but it is indisputably healing. The narrator comes to feel herself accepted by God (or Jesus), sheltered under his protection and guidance. There may be renewed periods of doubt—of self and of God, but they are usually resolved if the conversion has been authentic in the first place. One of the "signs" of transformation in the twentieth century, as earlier, is the release of new energies and abilities, some of which are likely to be directed toward the evangelization of others.

The remainder of this chapter and the next will explore the language of the twentieth-century narratives, examining both continuities and changes from earlier narratives. Chapter 6 will consider some of the rhetorical resources for the narratives of this century; chapter 7 will then look more closely at what these narratives meant to the women who spoke and wrote and heard and read them.

THE LANGUAGE OF SIN AND SUFFERING

As in earlier narratives the prospective convert must move from a state of indifference, carelessness, and—increasingly in the twentieth century—ignorance of the matters of salvation to overriding concern for them. To accomplish this she must go through a period of worry and anxiety. The misery that usually initiates conversion in a later narrative is of many kinds: the death of a child, a bad marriage or succession of them, serious sickness or injury, a deeper and deeper descent into alcoholism, drugs, crime, or prostitution. Some of these miseries resemble nineteenth-century ones; those involving criminality and addiction are more common to the twentieth century. As in the nineteenth century, prospective converts are often rebels. Open rebellion against parents and authority of all kinds, often accompanied by an ungovernable temper, is a recurring theme. The sinful, both male and female, often betray a trouble-seeking, aimless restlessness. One woman accused herself of "rebellion, pride, a stubborn will, assertion of self" and "rebellion against God." Like not a few other children of pastors, she also revolted against her minister father. Another woman recalled her girlhood "locked in a battle of wills" with her mother.[15]

The most spectacular miseries—the kind that send the narrator to prison or the gutter—have made for the most dramatic narratives. As one narrator observed, "The reformation of those who have been steeped in vice and crime always arrests attention."[16] This is doubly so in the case of women, who are not normally associated with vice and crime. The jailhouse narrative of Susan Atkins, one of the women in Charles Manson's murderous family, fits into this category. Rescue missions attract attention with the stories of converted female drug addicts and prostitutes.

Of course, women in the nineteenth century often indicated they felt anger and rebellion, but, unlike their later counterparts, they were less likely to act it out. One recent narrative tells of a young woman named Sue who, as a consequence of devastating childhood circumstances, had developed an explosive temper. On one occasion she came close to killing an acquaintance who she thought had stolen her radio. She had developed a sexual liaison with a bank robber, whose criminal efforts she had assisted, and had ended up with him in jail.[17]

But not all conversion narratives from this century chronicle female violence and criminality; the greater number describe lives of quiet desperation: the teenaged girls who feel themselves too fat, ugly, or shy, the wives whose husbands silently walk out the door never to return, the women who can't believe their husbands love them even when they do not experience actual abandonment, the women with too many children and too few interests of their own. One day Joyce Stutt's husband announced that he no longer loved her. She was doubly devastated because, as she said, she had followed all the rules. She had been a "submissive Christian wife," a "good little Christian," "trying to please others, . . . living vicariously through their achievements and experiences."[18] Diana Bertholf, trapped in a deteriorating marriage, described her life: "My friendships had been poor and there were few people whom I trusted. I had been an alien in my own family, in my own peer group, and in my own religion [she was Jewish]. I never seemed to fit in; I never blended. I was always clashing."[19] Sometimes the teaching of conservative evangelical churches appeared to reinforce these women's sense of worthlessness. Katie Funk Wiebe reflected on the commandment to "love thy neighbor as thyself":

One was supposed to love others, but oneself? . . . During my developing years I so often heard preaching about death to self: "He must increase, I must decrease."

I went through young adulthood feeling that it was scriptural to hate oneself, that it was important to die to self, to become a "nothing" so that Christ could become everything. "Self" and "life" became almost dirty words. A Christian had no right to think of self-actualization. I watched Christians struggling toward the goal of becoming "channels only," "instruments," and "meek, insignificant worms" like Jacob.[20]

Even the single women with money, independence, and successful careers could still find life a "very heavy burden." Eugenia Price had achieved success as a writer but found herself miserable:

I had nothing whatever to say as a writer and I was very heavy. Not only was I at least sixty pounds overweight from so much sitting around cultivating gourmet eating and drinking tastes, but there was so much added "weight" around my heart. . . . Things were heavy for me. In spite of periodic financial success the debt grew heavier and the lies to the creditors grew in proportion to the debts. Naturally I blamed life and that added a heavy load of resentment. I had what I always thought I wanted and then didn't want it enough to accept the responsibility for it. I deceived my parents and one friend in particular. And I hated myself—heavily. But saw no way to change and so eventually dodged behind the thick (heavy) wall of neuroticism and declared more loudly than ever that I loved things just as they were.[21]

What unites all the troubled narrators, besides their pain, is their sense of being unloved and unlovable, of isolation, abandonment, and hatred turned inward. Shirley Boone's preconversion estimate of her self-worth is typical: "I was so supercritical of myself—my figure, my lack of fashion sense—my unworthiness to be Pat's wife—that I could scarcely believe that anyone—even God—could love me."[22]

Yet, though they testify to plenty of psychic and physical suffering and to an all-too-intense awareness of their shortcomings, they do not draw as heavily on the language of sin and eternal punishment as did their predecessors. For instance, they rarely talk as earlier converts did of being suspended over a bottomless pit or of their fear of fire and brimstone. Hell is almost always interior now, or it is to be found in the ordinary world. Elizabeth Burns's description of her psychic pain before conversion, quoted earlier, is not unusual. Another convert recalled her bad times: "To live in terror is to live in hell on earth, and such was my life for seven years." Converts seldom describe themselves in the old designations for sinners such as "vessels of wrath"; they rarely speak of themselves as "worms," as harboring the "old Adam" or possessing a "carnal nature." They speak less persistently of being "convicted" of their sin. Even in the late nineteenth century Henry Drummond reported seeing "very few evidences of the agonizing conviction of sin which was so characteristic a feature of similar movements in the past."[23] Narrators speak freely enough of their undesirable character traits. But the danger is more that they will be condemned to unhappiness in this world rather than that they are threatened with eternal punishment in the next.

At the same time, there are continuities between 1880 and 1980. The threat of eternal damnation has not entirely vanished, nor do references to hell seem wholly rhetorical. One twentieth-century narrator grew up thinking of herself as a "damned soul" (although to be sure the sense of being damned came as much from her social isolation as from her religious convictions).[24] Another writer talked about "our mad hurtling to eternal destruction."[25] Sin has remained a common word in twentieth-century narratives up to the present; it is often the designation narrators give to such preconversion failings as restlessness, possessiveness, jealousy, rebellion, anger, pride, and self-centeredness. Susan Atkins probably had more ample reason than most narrators to apply the word "sin" to her past deeds. As she started to feel guilt about her participation in the Manson murders she imagined that "my mind was clogged with a huge mound, right in front of me. It was a massive pile of dirt, garbage and filth. There in front of me I saw twenty-six years of sins."[26] Satan remains a lively antagonist in narratives of recent decades. One narrator wrote, "The closer I get to Christ, the harder Satan tugs at me."[27]

Yet, despite the continued presence of sin and the devil in late–twentieth-century narratives, their existence has become somewhat problematical; these ideas do not claim nearly the universal assent they did in the early nineteenth century. A significant portion of Americans have come to dissent vigorously from the notion of sin and in particular of a hell of eternal suffering presided over by the devil. Influenced by a powerful cultural relativism, they would also avoid absolute positions on many moral questions. They might regard verbal expression of their anger toward a spouse or parent as healthy rather than blameworthy, and might condone the idea of a couple living together outside of marriage. Probably they would be less likely to hold an individual wholly responsible for her wrongdoing, but rather would place some of the blame on environment, genes, or society. Few of them would regard ideas and thoughts in and of themselves as necessarily wicked. Lost, then, is an older consensus about what constitutes good and evil. This moral ambiguity raises questions for conversion narratives that purport to chronicle movement from sinfulness to blessedness, unless of course the narrator confines herself to a subculture that recognizes absolute definitions of good and bad.

Even in those subcultures, however, the notion of original sin has waned; to many twentieth-century people it seems an unfair notion and seldom figures in recent writings. Most conservative evangelicals would continue to argue that all human beings are sinners, but not so much because they inherit the sin of Adam and Eve—who disobeyed God and were driven from the Garden—as because, being human, they are simply naturally imperfect. As one narrator put it, "sin is simply falling short of God's best or God's perfection." She was echoing Romans 3:23, "all have sinned and come short of the glory of God," a favorite verse of modern evangelicals. Another narrator expressed a similar idea when she defined sin as "a state of brokenness and separation from God."[28] A manual advised, with some disregard for the old orthodoxy, "You are not responsible for the sin of Adam and Eve, you are responsible for your own."[29]

It seems that many twentieth-century narrators, in contrast to earlier prospective converts, learn to talk about "sin" only after their conversions. We might even say that twentieth-century delinquents who come under evangelical influence are trying to find themselves linguistically as well as morally, spiritually, and psychically; they are groping for language to make sense of their past experiences as well as of their futures.

This ignorance of the language of sin is most often a characteristic of twentieth-century converts who have grown up outside the evangelical orbit, but it also applies even to those who have been raised by devout parents in conservative Protestant households. Joni Eareckson, who had grown up in the conservative Reformed Episcopal church, claimed she had only a vague idea of the meaning of sin and sinfulness until she was a teenager, and even then she did not learn to apply the concept to herself until she attended a Young Life weekend. There a camp speaker described sin at some length. Eareckson recalled thinking, "Me, a sinner? I'd never really understood what the word meant. However, now I saw my rebellion in the light of God's perfection. I knew I was a lost sinner, no matter how strange it sounded."[30] Long after her conversion, another narrator was still having difficulty accepting "the fact that I am a sinner."[31] In the nineteenth century a convert would have thoroughly reconciled herself emotionally and intellectually to the idea she was a sinner during the period of conviction; such recognition in fact lay at the core of the conversion process. By the twentieth century, however, the notion of oneself as a "sinner" could be perennially troublesome, even long after conversion.

At the same time there are astonishing continuities between older and more recent narratives. The old-fashioned concept of "legalism" (the mistaken idea that one can *earn* one's salvation—as opposed to having it granted by God—by following Old Testament law or other behavioral precepts) appears surprisingly frequently. Susan Atkins described another convert as one "who had once known the Lord, but had slipped into the clutches of legalism."[32] Another narrator expressed relief that she had escaped "the bondage of religious legalism."[33] A 1971 conversion manual cautioned against the "legalists" who "would like to take all freedom away from the Christian, and put him under interminable 'thou shalts' and 'thou shalt nots.' "[34]

Even more striking is the survival of the words "convict" and "conviction" (in the sense of "accuse" and "accusation") in the twentieth-century narratives. One narrator wrote, "God began to convict me of these faults [a quick temper]."[35] Another recalled, "When the Holy Spirit convicted me, I rebelled even more."[36] Still another related that "The words remained to convict me." Another said, "I . . . was convicted that we had argued about a trifle."[37] Kathryn Kuhlman's biographer referred to the "convicting power of the Holy Spirit" in Kuhlman's life.[38]

At the same time the meaning and context for "conviction" has altered subtly. In the nineteenth century conviction was a recognizable stage—the "period of conviction"—associated mainly (though not always) with the time before conversion, when narrators first realized the full extent of their sinfulness.

Converts in this century seldom go through a formal *period* of conviction, and they speak of being "convicted" on a number of occasions, both before and after conversion, by Christ as well as the Holy Spirit (the traditional convicting agent). Furthermore, the condition of being under conviction can be escaped by appropriate remedial action—doing the right thing. At times, as in the following quotation, the term "conviction" is used as a more secular-minded woman might refer to her conscience; its duration—like that of most bad consciences—is generally much shorter than most nineteenth-century periods of conviction. As one recent convert warned another, newer convert: "Now, don't think you won't ever do anything wrong again, because you're still human. You'll make mistakes, but Christ won't let you get away with them. He'll point them out to you—you'll feel—well, we call it 'convicted.' "[39]

Though the sinful heart is a less constant presence in recent narratives, the language still persists to be drawn on by those who wish. One narrator obviously found it a treasure trove and borrowed extravagantly from it. He spoke as did earlier narrators of "stony," "stubborn," "broken and contrite," and especially "hardened" hearts. And, faced with a "tough" heart, he prayed, "Touch this heart that is so hardened against Thee, and melt it with thy loving presence."[40] Evangelist Billy Graham and his converts have often referred to God "entering," "coming into," or "changing" their hearts, or of "inviting" him into their hearts. They also spoke occasionally of their "hard" hearts: "I still hardened my heart toward Him."[41]

THE LANGUAGE OF CONVERSION

Some twentieth-century converts have written with relish about the event of conversion, describing visions, dreams, and conversations with Jesus Christ. Susan Atkins, for example, imagined that Jesus was asking her to open a door she suddenly could picture in her mind. When she opened it,

> The whitest, most brilliant light I had ever seen poured over me. I was standing in darkness, but the light pushed the darkness completely out of sight. It vanished behind me. There was only light. And in the center of the flood of brightness was an even brighter light. Vaguely, there was the form of a man. I knew it was Jesus.
>
> He spoke to me—literally, plainly, matter-of-factly spoke to me in my 9-by-11 prison cell: "Susan, I am really here. I'm really coming into your heart to stay. Right now you are being born again and you will live with me in heaven through all eternity, forever and ever. This is really happening. This is not a dream. You are now a child of God. You are washed clean and your sins have all been forgiven." . . .
>
> For the first time in my memory I felt clean, fully clean, inside and out. In twenty-six years I had never been so happy.
>
> I have no idea how long I lay awake in the night. When I did slip off into unconsciousness, I slept soundly for the first time in many years, free of nightmares—unafraid and warm.[42]

Liz Burns's conversion as she described it, while more ambiguous in its meaning, was also dramatic and brought radical change into her life. On the whole, however, the nineteenth-century trend away from the expenditure of verbal energy on the moment or moments of conversion has continued. There are a couple of possible reasons for this. First, for many converts the event of conversion has become only one of several possible high points to punctuate one's religious life. And, even if it has been the initiating event, it has not necessarily been the most vivid or memorable of the high points. Once converted, a believer might well go on to experience the reconsecration of sanctification and, less universally, the baptism of the Holy Spirit and divine healing. These newer experiences became widely sought or available only in the late nineteenth century—or, in the case of the pentecostal experience, in the early twentieth century. Once available, however, they heralded a series of close encounters with the persons of the Trinity, especially Jesus Christ and the Holy Spirit, that might well continue all one's life, diminishing the significance of the original event of conversion.

A second reason that the event of conversion has declined somewhat in prominence is that the late nineteenth and twentieth centuries have tended to emphasize the "decision" for Christ and increasingly the decision has been made in a public forum not conducive to the experience of dreams and visions. (And it might be said, too, that the twentieth century itself has not been particularly hospitable to revelations by religious dreams and visions, which even the devout tend to regard with some skepticism.)

Thus, since conversion has often received only brief narrative mention, it has lent itself even more frequently to formula than earlier. Narrators have drawn on a small store of phrases to signify this event. Two formulas recur in great number. First, probably the most persistent one-sentence signification of conversion has been for a narrator to say that she had "accepted Christ as her personal Lord and Savior" (or, less frequently, "as Lord of her life"). Second, narrators have spoken repeatedly of "surrendering," "yielding," or "giving" themselves or their lives to Christ. Male as well as female narrators have used this formulation, but it is particularly striking in connection with women, who are normally seen as "yielding" or "surrendering" themselves sexually. Also common, narrators have spoken of having "asked" or "invited" or "received" Jesus Christ (or the "Lord Jesus") into their lives (or sometimes their hearts). They have also recalled "finding," "meeting," "coming to know," or "turning to" Jesus Christ, or they describe themselves as having been "converted," "saved," "born again" or "become a Christian" (the last formula is possible because converts perceive so much of the culture as either not Christian at all or as not *truly* Christian in the sense they mean it). All these formulations come from the point of view of the convert. Another set of phrases has originated with evangelists in their role of agents in the conversion of others. They have reported "leading" or "winning" or "bringing" someone "to Christ," or sometimes "reaching" someone "for Christ."

There are several observations to be made about these ways of describing conversion. First, the heart is less likely than in the nineteenth century to be an actor in the transaction. "Receiving a new heart" has been a relatively uncommon way of speaking about one's conversion, although narrators still routinely talk about the Holy Spirit or Jesus entering or coming into their hearts, or they may speak of inviting him into their hearts. The recent diminution in the heart's role may result from its close association with the emotions, the very association that accounted for its popularity in the nineteenth century.

Second, the convert usually speaks in the active voice; she *accepts* Christ as her savior rather than is *accepted by* him. Even when she "yields" or "surrenders"—actions that suggest passivity—she describes herself as making the decision, initiating the essential movement in the transaction. She is seldom *forced* to yield or surrender. In fact, she is rarely *acted upon*, unless sometimes by evangelists. The God who ravishes or enthralls has been left far behind; even the Holy Spirit has ceased to "strive" with the sinner, or to "break" her heart. Jesus, it is true, still knocks, in an allusion to the well-loved passage from Revelation, but the would-be convert must decide to open the door of her being to him. Thus, she seems, to a larger degree than formerly, responsible for her own conversion (though not for saving grace, which only God can confer); the emerging Arminianism of the nineteenth century has become a firm fixture of the twentieth.

Third, some of the usual early–nineteenth-century formulations are absent. Converts rarely refer to conversion as a matter of gaining a "hope" or "assurance" of salvation; the uncertainty or tentative note appropriate to an earlier time has been replaced by assurance. In fact, the reference to being "saved" has become less pervasive as the century has passed, probably because the question of one's soteriological status has diminished in importance. Narrators also rarely refer to a "new birth," a common nineteenth-century phrase, though of course they allude to the same idea in different words when they speak of being "born again."

If the formulations for conversion have changed somewhat, many of the agents that help bring it about have remained strikingly the same. Potential converts reach the point of "accepting Christ as their Savior" through the ministrations of a converted friend or relative, through hearing someone else's testimony to conversion, through reading a devotional book, pamphlet, or scriptural verse, or through attending a conference, sermon, or revival. As narrators once experienced conversion in nineteenth-century seminaries and colleges, now they do so in self-styled "Christian" or "evangelical" schools and in Bible institutes. New agents, however, have also made their appearance. In the twenties radio preachers made their first converts. Several decades later, televangelists such as Pat Robertson, Jim Bakker, Robert Schuller, and Jimmy Swaggert took advantage of television to win souls.

THE "FRUITS" OF CONVERSION

Once converted, narrators have enjoyed some of the same consequences as their nineteenth-century counterparts. Most notably, narrators have told of being propelled into a life of Christian service: entering the pastorate (mostly in the case of men), becoming foreign missionaries, Bible and Sunday school teachers, and lay evangelists. Converts have had more lay organizations to choose from than formerly: the YMCA and YWCA, the Salvation Army, Christian men and women's clubs, Christian businessmen's organizations, and groups for high school and college students such as Youth for Christ and Intervarsity. In many of these organizations converts have been able to work as paid professionals.

Another consequence of conversion, as earlier, is a character change. As in the nineteenth century the convert is expected to become "Christlike": humble, uncomplaining, unselfish, loving, tolerant, slow to lose her temper. Certain "Christlike" qualities no longer receive unqualified praise, however, even for women, for instance, meekness. (It is often better to be "bold for Christ" or "on fire for souls.") Usually the convert is expected to give up certain of life's "entertainments": drinking, smoking, gambling (including card playing), and dancing. Many of these "worldly pleasures" are activities traditionally renounced by converts, except that in the nineteenth century women had fewer occasions to abandon them, seldom having indulged in them in the first place. And new entertainments have been added to the proscribed list: drugs, movies (except for approved, "wholesome" ones), some kinds of jazz and rock, many television shows.

The designations for those who serve "their Lord" have changed slowly. Christian workers are less likely be be called God's "instrumentalities." Sometimes they continue as his "vessels," probably owing to the continued popularity of the King James phrasings. In the most old-fashioned circles they continue to be "watchmen on the wall"—though this designation, with its military connotations, less often applies to female Christian workers. Converts are occasionally "washed in Christ's blood," but they are less often "robed" or "clothed" in "his righteousness" than in the nineteenth century. The convert continues to be a "child of God," or even a "babe in Christ"; these are popular ascriptions no matter what the convert's age or sex. Converts who manage to retain or renew the first joy of conversion are often described as "radiant," "earnest" Christians who lead "wholesome" lives.

An interesting new element in the language of the convert is the constant reference to a "*personal* relationship" with Christ or to Christ as one's "*personal* Savior." (We have already noted the frequency of the formulation, "to accept Jesus Christ as one's *personal* Savior.") The idea is expressed in many ways. One narrator realized that "Jesus died for me, *personally*"; others referred to their "*personal* knowledge of Jesus Christ," or to knowing him "*personally*," or to "being loved by a *personal* Jesus" (my emphases). As these quotations suggest, the idea of a personal divinity was marked by a preference for Jesus Christ the Son over the God the Father. The Father was largely inscrutable, but the Son could be known from the gospel narratives. As the heroine of a 1930 novel explained, she couldn't know God the Father, but Jesus Christ is a "Person": "I must know the Person to love Him," she insisted.[43]

The allusions to Jesus as a personal savior and the many variants of this idea seem to contain a couple of intertwined meanings. First, the argument is that God is a person, not an impersonal force nor a doctrine, and he shares many of the more positive characteristics we associate with human persons, such as the ability to love and care deeply. Second, the adjective "personal" refers back to the worshiper: God, a good democrat, acknowledges and responds to each human being as a *person*, as a unique and valuable individual. He does not see humanity in the mass but rather recognizes that each person is different, with his or her own important needs and concerns.

It is difficult to pinpoint exactly when the adjective "personal" first appeared in this connection; it occurred occasionally in the nineteenth century, for instance in the sermons and writings of Dwight L. Moody. On the other hand, it is absent from a 1909 report on a series of Boston revivals, though the report abounds in so many other brief formulations for conversion that we might reasonably expect to meet it.[44] In 1922 William Jennings Bryan, the darling of conservative evangelicals, wrote about the necessity for belief in a "personal" God, rather than one who was "remote" and "distant." By 1930 the notion of a personal God and a personal relationship with him had become stock language for converts.

Why has this ascription come into such prominence in the narratives in recent decades? In part it is probably a reaction to the prominence of scientific theories that either have ignored the question of God's existence or reduced the deity to the status of an impersonal force in nature; in particular it was a response to the theory of evolution in which God, if he appeared at all, had only a remote, hands-off role in the history of natural and human affairs. The insistence on a personal relationship with God was also a culmination of the rising tide of reaction to Calvinism. Calvinist theology had emphasized the sovereignty and transcendence of God, his glory and his majestic distance from human concerns. Those who rebelled against Calvinism desired just the opposite: a divinity who was loving, caring, and immanent in daily human life, who involved himself in even the most minute concerns of his children.

The desire for a closer relationship with a *person*—usually Jesus Christ— is signified in a number of ways. In the twentieth century Jesus is often called a "Friend" or "Companion." He is addressed more colloquially and informally than in the past. Narrators often speak to and about him simply as "Jesus." They sometimes conclude prayer requests to him with "thank you, Jesus," rather than the more formal "amen." A prospective convert noticed that her born-again correspondent "almost always used the name 'Jesus,' not 'Christ.' Even on paper this seemed to make a difference."[45] The "difference" was that Jesus seemed closer, more alive, more accessible. Often he has become the partner in an intimate conversation. Converts customarily report that they "spoke to the Lord about" or "had a talk with the Lord about" a worry or concern; the worry did not need to be a major one. One nonconvert observed that a converted acquaintance "talked about God as if he were someone she knew very well. A Friend. Someone who cared about you." Conversely, her dilemma was that to her "God was someone or something vague, someone too busy with more important problems to pay attention to hers."[46]

In the more informal atmosphere of twentieth-century worship and prayer it has seemed suitable to bring slang into transactions with "the Lord." In an introduction to a conversion narrative, Catherine Marshall writes familiarly, "He 'gets a charge' out of seeing these rescued ones grow so fast in the faith that they overtake and overrun us plodders in the Kingdom."[47] A businessman can signify his conversion in businessman's language: "I'll buy it." A manual counsels, "put your life under new management."[48] In fact, as befits a close, good-natured companion, the Lord enjoys a joke or a humorous approach and is willing to laugh gently at his fractious flock, stances that were rare in earlier centuries. After an earthquake Dale Evans Rogers remarked to God, "You certainly shook us up with that one!"[49] Jennifer Vanderford confides that "One day I prayed one of those 'tell the Lord what to do prayers.' " She asked that two people she was furious with not drop in to visit her. "You've promised not to put on us more than we can bear; and, Lord, you know that would be more than I can bear! so please don't allow these people to visit. Okay, Lord? Amen." Despite her exhortations, the two undesirables appeared anyway: "I thought, 'I need to talk to the Lord about this!' I said, 'Now Lord,' (I should know by now not to begin a prayer with 'Now Lord'!) 'I'm simply not going to the door! I asked You not to let this happen!' " Later the same narrator, in a dark moment, expostulated, "Lord, if you don't guide us, we're doomed." She heard the Lord respond, "Poor Jennifer, I was wondering when she would give up and trust Me completely."[50] Similarly, Catherine Marshall pictured Jesus as "a trifle amused at my too intense seriousness about myself."[51]

One "fruit" of conversion is the obligation for converts to tell their stories— to testify, to witness, to "share their faith." Again and again narrators refer to this responsibility. One convert compared herself to the demoniac whom Jesus instructed to "tell the people what I have done for you." Another quoted Psalm 26: "I say publish with the voice of thanksgiving and tell of thy wonderful works." A third expressed confidence that "by my example, people would be able to know how good God is and how he heals." In an aside to readers meant to draw them in she added the hope "that you can gain strength from my story; I pray that it will be a blessing to you. . . . I know, it has happened to me."[52] Yet another convert wrote directly to readers, "You can be convinced that eternal life is available to you by looking at my eternal life and believing that if this wonder is for such as I, it can be for such as you, too."[53]

The obligation to tell one's story may be much the same as in the nineteenth century, but the conditions in which this "witnessing for Christ" is done have altered substantially. Nineteenth-century narratives suggest that witnessing was done more easily, naturally, and spontaneously than in the twentieth century. Despite the convention of the scoffer, those who told the stories of their conversions were accustomed to a receptive and understanding audience; they benefited from living in a culture that was fundamentally Protestant and evangelical and accustomed to the notion of conversion. Often those who remained unwilling or unable to be converted felt guilty, anxious, and out of step. Rarely did they need to be told what was at stake in rejecting or postponing the "new birth"; they knew full well they were not only flouting society's norms but also endangering their immortal souls.

As the nineteenth century gave way to the twentieth, however, a religiously much more diverse culture began to present formidable obstacles to Christian witness. If the potential convert had grown up outside Protestant evangelical circles, her conversion required more thorough instruction. Lacking society's automatic collaboration, it also required more effective persuasion. The danger increased that the one who told her conversion story might incur ridicule, not only from former companions in sin but also from the society at large. Conversion to be successfully induced required of the evangelist greater skill, thought, and tact. It also demanded the courage to face the possible rejection of one's efforts, for the twentieth-century culture turned out to abound with scoffers. These difficulties are often reflected in the narratives, which begin to deal self-consciously with problems of credibility, effective expression, and the narrator's stance toward a sometimes hostile world.

Thus, a convert described a friend's warning, "Now, Regina, don't get fanatical, you'll lose all your friends." Dale Evans Rogers recalled that when acquaintances heard she had been converted, many assumed she "was on some sort of 'religious kick.' "[54] When another convert told her husband she had become a Christian, he exploded, "You're nuts. People who believe in Jesus are a bunch of hypocrites. Forget it." The same convert anticipated the reaction of her agnostic (and probably liberated) friends: "They wouldn't understand my humbling myself in front of God."[55] Even a seasoned convert who often spoke of her experience before audiences recalled encountering "those who openly jeer, who assail with bitter words, and rise up in open rebellion."[56]

Of course, as the somewhat formal and old-fashioned sound of the last quotation suggests, twentieth-century narrators *could* draw on a rhetorical tradition which portrayed Christianity as unjustly scorned and God as mocked. Not only was it reassuring to see twentieth-century scoffers as part of a long lineage of wicked folk (starting with the Romans who threw Christians to the lions) who were bound to be confounded in the end; whatever the reality, it was also useful to cast those scoffers in roles as loners and outcasts.

Converts in their enlarged roles as teachers and persuaders had to teach not only the necessity or desirability of conversion but also the centrality of other experiences that were relatively unknown until the late nineteenth century. The next chapter describes the narrative languages they created to describe these new events.

FIVE

Finding Words
for New Experiences

Several new experiences—each with its own distinctive discourse—trans-formed the conversion narratives of the twentieth century, chief among them holiness and pentecostalism. Advocates of holiness or sanctification taught that Christians could achieve or at least approach "sinless perfection"; holiness was variously regarded as an experience (one entered into holiness or was sanctified in a short span of time, usually moments or hours), a way of life, and a doctrine.[1] Holiness was an old idea. Adherents claimed that it was scriptural, and in some sense it was (see, e.g., Lev. 20:7: "Sanctify yourselves therefore, and be ye holy"); some advocates drew on Walter Marshall's *Gospel Mystery of Sanctification* (1690). Still others looked to John Wesley, who had advanced holiness, though this particular teaching had vanished from the Methodist manual of practice, *The Discipline*, by the early nineteenth century. In the 1830s two American Methodist sisters, Phoebe Palmer and Sarah Lankford, revived the teaching through their weekly "Tuesday Meeting for the Promotion of Holiness." During the second half of the nineteenth century the idea spread to other denominations. In England the teaching was institutionalized in the Keswick meeting, started in 1875. By the late nineteenth century many of the major American Protestant leaders claimed to have undergone an experience of holiness or sanctification; Dwight L. Moody, A. J. Gordon, A. B. Simpson, Hannah Whitall Smith—and many in the pews as well—professed the experience. Holiness teachings early found their way into African-American Protestant circles as well, as, for instance, the narratives of Jarena Lee (1843) and Julia A. J. Foote (1886) attest.[2]

Basically, entering into holiness or being sanctified meant letting God take over one's entire life, in all its dimensions. This "surrendered" attitude often entailed living what was called "the life of faith," in which the Christian committed herself to serve the Lord and let him worry about how she was to survive economically. Increasingly, holiness came also to involve the related belief in divine healing. Letting God manage one's life meant letting him take care of one's health as well.

Ultimately to some, divine control of one's life included even control of one's language, one's tongue. This was one of the core ideas behind pentecostalism as it emerged in the late nineteenth and early twentieth centuries. Initially, however, reference to "Pentecost" usually suggested simply a very intense experience of the Holy Spirit, a revival of interest in the Third Person of the Trinity. Shortly after 1900 pentecostalism came to focus particularly on glossolalia, that is, the practice of speaking in tongues (either an unknown one or at least one unknown to the speaker) under the inspiration of the Holy Spirit. The scriptural warrant for "tongues" was Acts 2:4, which describes the day of Pentecost: "And they were all filled with the Holy Ghost, and began to speak with other tongues, as the Spirit gave them utterance."

For most of the twentieth century, pentecostalism has been confined mainly to those in the "pentecostal" denominations, most notably the Assemblies of God. Pentecostals came primarily from the lower or lower middle classes and were disdained by other Protestants as ill educated and overly excitable. Pentecostalism has strongly attracted blacks. The experience has also had a strong appeal for women, who, rather than having to struggle for a place in a church's male power structure, could claim religious authority by virtue of their experience of the Spirit. It was not unusual for women to become pentecostal ministers long before they could achieve ordination in most orthodox denominations. Aimee Semple McPherson, founder in the twenties of the Foursquare Gospel Church, achieved considerable fame and notoriety through her prominence in the tongues movement. In part because of the social and gender identifications of pentecostals and in part because of the high emotional excitement associated with the experience—so threatening to orderly religious and denominational life—most other conservative evangelicals frowned upon the practice. They acknowledged that the "gift" of speaking in tongues had characterized biblical times but insisted they did not expect to see a genuine recurrence of such gifts in the present.

Pentecostalism, a persistent if widely scorned strand of American religious life in the early twentieth century, enjoyed a revival between the end of World War II and the mid-fifties, especially in the evangelistic ministries of William Branham and Oral Roberts. For these men, who toured the country holding large tent meetings, the "gifts of the Holy Spirit" meant not only speaking in tongues but also divine healing, that is, the practice of asking God to cure sickness and believing he actually would. The revival dwindled briefly, only to rekindle in the sixties. This time pentecostalism was no longer confined to the traditional pentecostal denominations but also affected a significant minority of Protestants in the mainline churches and even Roman Catholics. In its most recent, more catholic, manifestation, pentecostalism has often been called "neo-pentecostalism," or the "charismatic movement." Belief in the "gifts of the Spirit," extending to such matters as prophecy and demonology as well as glossolalia and divine healing, gained a popularity and respectability they had never enjoyed before.[3]

Obviously, if these new experiences were to be incorporated into narratives, they required new vocabularies for their expression. These they received—partially new, partially derived from the Bible, and partially adapted from already existing language for spiritual experience.

EXPRESSING HOLINESS

From the mid-nineteenth century on the experience and language of holiness entered increasingly into conversion narratives. Narrators began referring not only to their conversion and its consequences but also to that later climactic event known as holiness or sanctification. By the mid-twentieth century the language of holiness had pervaded so many of the narratives that some recent narrators have used the rhetoric without alluding to the doctrine, and indeed without even invoking the words "holiness" or "sanctification." Thus, believers have used shorthand designations for the sanctified life. They have called it a "life of rest" (that is, rest from worry and care, because everything was left up to God), or sometimes "the victorious life" (i.e., victory over sin), or a "life of fulness" (echoing a frequent scriptural term, e.g., "filled with all the fulness of God"—Eph. 3:19).

Recent narrators have sometimes treated sanctification as equal in importance to conversion itself. To judge from some of the narratives, in fact, the experience of holiness has changed their lives more fundamentally than conversion. As motives for tacitly devaluing conversion, narrators may have begun to feel that conversion was too easy, too inexpensively obtained, and therefore less than emotionally satisfying. Despite an initial period of elation, the supposed fruits of conversion could turn out to be elusive. One could undergo conversion and still quickly revert to sin and spiritual lassitude. Indeed, one could be downright mistaken in one's claim to conversion. Talk and gestures were cheap. Already in about 1915 Elizabeth V. Baker was contrasting her father's earlier soul winning activities with the efforts she saw around her. Her father's achievements, she said, were "Not like modern revivals so-called, where men sign cards and are taken into Church fellowship," but rather were achieved "through mighty soul travail when the unsaved were taken upon his heart, and held before the throne in an agony of desire and prayer."[4] A 1935 observer noted that "We today calculate conversions by raised hands or signed cards or seats occupied in the enquiry [*sic*] room." This was all very well, he conceded, but some of these "conversions" would turn out to be false, and their consequences would not be felt much beyond the revival that brought the raised hand or signed card in the first place.[5]

The experience of holiness resolved this dilemma of "cheap" grace; holiness was not only an event in time, a few moments when one became "sanctified," but also a way of life. Sanctified believers *acted* differently, so that even children and animals were supposed to be able to discern the change. The sanctified betrayed little anxiety and worry about the minor or major troubles of their lives. They simply shifted their problems onto the Lord; he either brought about a solution, pointed the way to one, or gave believers the strength to suffer, endure, and learn from what could not be changed. Believers who had lost a purse, for example, only needed to pray about it and, if the Lord was willing, the article would show up. Those troubled about a course of action would often be led to the "answer" in just the right biblical passage. Or they might encounter a person who unwittingly indicated a direction. If conversion sometimes seemed cheapened by the methods of mass evangelism, one could turn to sanctification for a more authentic experience and a deeper piety. For better or worse, holiness raised the spiritual ante by increasing the expectations and rigors of the religious life.[6]

Some holiness adherents claimed that sanctified persons ceased to sin, that is, sin ceased to wield real influence over their lives. As one successful seeker after holiness put it, "I knew God was working in my life to save me not only from the past penalty of sin, but also its present power, . . . "[7] Other more Calvinistic adherents took a more cautious position; they taught that the state of sanctification helped believers to *counteract* the temptation to sin in the present. Both claims differed from those made for conversion: when believers accepted God's offer of grace and were converted they were simply "justified," that is, they were released from the penalty of their past and future sins; they were rescued from eternal punishment, but not from the disposition to act sinfully in this life. They were "redeemed" sinners, but *sinners* they remained.

The altered understanding of sin and grace that emerged with holiness obviously required a different language. Those who wrote about holiness typically drew upon a special vocabulary. First, they were likely to quote certain biblical texts, chief among them, "Be ye therefore perfect, even as your Father which is in heaven is perfect" (Matt. 5:48). Another favorite passage was Galatians 2:20: "I am crucified with Christ: nevertheless I live, yet not I, but Christ liveth in me." This passage was one of the prime sources for the holiness claim that when believers were sanctified their old selves "died," disappeared ("I am crucified with Christ"). It was also a locus for the conviction that when believers experienced sanctification, Christ began to "live," "abide," "take up residence," and "dwell" in them (sometimes it was said he became "indwelling" in them or simply that he "indwelt them"). Usually Christ was said to accomplish this indwelling through the agency of the third person in the Trinity, the Holy Spirit. Thus, one narrator put it, "Jesus Christ [came] to indwell me in the Person of the Holy Spirit."[8] Several other biblical texts appeared to affirm this idea of "Christ in us," and also to encourage the choice of "dwell," for example, John 6:56, "He . . . dwelleth in me, and I in him," Romans 8:11, "by his Spirit that dwelleth in you", and 1 John 4:12, "If we love one another, God dwelleth in us, and his love is perfected in us."

Certain other biblical verses were regarded by sanctified believers as containing divine "promises" that made a life of holiness possible. Probably the one they most often cited was the last verse of Matthew: "lo, I am with you always, even unto the end of the world" (28:20). Another example of such a "promise" was Luke 1:74–75: "that he would grant unto us, that we being delivered out of the hand of our enemies might serve him without fear, in holiness and righteousness before him, all the days of our life." Sanctified narrators customarily spoke of "claiming" promises such as these, or, alternatively, "stepping out on" or "resting on" these promises.

A hallmark of sanctification was for the believer to speak of relying wholly on God, rather than on herself. To be sure, this was traditional Christian teaching, except that holiness advocates meant total reliance on God in their mundane affairs as well as in their life crises.[9] The sanctified woman was to give up all effort and struggle and let God act in her life. Her will was to operate in harmony with his ("Not my will but Thine"). Frequently, sanctified persons used the word "surrendered" to describe their new attitudes; they asserted that their souls or hearts were "surrendered" to God. There is potential for confusion here: the word "surrender" was often used by believers when they described the experience of conversion as well. Usually the context indicates which kind of "surrender" is meant. In addition, when believers used the word "surrender" to refer to sanctification they often intensified it: the believer was not merely "surrendered" but *"wholly"* or *"completely"* or *"totally"* surrendered. In addition to surrendering themselves, believers might also "surrender" a gravely ill child or spouse to God, that is, they willingly turned over that person's fate into God's hands. They also "surrendered" their "burdens" to God, for instance, their doubts, their failures, their temptations, and the other undesirable circumstances of their lives. When one narrator wrote, "I 'surrendered' having to make an appearance at a radio station in my wrinkled suit," she meant that she was bowing to the necessity of having to show up for her appointment looking rumpled. Although she didn't *like* to appear in a disheveled state, she acquiesced in God's will.[10]

The sanctified used other phrases to express this idea of utter reliance on God: the "wholly yielded heart," for example, was one that was completely surrendered to God; sanctified persons were also said to be "totally dependent" on God. One narrator wrote, "My whole dependence must be on him [God]." Believers might express their closeness to God or their unity with him by speaking of "a closer walk" with him. One narrator welcomed what she called "a moment-by-moment walk in fellowship with him."[11] Completely surrendered believers, drawing from an abundance of biblical passages, would often talk about putting their "trust" in God or "trusting all" to him. Echoing 2 Cor. 12:9 ("my grace is sufficient for thee"), they would say that entire dependence on God was possible and desirable because his grace was "sufficient."

One of the things for which the sanctified person trusted God was an answer to her prayers. She might assert she looked to a "prayer-answering" God. He did not respond to prayers automatically, of course. The thing or action prayed for must be appropriate for the petitioner. Sanctified persons who did not get an expeditious answer to their prayers were advised to search their hearts and consciences to discover any secret sins they might still harbor or any parts of themselves they might be holding back from complete surrender to God. For instance, a woman whose husband had died appeared to be completely "yielded" to God: she accepted his death as the will of God. Eventually she prayed that the Lord might give her a useful ministry, but time passed and nothing happened. At length she realized that God had failed to respond to her prayer because she had withheld part of herself from him; unwilling to give up all of her past life with her husband, she had continued to live in the house the two of them had shared. Once she was able to surrender even the house and its precious memories, God sent her a prosperous ministry.[12]

In addition to expecting God to answer their prayers, sanctified persons also trusted him to provide all their material and spiritual necessities. He would "supply" courage to deal with a loved one's death or a painful illness; he would heal sickness (if that was his will); he would send money as needed, particularly if it was meant for religious causes; he would direct a sanctified person to an advertisement for the rental house that was needed. One woman learned "to look to the Lord in confidence for the little things as well as the big."[13]

Sanctified believers have habitually spoken of God's "leadings," that is, God's guidance in their lives. This idea was not of course new: Christians had long referred to God's plan or purpose or will for them, especially when they considered life's most important decisions. They might assert that God was "leading" them to marry a certain person or to go to China as a missionary. New England Puritans had spoken constantly of God's "providences." What sanctification did was to intensify this sense that God was telling them what to do and to extend the conviction of his guidance to the smallest details of their personal lives. They might say, for instance, "I felt led to buy a newspaper," or "The Lord led me to visit my aunt." A camp meeting speaker lost his prepared speech on the way to the camp; rather than fuming at his own stupidity or scrambling madly to rewrite the speech, he remained calm: "I accepted the loss as God's leading that in camp we must trust *all* to Him, and that He would say what should be said, through me or through others." What he meant was that he planned to speak extemporaneously, confident that when the time came the Lord would provide the right words.[14]

Because sanctified persons were so thoroughly convinced of God's "leading" in every area of their lives, they developed a multitude of ways of referring to God's will or plan for them. They would assert, for instance, that God "is at work in our lives [or in my life]"; "This is the Lord's doing," they might say, or "it was of the Lord." They would speak of their own actions as "in the Lord's will," that is, their actions were in accordance with divine will. Frequently they would announce that "God spoke to me" or "God spoke to my heart," or they might say "the Lord is telling me to do it." It was common for them to claim that the Lord "spoke" to them through a Bible verse that they heard, read, or remembered. When a contemplated course of action became possible they would declare that "the Lord had opened the way," or simply that "the way opened." One young evangelical, Jim Truxton, hoping the woman he loved would be able to visit him in California, wrote her that he was "confident that if this is the will of the Lord he will make a way, so long as we are alert to the means he provides." The narrator went on to explain, "Jim was endeavoring to be alert to God's leading both for Betty and himself." Betty was offered a ride and on the basis of that decided that her relationship with Jim must be "in the Lord's will."[15]

A life of holiness entailed a strenuous life of perfectionism. As one writer put it, "The Spirit comes in to master the life so that self goes and every passion and power and prejudice is brought under divine control."[16] Ideally, the sanctified person was all the things a converted person was supposed to be, only more steadily and intensely. She was sweet-tempered, slow to complain, humble, loving, cheerful, and tolerant of the faults of others.

Holiness advocates were loath to describe the nether side of sanctification. True, surrendering their lives to God removed many of the ordinary causes for human stress and anxiety. At its best the experience brought them peace and serenity—"rest," as adherents claimed. But no human being could manage to remain completely surrendered all the time. It was difficult to stay unruffled while facing a spouse's wrath or watching one's own child suffer. Holiness was said to permit a cessation of human struggle; many times it apparently did so. But one still needed to expend enormous effort in order to remain surrendered. For human beings—even sanctified ones—it sometimes took prodigious struggle to refrain from struggling!

Notwithstanding the paradoxes in holiness language—struggle and utter cessation from struggle—it's hard to miss the fact that this was a rhetoric about extreme dependence on a male Person. On an all powerful Father? On a Husband? It takes little imagination to understand its attractiveness to many women (and of course also men, but *especially* women). Nor is it difficult to comprehend the disgust which holiness teachings would elicit in those who have worked for and called for greater autonomy and self-reliance for women. But the issue is complex: the fact that the utter dependence is upon *God* rather than upon human males alters the usual dynamics of female submission, as we shall see in chapter 7.

YIELDING ONE'S TONGUE

Holiness has been a novel episode in the conversion narrative, in need of a new vocabulary; pentecostalism has been viewed as an even newer and stranger experience. Some who have undergone it have been unable to name or categorize it at the time; as a child, one narrator

> was standing in her father's orchard in Ohio one day, looking up through clouds of white blossoms to the blue sky overhead, when suddenly she had an overwhelming experience of the presence of God. She opened her mouth to talk to Him in the unself-conscious way of children, but the sounds which came out of her mouth were not English, and though she prattled along fluently for a while, her lips would form no sensible words at all.[17]

In fact, holiness was not nearly as difficult to integrate into the pattern of conversion and spiritual growth, since it involved mostly an intensification and elaboration of old themes already common in devotional literature. A decorous experience, it could be fairly easily assimilated into middle-class religious experience. Pentecostalism was another story: it often involved speaking in unknown languages in public, not infrequently at the top of one's lungs; raising one's arms skyward and shouting "Praise the Lord"; and emulating the worship practices of blacks or poor whites. Understandably, it took a while to catch on among middle-class white evangelicals.

For its first five decades, then, pentecostalism was confined generally to the lower castes of American society and thus was defined by those castes. Such folk tended to espouse biblical literalism, and so their attempts to describe the pentecostal phenomenon leaned heavily on scriptural phrasing. They had other reasons to appeal to biblical undergirding as well: often under attack from nonpentecostal fundamentalists, they doubtless derived comfort from quoting Scripture to support their beliefs and practices. Then again, the experience was difficult to express in ordinary language and biblical formulas were for this reason most welcome. Even in the past decade or two, when pentecostalism has become more respectable and more widely practiced, guides to the experience still typically begin with a survey of what the Bible has to say on the subject of "tongues" and on the activity of the Holy Spirit in the believer.

The precise temporal and logical relationship between the experiences of holiness and pentecostalism is unclear and has been a vexed topic since the early twentieth century. Often the same person undergoes both—and often holiness comes first—but a given narrator tends to give priority to one or the other. Pentecostals have customarily referred to their experience as a "baptism in" or "baptism with" the "Holy Spirit," a phrase used several times in the gospels: Jesus, it is promised, will "baptize" his followers with "the Holy Ghost." Less frequently the baptism is with "fire," presumably because in Acts 2:3 "cloven tongues like as of fire" hovered over the heads of those who were being filled with the Spirit. Marjorie Holmes experienced the Holy Spirit as a flame: "I prayed for the Holy Spirit to come into me, Lord. I prayed for the fullness of its fire, destroying the old proud, rebellious, selfish, foolish me. And the sweet fire came and I was purged for a time. For a time, I was freed."[18]

In addition to describing being "baptized in the Spirit," pentecostals speak in scriptural fashion of "receiving" the Spirit; they are also "filled with" the Spirit (see Acts 2:4). The Holy Spirit is sometimes said to "fall upon" a person (Acts 10:44: "the Holy Ghost fell on all them which heard the word"), though the description probably suggests too much force and violence for some pentecostals. More gently, the Spirit also is said to "proceed from God" and to "come upon" the believer (Acts 1:8).

The usual King James designation for the third person of the Trinity is "Holy Ghost." As might be expected, twentieth-century pentecostals have adopted this usage—especially when they want to sound a little raw or stark, as befits exponents of the "old-time religion." But many pentecostals seem to prefer the softer term, "Holy Spirit." They also commonly call the Holy Spirit "the Comforter" (John 14:26). While under the impact of the experience, pentecostals often raise their hands toward heaven (see 1 Tim. 2:8—"lifting up holy hands"). Once believers have received the Holy Spirit, he remains to dwell within them; they continue to be "quickened" by him, to be "Spirit-filled" and "Spirit-led." But however intense the initial baptism in the Spirit, believers periodically need to undergo a "new inflow of the Holy Spirit."

Pentecostals often perceive the reception of the Spirit as an intense sensual experience. No two baptisms in the Spirit are identical, but believers customarily write of floating, or of feeling physically washed clean. Frequently they respond to the coming of the Spirit by weeping or laughing or singing. They recall themselves trembling, quivering, or stammering. They report feeling the Spirit "flow in" (the "inflowing of the Spirit"), as if it were water, light, fire, warmth, or electricity. Early in the twentieth century water in the form of rain was a frequent image, for pentecostalism was spoken of as the "latter rain" movement. In 1910 a pentecostal writer advised metaphorically, "please don't come with umbrella or rain-coat. Just stay out in your common clothes in the latter rain, and let it wet you to the skin, let it go through the skin down into the bones and into the marrow."[19] This "latter rain" usage has become much less common in recent decades.

Certain themes recur in pentecostal utterance. Pentecostals repeatedly refer to speaking in tongues as "praising" God—or "praise" for him. Pentecostals who use their gifts, for example, of healing or praying "in the Spirit," to help others are designated as "channels." Often baptism in the Spirit is described as an inflowing of divine love.

Some narrators reduce their description to the simplest terms, saying only that they were "baptized with the Spirit and spoke in tongues," or, alternatively, that they "received the Spirit." Others narrate the experience at some length. Which they do may depend on the intensity of the experience and their facility with language, but perhaps even more on how they perceive their audience. If they address those already familiar with the experience (whether or not they have undergone it), they can use shorthand expressions; if, however, they are trying to educate their audience, to attract them to an experience novel to most of them, they may take the time and energy to search for vivid words and more complete explanation.

A twelve-year-old girl, after listening to others' accounts of the experience, herself underwent a baptism in the Spirit:

> I went into the chapel one day to pray by myself. I started telling God all about my problems and I asked Him to come into my life like He had to those drug addicts. Like a blinding light, Jesus burst into my heart. Something took over my speech. It made me feel like I was sitting down by a river that somehow was flowing through me and bubbled up out of me like a musical language.[20]

This narrator uses some stock language—"blinding light," "flowing." Her description is brief and apparently unreflective. The idea of Jesus "bursting" is perhaps less dignified than we are used to, but is characteristic of pentecostal energy and exuberance. She seems to make an attempt to get her audience to *feel* the sensation when she describes the "something" as bubbling "out of me like a musical language."

Agnes Sanford's day on a lake was expressed in a more complex way:

> I prayed for God's life to reach me through the rays of the sun. And even though I did not know the Holy Spirit, the Spirit of God entered in a way so defying understanding that I have never tried to explain it. Nor could I explain it now. I can only say that for a split second I lived consciously and awarely in the bliss of eternity. I saw nothing and I heard nothing, but I was so enwrapped and interpenetrated by the bliss of light that I thought, "If this doesn't stop I shall die!" And again I thought, "But I don't want it to stop!" It ceased, and I have no way of measuring the time of it, for I was living beyond time. But the holy fire burned within my head for some fourteen days. I did not know then that it was the baptism of the Holy Ghost . . . But no experience ever equaled in bliss this baptism of pure light and power that came to me from God.[21]

Sanford claims that she did not know how to name her experience at the time, that it was and is impossible to explain; it occurred outside of time. She appears to struggle for words to express the experience; she cannot reconcile the contradiction (she wants it to stop; she *doesn't* want it to stop). Yet, since actually she is recalling the experience *after* she has learned to name and categorize it, her claims that it is inexplicable and ineffable are a trifle disingenuous. By means of this rhetorical convention she presumably connects herself more closely to her uninitiated, uninformed, and potentially skeptical reader. By borrowing some traditional mystical elements—paradox, inexplicability, a spiritual response to natural surroundings—she helps to make her middle-class reader more receptive to her assertions about the Spirit.

Pentecostals view the experience of receiving the Spirit as the final step in a progressive surrender that may well have been going on since before their conversion; the baptism in the Spirit represents the extreme in "yieldedness" to God. When they receive the Spirit, pentecostals allow the Holy Spirit to supersede their intellects and wills; they let the Spirit take control of their tongues, their power of speech, which they consider a central part of their beings. They pray the prayer that the Holy Spirit puts into their mouths, that is, they pray "in the Spirit." According to their lights they could scarcely adopt a more "yielded" attitude.

And yet the consequence of such apparent passivity is far from helplessness; at the same time believers yield to the Spirit, they also receive "power." This is a word seldom emphasized in the narratives in connection with the experience of conversion or holiness, but it occurs insistently in conjunction with the pentecostal experience. The scriptural source for "power" is Acts 1:8: "ye shall receive power, after that the Holy Ghost is come upon you." Sanford above speaks of power; Shirley Boone, praying for the experience, pleaded, "Please, if this power is available to me, please fill me with the Holy Spirit." A church full of pentecostals is described as "full of the power of the Lord." A manual lauds "this wonderful power of the Holy Spirit." Rita and Dennis Bennett, prominent pentecostal writers, promise that "your life will begin to have real power" and that a "Spirit-filled" person will become "a channel for real spiritual power."[22]

Now to be sure, this "power" is seldom associated with "principalities and powers." It is from God and it ebbs as soon as one attempts to use it for one's own or another unworthy end. It is not a power readily translated into political, economic, social, or cultural arenas. It is described as strictly a "power for service." It makes for more effective prayer. Petitioners are more likely to receive or achieve what they pray for if they are filled with this power, even if they ask for very specific things. It also leads to successful evangelism: the "Spirit-filled" are able to offer the most effective testimony and win the largest number of souls, and they summon the greatest zeal in their efforts.

And yet such power has perhaps an unintended consequence: in the pentecostal subculture, of course, it inspires respect and confers authority over others. But even in the wider culture it can have consequences insofar as a possessor of "pentecostal power" is perceived as more serene, self-confident, stable, and secure, a better worker and perhaps also a better leader. Surely there is no hard and fast line between spiritual and secular power, even in twentieth-century America. Pentecostals make more explicit an idea that was only suggested by other conversion narratives—that surrender leads to power, and that the most complete surrender results in the most complete power. Clearly, then, such teaching about power is pregnant with possibilities for women, and chapter 7 will explore some of them.

Holiness and pentecostal experiences have become more necessary parts of the twentieth-century narrative. If we are talking about the period of time before the late 1960s, holiness is more universally expected than pentecostalism. Pentecostalism has become an increasingly frequent narrative ingredient in the past few decades, as more and more middle-class narrators either claim to have undergone the experience or feel constrained to justify its omission.

In what way do these new experiences change the patterns of the twentieth-century conversion narratives? First, they extend the temporal scope of the typical narrative. In the early nineteenth century when the event of conversion, together with its immediate "fruits," had been related, the tale was for the most part over. The heroine was free to die young. In the twentieth century there is more to tell; the process of "growth in grace" can be lifelong.

Sometimes the structure of the narrative has changed. The expected pattern of the nineteenth century tended to be a deep dark valley (conviction) followed by a high bright peak (conversion), followed in turn by a series of progressively less extreme valleys and peaks (periods of backsliding and renewal). Narratives that relate holiness and pentecostal experiences sometimes tend to resemble a series of quests, with each quest becoming more intense, more extreme, the result more rewarding. A narrator experiences an initial conversion but soon begins to wonder what else God might have in store for her.

Pentecostalism introduces the possibility of sensual, tactile experience into the narrative. As it is often described, it is a physical sensation, with clear connections—albeit not normally acknowledged—to sexual experience. When middle class evangelicals have turned to it, it has fulfilled their desire for more authentic, more stirring, more vital religious experience; it has signified their rebellion against middle-class religious conventionalities—against "squeamish bourgeois prejudices," as one pentecostal leader put it—and the boredom they have endured in their original churches. It seems to be the religious equivalent of white middle-class discovery of the blues sung by black convicts, or the espousal of "hillbilly" music by Ivy League academics. As such it has become a revitalizing element in religious experience and hence in the conversion narrative.

In a sense pentecostalism also represents a rebellion against rhetorical formula, since what the Holy Spirit may cause us to say is not predictable either in its timing or its content; it may not even be comprehensible in any ordinary sense. It can also be seen as a protest against the inadequacy of ordinary language—a literal interpretation of the stock protestations about the ineffability of intense spiritual experience. A leading pentecostal, for instance, is described as reviewing "all the things he had to be thankful for." Words eventually fail him and he breaks into tongues:

> suddenly in trying to express his gratitude he would reach a language barrier. English could no longer express what he felt. It was simply inadequate for the Being that he perceived. It was at this time that he would burst into communication that was not limited by vocabulary. His spirit as well as his mind would start to praise God.[23]

Yet at the same time pentecostalism reaffirms the primacy of language, even to emphasizing the expression of ecstatic experience in words (rather than, say, dance). And in the end some of its verbal exuberance yields to rhetorical formulas. Notice that in the quote above, for instance, "to praise God" had become a stock phrase for speaking in tongues.

No doubt the recent middle-class (and often suburban) interest in the experience has served to tame the rhetoric even further. Middle-class adherents claim (against some of the evidence) that pentecostalism is not predominantly emotional in its nature; they insist that when one speaks in tongues one is not "out of control." They also require that pentecostal utterance be orderly—that practitioners speak one at a time and that their language be "interpreted," so that it can communicate to others.

Holiness advocates and pentecostals often claim that they practice and preach a "full salvation." They are also convinced they tell a fuller, more complete story.

SIX

Establishing the Twentieth-Century Text

In the twentieth century the dissemination of conversion narratives has become a more complex process, given a pluralistic culture that hosts a number of different rhetorics, and even a large assortment of narratives of personal transformation. This chapter deals with the strategies—self-conscious and otherwise—that evangelical speakers and writers have devised to ensure a hearing in the twentieth-century Babel of American voices.

PROBLEMATIC RHETORIC

In 1928 an editorial writer in the *Moody Monthly* asked plaintively, "how can evangelists lead souls to make a decision for Christ when the latter know nothing about Christ and the salvation He wrought out for them on the Cross?"[1] As the experience of Christian conversion became less the norm in late nineteenth- and twentieth-century America, two important things happened. First, men and women began with increasing frequency to relate "out of church" conversions, that is, life-transforming experiences that had nothing directly to do with Christianity except for certain shared structural patterns and rhetorical elements (see chapter 8). Second, evangelists—would-be "soul winners"—began to adapt their attitudes and methods to the new situation in which a large portion of the population—churched or unchurched—no longer took it for granted that they must be "saved."

One of the evangelists' adaptations involved language: if conversion was no longer normative, neither was the language with which the experience was described. We have already taken note of Elizabeth Burns's uncertainties in describing (and even experiencing) her conversion. Potential converts like her could no longer be depended upon to know exactly what conversion was, let alone how to describe it, nor did they necessarily know how to address God or Christ in prayer. Again and again converts who had grown up outside evangelical traditions fumbled over wording. Wrote one woman, "I was so inexperienced as a Christian I didn't even know how to ask God for help."[2] Another, in her moment of "surrender," began a prayer, "I don't know how to say this, but, Jesus, please help me out of this mess. Please take over!"[3] As early as 1909 a lumberman participating in a series of Boston revivals apologized, "I can't talk Christ as they do here but I'll tell the story my way."[4]

Not least troublesome was the seventeenth-century text of the King James Version: "its language was hard for me," confessed Susan Atkins.[5] Even those who became well versed in the rhetoric of the Authorized Version and of conversion generally began to sound self-conscious about using scriptural language and sometimes felt the need to explain what they were saying. Twentieth-century writers have frequently put scriptural and other peculiarly religious language in quotation marks. Already in 1909 Harold Begbie set off "lost," used as a synonym for damned—"the sad, the sorrowful, the broken and the 'lost.' . . . " "Lost" in the sense he meant it had already become less than standard.[6] Later, Shirley Boone recalled telling a psychiatrist how in a dream she had seen people running "to and fro," "although," she added, " 'to and fro' isn't a phrase I'd normally use. To me it's scriptural phrasing."[7] Similarly, Eugenia Price reported that on one occasion "my prayers consisted of a long complaint to God (sometimes in the King James Version, sometimes not)."[8]

Ironically, this language, though increasingly foreign to many, had grown all too familiar in other circles. For them the trouble with evangelical rhetoric was not that it was alien and strange but rather that it was tired, hackneyed, and sometimes insincere. Tom Skinner, a black minister's son, disparaged the "platitudes" he had heard from white evangelicals and the "clichés" of the black church he had grown up in.[9] Even to the uninitiated, certain little-understood conversion phrases—"born again," "praise the Lord," "Jesus saves"—began to echo, sometimes unpleasantly, in the ears. As early as 1908 a writer on conversion remarked that

> Probably nothing has done more to foster the antipathy with which in many quarters the doctrine of conversion is still regarded than the vulgar notion that . . . there is a mill to go through, and that everybody must go in at the hopper and come out at the shoot, that unless you have had the regulation experience your conversion is not genuine.[10]

Part of the "regulation experience" was of course regulation language. The phrase "born again" has attracted pejorative uses. When in the 1988 election Democrats wanted to convey their skepticism about the sincerity of George Bush's new-found concern for the environment, they sneered at him as a "born again environmentalist." An earlier writer recalled how easy it was to fool evangelicals by parroting the right language, without experiencing any accompanying conviction: "I made up some story about how I had gotten 'saved' as a teenager, embellished it with dramatic details, and told it at one of the Christian sharing meetings. The response was unbelievable. Most of the girls were in tears. Everyone hugged me, said 'Praise God' and had a special prayer meeting of gratitude."[11] The formulaic quality of conversion narratives and of religious language in general was becoming a liability as well as a strength.

Occasionally, educated evangelicals have expressed discomfort about the impact of the shop-worn phrases on potential converts. Jean Dillard, a painter and convert from the Billy Graham crusades, complained,

> I know thousands of Christian whose lives have been changed through conversion speak a limited, warmed-over jargon because they are at a loss to express themselves in any other way. But I also know that it's this very same language usage that scares others away. To the non-believer, it smacks of a brand of Bible-beating, hellfire revivalism, alien to our times and to the fresh winds of ecumenism that are revitalizing our century.[12]

Dennis and Rita Bennett advised, "A good witness is not necessarily rushing in and saying: 'Are you saved?' or 'Do you know Jesus?' You may so frighten or offend the person that he may run away from God for years."[13] In relating her conversion experience, Lareta Finger worried, "It is hard to talk about feeling so greatly loved by God and not have it sound like a platitude."[14] Another evangelical convert wrote, "The Cross does not call me to be . . . an emotionless follower who parrots the right words." A pentecostal minister echoed her, cautioning his youth workers,

> We've got to be very, very careful that we don't become parrots. I try to keep my ear tuned for phrases—religious terms—that I've heard before. Then when I'm on the street I never use such a phrase without first saying a prayer that I can give it all the power it had when it was spoken for the very first time.[15]

Twentieth-century evangelical writers have also rejected the "unnatural," stilted, and old-fashioned discourse they associate with earlier evangelicals. Hannah Hurnard, describing her communications with her Lord, said,

> When we were alone together I never spoke to him in anything but everyday language, with complete naturalness and no artificial phraseology. As I walked on the hills or by the lake . . . I never dreamed of using formal language or of expecting his words to come to me (apart from the Bible itself) in anything but my everyday vocabulary. It was obvious he used one's mental faculties to receive the thoughts he wanted to give, and it was therefore natural to suppose that he would use the sort of vocabulary I had acquired in which to clothe those thoughts.[16]

The *Jesus Person Maturity Manual* advises Christians how to pray: "*Be Natural.* Tell Him you love Him, if you do. No fancy words. Drop all *thee's* and *thou's.* Pray in clear language."[17]

One development that helps explain the unease of a Dillard or a Hurnard is that during the twentieth century more and more conservative evangelicals have entered the educated middle class. Though their parents or grandparents may happily have accepted the "sawdust trail" language (or more probably didn't give it much thought), they no longer can do so. Nor are they comfortable to remain part of a linguistic subculture. And they are impatient with modes of narrative that depend too obviously upon conventions.

If nonevangelicals and even some evangelicals find the language of conversion either incomprehensible or repugnant, evangelicals face a potential problem. Their evangelistic task is to reach the largest possible number of people in order to "bring" them "to Christ." But if the traditional language has become a liability, how can this be accomplished? Evangelical writers have created new modes of evangelical discourse, which they often use in combinations. Certainly they have not abandoned the traditional rhetoric; rather, they mix it with new forms, and they preserve it for the people most likely to find cliché and formula comfortable—the least articulate, perhaps, or the shyest, maybe the poorest and least educated. The old conventions can appeal to those least inclined or able to find original language, words of their own.

For the more sophisticated, though, they also adapt the language of conversion and religious experience to some of the common conventions of twentieth-century discourse. In our litigious culture they may turn to legal language and talk about evidence, verdicts, and the need for a decision for Christ (see, for instance, the writing of Josh McDowell). They may take a scholarly, academic approach, with a liberal use of footnotes (here again McDowell). They may borrow the traditional language of mysticism and spiritual formation, language that is familiar to many Catholics, among others. They may turn to the rhetoric of business or of sports. Such choices are likely to be made with different potential audiences in mind.

Probably the most popular and universal language has been that of advertising, which, as a field with its special techniques and professional practitioners, has come into its own in the twentieth century, at the same time as evangelists have been searching for new approaches to their increasingly difficult tasks. Evangelists and advertisers have in fact become first cousins. Evangelists have often seen themselves quite explicitly as sales persons needing to research the markets for their product and then choosing the best methods and messages with which to "sell" to those markets. The technique of witnessing is central to both endeavors—especially the witnessing that can be done by a celebrity.[18]

The advertising impetus shows up in a number of ways in twentieth-century conversion narratives. First, it appears in the use of catchy and easily remembered slogans like those prized by Madison Avenue. Often these slogans rely on the bipolar nature built into conversion: before and after, darkness and light, sinner and saved, hell and heaven, lost and found, rebellion and surrender, bondage and freedom. Thus, narrators frequently contrast the "self-centeredness" of the unconverted individual with the "God-centeredness" of the convert, or the notion of being "self-satisfied" with that of being "God-satisfied." A British pastor well known in the United States was given to saying, "Our business is not to coddle the saints [i.e., the converted], but to collar the sinners."[19] Even the rhetorically scrupulous Liz Burns quoted a favorite word play of evangelicals: "Let go, let God."

Evangelicals, like advertisers, have turned to memory helps: Rita Bennett has come up with the " 'ABC's' of receiving the Holy Spirit": "Ask, Believe, Confess." Frank Buchman, founder in the 1920s of the evangelical Oxford Group, taught the "five C's" of the "changed life": Confidence, Confession, Conviction, Conversion, and Continuance. He fancied word plays that could serve as aids for recall: "J-E-S-U-S, just exactly suits us sinners." Members of a conservative evangelical church studied by Nancy Ammerman repeated a formula, J-O-Y, "Jesus first, Others second, Yourself last."[20]

Less obviously, professional evangelical writers began to turn out prose that, consciously or unconsciously, had borrowed techniques from advertising copy. Eugenia Price, for example, has resorted to clipped paragraphs, intentional sentence fragments, repetitious sentence structure, and unlatinate phrasing:

We can stop trying.
We can even cease the struggle to cease struggling.
It has been done for us.

Jesus could say, "Seek and ye shall find," because he knew we were being sought! He, Himself, was seeking us for Himself, is still seeking us for Himself.
When we receive Him, we find.
We find because we are found.[21]

While rejecting the selling techniques of advertisers who promise the "plus life"—something for nothing—Vicki Huffman uses just those techniques for her "higher" purpose: "The plus life. It's real. It's available. And it's yours for the asking."[22]

Evangelical writers have also turned to other rhetorical strategies. In her account of her young womanhood, *I Gave God Time*, Ann Kiemel Anderson employed poetry reminiscent of Rod McKuen. Baptized in the Sea of Galilee, she recalls

everything was new, clean. old things washed away.
the sun was shining in my eyes, on my face.
i was changed. different heart . . . new hope.
the voices were singing all around me,
    "freely . . . freely. . . . " i was singing too.
they were reaching for me . . . hugging me.
i didn't know why i was crying . . . i couldn't stop.
nothing would ever be the same.

i carried a new treasure of freedom in my heart.
no words. no tongues. just freedom.
the sins of my youth. the dreariness of the past year.

the weakness and imperfection of this human
clay . . . all cleansed.[23]

Other evangelical writers, in an attempt to participate fully in twentieth-
century discourse, speak variously in witty, cute, and cosmopolitan voices, their
allusions reaching beyond the usual religious sources. Though Huffman cites
the popular devotional writers, including Dwight L. Moody, she also alludes
to nonreligious sources such as *The King and I*: "Like Anna in Siam, whenever
you're afraid, you may need a tune to sing. Try a song about the King and you—
Psalm 56."[24] Her chapter titles convey some sense of her wider frame of reference: "The Children's Hour," "Cancel My Subscription," "All in the
Family," and "A Neapolitan World."

Twentieth-century narrators have also reached outside their particular religious tradition for phrases and formulations with more universal, sophisticated appeal. They have begun to refer to "mountain top experiences." While
presumably the phrase refers to Jesus' experience on the mountain, it has not
been employed by evangelicals until recently. An especially interesting example
is the phrase "dark night of the soul" to describe the period of misery and
anxiety preceding conversion. Evangelicals have used this formulation only in
the past few decades. The phrase apparently comes originally from the six-
teenth-century Spanish Catholic mystic, St. John of the Cross; it is the title of
one of his treatises. But in this century it was not frequently used by Protestants
or others until the 1960s. Possibly its contemporary renascence has had to do
with the "rediscovery" of the work of John of the Cross by literary scholars in
the 1950s, or with F. Scott Fitzgerald's well known remark, "In a real dark
night of the soul it is always three o'clock in the morning" (*The Crack-up*,
1936).[25] Besides its resonance for anyone who has known a "dark night of the
soul," the phrase would have additional attractions for evangelicals trying to
enrich their narratives and make them more widely appealing; not only is it
venerable and classically Christian, but also sophisticated in a literary sense.
Its association with Fitzgerald, one of the most cosmopolitan of the twentieth-
century writers, cannot hurt either.

Yet even these new departures in language and technique depend no less
upon the use of formula than the traditional rhetoric. For evangelicals the "dark
night of the soul" has quickly become a stock phrase. Along with her unortho-
dox rejection of capitalization and her sentence structure, Anderson includes
very traditional expressions: "everything was new, clean," "old things washed
away," "i was changed," "the weakness and imperfection of this human clay,"
"all cleansed." Similarly, Price, despite her homage to advertising technique,
builds on a quotation from the King James Version and depends on the familiar
evangelical notion of seeking and finding. Through their blending of the new
and the old, then, narrators have hoped to capture the attention of twentieth-
century audiences and thereby speak to the souls of the better educated and
more sophisticated.

MANUALS AND GUIDES

The strategies used to reach potential converts who are likely to be ignorant of or indifferent to traditional conversion narratives have been delivered through a growing body of literature, including manuals and guides. To an even greater degree than their nineteenth-century predecessors, twentieth-century Protestants have been able to draw upon a wealth of instructional sources as guides for creating their conversion narratives.

Many of the older models and guides continue to inspire narrators; in recent decades particularly, some of the classics have been reissued in new editions. But converts have also needed to reach beyond the classics, as they have found the older language less readable and the old theology no longer relevant. Many converts of this century, unlike their earlier counterparts, have sought instruction in experiences such as holiness and pentecostalism and, since the older guides are largely silent on such topics, they have looked to newer manuals and models.

As earlier, biographies and autobiographies are significant sources of inspiration. Some standards from the nineteenth century have slipped from sight: William Cowper's and Jonathan Edwards's accounts of their conversions (interest in Edwards's life and writings has of course continued and even increased, but on a scholarly rather than on a devotional level). But other classics persist: John Bunyan's *Grace Abounding* and of course *Pilgrim's Progress*, David Brainerd's biography, and John Woolman's journals. After several decades of neglect, Madame Guyon's *Life* has recently reappeared in print. Among nineteenth-century biographies and autobiographies, the lives of foreign missionaries are favorites, for instance, those of Amy Carmichael of India; J. Hudson Taylor (who began the China Inland Mission); Adoniram, Ann, and Sarah Judson; Lottie Moon of China; Mary Slessor of Calabar; Rosalind Goforth of China; and Malla Moe of Africa. The life of the wealthy missionary William Whiting Borden, who graduated from Yale and died shortly after in 1913 in Egypt, is a special favorite. Elisabeth Elliot, a leading evangelical author, testified that the "biographies of missionaries—Hudson Taylor of China, James Fraser of Lisuland, David Brainerd of early New Jersey, Raymond Lull of North Africa—influenced the course of my life. Sometimes if we catch the music that other people march to, we can fall into step."[26] The life of Amy Carmichael, she recalled, was a biography of special importance to her.

Interestingly, Elliot has noticed a problem encountered by educated evangelicals in reading missionary biographies, especially nineteenth-century ones. The missionary writers, she observes, tend to tell their supporters on the homefront, who contribute the bulk of the funds for foreign missions, what they think those people want to hear. Accordingly, they exaggerate the successes of missionary work and sentimentalize the activities of the missionaries, sometimes making it difficult for twentieth-century evangelicals to take their work seriously. Elliot pokes fun at the language used to describe foreign missions and missionaries; she refers to a woman missionary who "died after fifteen years of hard work—generally called 'labor' if a missionary does it. (We all know that missionaries don't go, they 'go forth,' they don't walk, they 'tread the burning sands,' they don't die, they 'lay down their lives.' But the work gets done even if it is sentimentalized!)"[27] Despite these difficulties, old biographies and autobiographies get revived nonetheless, and some get rewritten for twentieth-century audiences.

Other nineteenth-century "giants" in the faith attract numerous biographies: Henry Martyn, Charles Spurgeon, Robert Murray McCheyne, Frances Ridley Havergal (the hymnwriter), Dwight L. Moody, Andrew Murray, A. J. Gordon, Charles G. Finney, and Reuben Torrey. V. Raymond Edman, in *They Found the Secret*, chose to tell the pre-1900 stories of Hudson Taylor, John Bunyan, Frances Havergal, Charles G. Finney, A. J. Gordon, Dwight L. Moody, and Andrew Murray.[28]

Manuals and guides have remained perennially favorite methods of inculcating conversion rhetoric. Some seventeenth- and eighteenth-century standbys, it is true, including even Philip Doddridge's *The Rise of the Soul*, have dropped from circulation.[29] But two late nineteenth-century holiness writers have enjoyed particular popularity since their original publication in the 1880s: Hannah Whitall Smith (1832–1911) and Andrew Murray (1828–1915). Smith was a Quaker brought up in Philadelphia. Through speaking tours she and her husband, Robert Pearsall Smith, helped spread holiness teaching in the United States and Great Britain in the 1870s. Smith's most widely read book, *The Christian's Secret of a Happy Life* (1883), was addressed to converted Christians who found themselves troubled and lukewarm in their faith. Smith's "secret" was essentially the good news of holiness—the assertion that Christians need only surrender themselves completely to the Lord and trust him wholly. Like children, they can leave all their problems—their "burdens"—with their Lord and stop struggling to solve them by themselves. As her title suggests, Smith claimed that Christians could expect to find happiness in this earthly life, whether or not outward events and circumstances favored them. Traditionally Christians had been taught not to *expect* happiness in this world, but Smith offered assurances of it. The more troubles one had in life, she counseled, the more dependent one needed to be on God, and the more dependent one was, the closer one could feel to him. And whatever one's outward circumstances, closeness to God brought peace and contentment. Smith explained how Christians could surrender fully to God, by determining his will and merging their own with his. And she described how, from the study of God's word and from the guidance of the Holy Spirit, they could determine with certainty what his will was.

Christian's Secret was a modest bestseller during the 1880s, when it appeared in eleven different editions or reprints. More editions, including a London one, came out during the early twentieth century; then between 1916 and 1941 there were no new versions. The book enjoyed a brief publication renascence in the 1950s and early sixties, then went through another short eclipse.

Recently paperback versions have become readily available in Christian bookstores.

Many twentieth-century narrators have spoken of the impact the discovery of Hannah Smith made upon them. Dale Evans Rogers read her in the fifties; Catherine Marshall struggled for almost thirty years with Smith's chapter 12 ("Is God in Everything," even the evil that happens to us, a question that Whitall answered affirmatively); Elisabeth Elliot, who provided the introduction to a 1985 Word Book edition of *Christian's Secret*, testified to its value for her when she first read it in 1978. She had long had the book in her library: her copy originally had belonged to her great grandfather; her father had carried it with him into World War I, and her mother had recorded reading it in 1938. Said Elliot, "Again and again I have heard people speak of it. Many of them say it has helped them more than any other book to live the Christian life."[30] The book is currently familiar enough among evangelicals that a recent manual for young people could employ a word play in its title: *Unhappy Secrets of the Christian Life.*

Andrew Murray, another late–nineteenth-century writer favored by twentieth-century converts, was a South African pastor who visited the United States several times. He wrote a number of devotional books, but probably one of his most influential has been *With Christ in the School of Prayer.*[31] (Another important one has been *Abide in Christ*, whose title indicates its central message.) *With Christ* consists of thirty-one short lessons, each opening with a biblical quotation that deals with some aspect of prayer. The book's central argument is that God answers prayer, that prayer is "always availing," that prayer *makes a difference* in world events, great and small. The notion of receiving a response to prayer presupposes a petitioner who is in "a personal, loving relationship" with God, knows how to determine his will, and then obeys it faithfully. In short, the pray-er is wholly surrendered to God—"sanctified." Murray's text, like Hannah Smith's, is at base a guide to achieving the fruits of sanctification.

Murray's influence can be traced through the twentieth century. The Bible Teachers Training School, opened in 1901 in New York City, used Murray's *With Christ* for decades as its central manual of prayer. In 1977 Susan Atkins praised Murray for his teaching about obedience to Christ; in the same decade Joni Eareckson quoted a Murray formula approvingly: "by God's appointment, in His keeping, under His training, for His time."[32]

In the past three or four decades several devotional writers have moved into prominence. Narrators constantly cite Catherine Marshall's books (*A Man Called Peter, Beyond Ourselves*, and *Something More*). They also pay homage to Eugenia Price, whose spiritual autobiography, *The Burden is Light* (1955), has been a best seller; evangelical readers have also drawn upon her *Early Will I Seek Thee*. Again and again narrators mention Corrie ten Boom, Ann Kiemel Anderson, Elisabeth Elliot, and, more recently, Hannah Hurnard. Billy Graham has of course been a primary source, especially his *How to Be Born Again*. Narrators also refer to the writings of Edith and Francis Schaeffer, who for many years carried on a ministry with young people, especially college students, from a base in Switzerland. Their piety, combined with their cosmopolitanism and their concern for culture, has made them respectable among younger and better educated evangelicals. Manuals by lesser known writers abound: Barry Wood, *Questions Non-Christians Ask* and *Questions New Christians Ask*; Josh McDowell, *More Than a Carpenter*.

As evangelicals have learned to seek union with God by means of the practice of holiness and of charismatic gifts, they have turned in appreciation to mystics and writers on mysticism. They have, for instance, rediscovered Thomas à Kempis's *Imitation of Christ* and Brother Lawrence's letters and his *The Practice of the Presence of God*, and they have embraced Evelyn Underhill's *Mysticism* (1910). Underhill was in fact not an evangelical but rather an Anglican who came close to converting to Catholicism.

As the choices above suggest, American evangelicals have been willing to go outside of Protestant evangelicalism itself for inspiration and guidance. Those in search of "reasonable" and eminently respectable arguments for Christianity have turned increasingly to C. S. Lewis, particularly to his apologia for his faith, *Mere Christianity*, and his *Screwtape Letters*. The more educated a narrator the more likely she is to cite Lewis as a spiritual and intellectual resource. As in the case of Underhill, the circumstance that Lewis was not an evangelical has not limited his importance to evangelicals.

Pentecostals and charismatics have their own classics: David Wilkerson's *The Cross and the Switchblade* (1962); John Sherrill, *They Speak with Other Tongues* (1964); Rita and Dennis Bennett, *The Holy Spirit and You* (1971); and Andrew Murray, *The Full Blessings of Pentecost*. Since the sixties Wilkerson, an Assemblies of God minister, has conducted a ministry among the youth of urban ghettos; the Bennetts are Episcopalians who have carried on a charismatic ministry in Washington state; and Sherrill was a religious journalist who experienced a baptism in the Holy Spirit while reporting on pentecostalism.

With the exception of hymns, evangelical Protestants of this century seldom emphasize poetry as a source of religious inspiration. One notable exception is Francis Thompson's "The Hound of Heaven," published in 1893. Converts as diverse as Dale Evans Rogers, Joy Davidman (the wife of C. S. Lewis), Ruth Bell Graham, and the hero of a 1930 novel cite this poem as an inspiration in their conversions or the conversions of those close to them. Thompson (1859–1907) was a reformed opium addict and an English Catholic. It may seem surprising that evangelical women have turned to a *Catholic* poet. Among evangelicals this attraction to Catholic writing is in fact no longer unusual; they have turned regularly to English Catholics such as Thompson and G. K. Chesterton. Indeed, educated evangelicals have recently tended to become Anglophiles (witness the attraction to C. S. Lewis), in part because they relish the culture and cosmopolitanism of the English religionists. In the case of English Catholics, they may regard them as allies, since English Catholics must, like themselves, contend with modernism and minority status in their own culture.[33]

Though "The Hound of Heaven" is by a Catholic poet, it is largely atheological and undenominational. It contains no predominantly Catholic presences, such as the Virgin. Its central figure, the "hound," who pursues the poet unremittingly, represents Jesus Christ. The poem contains several themes familiar to Protestant evangelicals. Its poet speaks of his fear that yielding to the hound will mean renunciation of all earthly pleasures and interests ("Yet was I sore adread / Lest, having Him, I must have naught beside") and so he flees the hound. He finds, however, that all the usual sources of earthly human happiness fail him and turn out empty and unsatisfying. At length the poet recognizes that human beings separated from God are without any merit of their own—"clotted clay," "little worthy of any love." Perhaps most attractive of all to evangelicals is the poem's depiction of a God so persistent and insistent in his love that for years and years he refuses to give up in the face of the poet's determined rebellion and stubbornness. (Not only the words themselves but also the driving rhythm of the poem convey the unremitting nature of God's love.) In the end the poem probably succeeds with American evangelicals because it is a conversion narrative with all the best elements of such a narrative: a hardened sinner who refuses to yield to God, a loving God who declines to give up on the sinner, and, finally, a glorious conversion that transforms the sinner's misery to joy.[34]

CONVERSION NARRATIVES AND THE BIBLE

If the conversion narrative has no longer been as widely normative for the twentieth century, neither has the Bible. Americans have not regarded the Scriptures with their former universal reverence and fascination. The wide acceptance of higher critical study of the Bible, which treats the book as a human document rather than a divine one, has wrought these changes in attitude, as has the knowledge explosion of the past century. Biblical knowledge has simply become a smaller part of the whole body of human learning. In particular the hallowed version of the Bible, the King James, has receded in importance as American English has diverged further and further from the formality and usage of the seventeenth century, and as a number of new, "modern" versions have become available.[35] Fewer Americans grow up "knowing" their Bibles, and an even smaller number arrive at adulthood with the cadences of the King James in their ears.

Perhaps because knowledge of and reverence for the Bible can no longer be assumed, study of the Scriptures in this century has become more of an industry than ever before, particularly in the evangelical subculture. Many converts undertake Bible study with a self-consciousness and a degree of deliberation that would have been unknown to nineteenth-century Protestants. Intensive Bible study, once largely a ministerial activity, has been extended to lay persons; in fact, it has become preeminently a lay person's endeavor. A whole group of schools—Bible institutes and colleges—which deliberately place study of the Bible at the centers of their curriculums, has come into being. Bible teachers boast of any number of systematic and efficient *methods* of studying the Scriptures. As a matter of course many converts become involved in Bible study groups and Bible conferences; often on their own they engage in daily Bible study sessions; it has become part of many an evangelical's routine to engage in prayer and Bible study early in the morning.

Many converts zealously commit Scripture to memory. One narrator wrote that "I memorized Scripture doggedly, trying to fill my mind night and day with the Word of the Lord."[36] One advantage of such copious memorization is that when in need one is likely to be able instantly to recall a relevant verse. Struggling with the trauma of a birth-deformed baby, Jennifer Vanderford consoled herself by recalling long passages from the Psalms. Converts engage in a very personal appropriation of Scripture; they continually apply the Bible to their own problems and concerns. In one institution for troubled teenage girls, the girls were encouraged to regard Bible study classes as "conversations between the girls and teachers. . . . In this atmosphere the Bible was no longer an intellectual exercise; it became the key to life itself. If a girl had a problem, she could find its solution in God's own words."[37] One narrator told of a list of Bible verses obtained at a Sunday school class; each verse applied to a different life situation, and the narrator took comfort in appealing to them during her daughter's fatal illness. In the twentieth century it has been common for converts to adopt what they call a "life verse," a biblical passage that "spoke" to them with particular meaning. One convert, for instance, chose Mark 10:29–30 as her life verse, another Phil. 3:13–14. A husband and wife pair selected Jeremiah 33:3. When signing letters, converts often have added the references to these texts after their names, the way another correspondent might append "M. D." or "Ph.D.": Jane Smith, Ps. 37:4.

Narrators cite certain passages as instrumental in their conversions. Women converts turn to the prodigal son parable. Even more often, they refer to the knocking passage from Revelation: "Behold, I stand at the door, and knock: if any man hear my voice, and open the door, I will come in to him . . . " (3:20). As a small girl Corrie ten Boom was converted through this verse. As earlier, one has only to open the door and let him come in to one's "heart" or "life," and conversion is accomplished. Another frequent conversion verse is "Him that cometh to me, I will in no wise cast out" (John 6:37).

Other favorite passages apply to the life of the narrator after conversion: Jesus promising, "Lo, I am with you alway" (Matt. 28:20), "Come unto me, all ye that labour and are heavy laden, and I will give you rest (Matt. 11:28)," "my grace is sufficient for thee" (2 Cor. 12:9). Frequently the convert murmurs, "Not my will, Lord, but thine be done," especially if she has been influenced by holiness teaching. Constantly applied to one's human, imperfect condition, even postconversion, is the admonition "All have sinned and come short of the glory of God." The convert often refers to "the peace which passeth understanding." The vocational question that often comes up once conversion is accomplished—the decision, that is, how best to serve God—is commonly framed in scriptural language: "Lord, what will You have me do?"

In addition, narrators show their reverence for Scripture, especially the King James Version, by adopting "biblical" prepositions. Occasionally they talk about believing "on" the Lord Jesus Christ.[38] Or they say someone was "used *of*" (rather than "by") God, or that something was "known *of*" and "chosen *of*" God (again, instead of "by").[39]

Indeed, as the Bible has suffered more and more neglect in the general culture, it has become the object of almost feverish study and veneration in the evangelical subculture. Certainly one function of the modern conversion narrative—in addition to its traditional purposes—is to foster in readers and hearers familiarity with the Bible. It keeps alive the echoes of the King James, the version of the Bible that is somehow the "true" one for evangelicals, even for those who accept the utility of other updated versions.

SINGING THE NARRATIVES

The older conversion language, then, gets remembered and retained in a number of ways: through classic narratives and manuals that are still read, through the continued study of the King James Bible, and through oral testimony; it is transmitted also through hymns and gospel songs. In fact, music may be the "purest" source of traditional language; while there are current narratives and modern translations of the Bible to supplement the older ones and thus foster the blending of newer and older rhetorical traditions, there are few current hymns whose popularity even begins to rival that of their nineteenth- and early–twentieth-century counterparts. Evangelicals in this century have sung an eclectic mixture of hymns; however, most of them are at least fifty years old, usually older. They have preserved the hymns of Charles and John Wesley, Isaac Watts (1674–1748), John Newton, and William Cowper (1731–1800); especially they have cherished the gospel songs of Fanny Crosby (1820–1915—"Safe in the Arms of Jesus," "Rescue the Perishing," "Saved by Grace"), Philip P. Bliss (1838–1876—"Let the Lower Lights Be Burning," "Almost Persuaded," "Hold the Fort"), William B. Bradbury ("Jesus Loves Me"), and Ira D. Sankey (1840–1908—"The Nine and Ninety"). They have also continued to sing the songs of turn-of-the-century writers such as Charles Gabriel (b. 1859) ("Since Jesus Came into My Heart," "Sail On"), A. H. Ackley, and George Bennard ("Old Rugged Cross"). The best-loved hymns of the Billy Graham crusades have been not modern compositions but rather "Just As I Am, without One Plea" (written by Charlotte Elliott in 1834, with a tune by William Bradbury) and Fanny Crosby's "Blessed Assurance," from the mid-nineteenth century.

Evangelical hymns usually have lively rhythms, often using syncopation and dotted eighths in combination with sixteenth notes. The melodies are easy to pick up and remember, especially the repeated refrains. The harmonies are simple. Gospel hymns have been close relatives of secular songs. For instance, George Frederick Root's "The Little Octaroon" was later given new words and became the gospel song, "Ring the Bells of Heaven."[40]

Hymns and gospel songs teach the older rhetoric. They retain nineteenth-century usage and King James phrases: "tarry," "vale," "billows," "abide," "tidings," Jesus as one's "everlasting portion," and the guilty as "perishing." They constantly quote Scripture: "I'll walk the vale with Him, / Or 'meet Him in the air' "; " "He that believeth on the Son,' saith He, "Hath everlasting life' " (John 5:24); "For him that cometh, He will not cast out"; "Then shall the dead in Christ arise, / Caught up to meet Him in the skies," "Come unto me and find rest ye heavy laden." More than any other form of evangelical rhetoric, hymns even preserve the biblical constructions: prepositions—"on Him believe" (from "Why Not Now?"); choice of words—"whosoever," "wheresoever," "thee"; and word order that echoes that in Scripture—"where joys immortal flow" and "Grieve not the Spirit lest He should depart from thee."

Hymns contain numerous fragments of conversion narratives: "Lead me from the shadows to marvelous light," sings E. E. Hewitt in her hymn "Wonderful Power." Elizabeth Prentiss teaches, "Once earthly joy I craved, Sought peace and rest; Now thee alone I seek, Give what is best" ("More Love to Thee," ca. 1856). And Ina Duly Ogden promised, "No matter how dark is the stain of your sin, / His love still entreats you to come; / In Him to find healing, new life to begin" ("Wherever You Wander, Come Home").

Hymns convey the main themes of late–nineteenth-century theology, which has changed little among conservative evangelicals since they were composed. They tell of an intimate relationship between the individual and Jesus, who is a tender and loving Savior. He is above all a Friend ("What a Friend I Have in Jesus," "I've Found a Friend," "Jesus Is All the World to Me.") In "In the Garden" (1912) Jesus "walks with me, and He talks with me, / And He tells me I am His own, / And the joy we share as we tarry there / None other has ever known." He yearns over us until finally we turn to him: "He moved my soul to seek Him, seeking me; / It was not I that found, O Savior true; / No, I was found of Thee" ("I Sought the Lord," by George W. Chadwick (1854–1931); cf. "Hound of Heaven"). The ideal attitude of the believer is surrender (see the hymns "I Now Surrender" and "I Surrender All"). Fanny Crosby's popular hymn "Blessed Assurance" sings of "perfect submission." Charlotte Elliott's "Have You Counted the Cost?" exhorts, "While the door of mercy is open to you, / . . . won't you whisper, I yield." The reward of this surrender is union with him: "I'm His and He is mine" ("It's Real"). The scriptural word "abiding" is recurring: "He abides in us still": "Jesus so sweetly abides within"; "in me abide"; "in Christ abiding," "bid Him come in to abide."

The words "abide" and "abode" often signal the holiness experience. Hymns contain other references to holiness as well: "thou wilt supply our need," "On my dear Savior I'll cast my ev'ry care," "Standing on the promises" (a hymn title), and "I must tell Jesus all my trials." In the early–twentieth-century hymns the Holy Spirit began to figure more prominently: "Spirit, now melt and move / All our hearts with love, / Breathe on us from above / With old-time power" (Paul Rader, "Old-Time Power"). Charles H. Gabriel's "Pentecostal Power" pleaded with God to send "the old time power": it urged, "With cleansing, purifying flame / Descend on us today."

Though few hymns warn of hell or judgment, "sin" and the misery it causes are pervasive presences, and preconversion individuals are definitely "sinners," described by many of the familiar nineteenth-century adjectives: they are "guilty," "vile," "helpless," "unclean," and "ruined." More kindly, the sinner of the hymns becomes a "wanderer," a "lost sheep," one who has "roamed" and "strayed" and labors under heavy "burdens." Satan, the "tempter," armed with his "darts," lurks nearby. Jesus' blood, which has the power to wash and cleanse sin and to make white as snow is constantly celebrated: "For all my sins His blood will atone, / Flowing o'er till ev'ry sin is covered" ("I Am Coming Home"), "the crimson flood that washes white as snow" ("Only Trust Him"), "When the Bridegroom cometh will your robes be white, / Pure and white in the blood of the Lamb" ("Are You Washed in the Blood of the Lamb?").

Heaven in the nineteenth-century style remains a popular hymn subject in the twentieth. It is Canaan, the promised land, the "beautiful, beautiful shore," and it contains many "bright mansions," the great white throne, denizens robed in white and crowned with victory, the music of bells and harps, angels, and golden streets; above all, it is our "home." In contrast, life here on earth is hard and unpleasant, though worldly woes are sentimentalized; life is a voyage on a stormy sea (e.g., "Sail On"), or, alternatively, an empty, unsatisfying collection of "vain" and "worldly pleasures."

Testimonies to the effectiveness of hymns in aiding conversion are pervasive. A former Mrs. America attended a Chicago meeting of the Billy Graham Crusade, where she heard Cliff Barrows, Graham's songleader, practicing with the choir. She was "suddenly exalted. 'I sensed a great Presence,' she says, 'and the song went through my mind, "Are ye Able?" ' She shut her eyes, looking inward and praying, 'Lord, only you know whether I am able, but I am willing.' " Mabel Duvall recalled turning to the televised Graham Crusade simply to hear the "unforgettable voice" of George Beverly Shea, another Graham songleader. She heard Graham's sermon and then, she remembered, "My heart seemed to be melting like wax under the warming strains of 'Just As I Am, Without One Plea.' " Similarly, a woman in Minnesota heard Shea sing "My God and I" and "Just As I Am" and recalled how she "broke down in tears, knelt by the side of my bed and dedicated my life to Christ."[41] In one of the most extreme cases, a youth about to jump to his death from a building was saved by hearing "The Old Rugged Cross." "He turned his life over to Christ, and later he received the baptism of the Spirit."[42]

The twentieth-century sources for evangelical rhetoric are staggering in their number and variety: radio and television, the lecture circuit with its multitude of church and Bible conferences, magazines and journals such as *Christianity Today* and *Moody Monthly*, numerous Christian publishers: Word Books,

Fleming H. Revell, Logos, Eerdmans, Tyndale House, Moody Press, and Zondervan, to mention only a few of the most prominent. Even secular publishers perceive a market for conversion narratives and devotional manuals. For instance, Doubleday produced Marjorie Holmes's *Who Am I God?* and Laura Hobe's *Try God*, Macmillan the biography of Joy Davidman, and McGraw-Hill Catherine Marshall's devotional as well as fictional volumes. The paperbacks issued by the evangelical presses are relatively inexpensive, and a conversion narrative, if it catches on, can reach millions of readers. Even if it does not become a bestseller, it still will find its way to thousands of readers.

Women have figured prominently among the narrators. As a consequence they have gained potential access to a public larger than their nineteenth-century sisters could ever have dreamed of. And they have become celebrities among the devotional writers of this century—especially Catherine Marshall, Elisabeth Elliot, and Eugenia Price. Since the mid-nineteenth century women have authored a substantial number of hymns; the most successful among them—Fanny Crosby, Charlotte Elliot, and Ina Duvey Ogden—have received an enormous hearing. Women, then, have taken an important part in establishing the religious narratives of this century and therefore have had a decisive role in defining the roles for evangelical women. But ironically, women narrators have come into their own at a time when the narratives, though numerous, bear an ambiguous relationship to their potential publics: a substantial number of Americans are simply unacquainted with the language of conversion; others think it is bizarre; yet others dismiss it as clichéd, unoriginal. Those parts of the narratives that still draw on nineteenth-century prose sound old-fashioned and sentimental. What do these problematic aspects mean for those women? In embracing the language of conversion, do they run the risk of "ghettoizing" themselves linguistically? Will they have difficulty communicating with other women who do not share their experiences?

In a sense, of course, many evangelical women wish to be "ghettoized," or at least separated from the world. A distinct language obviously advances this goal. And adaptation raises other dangers besides that of assimilation to "the world." The traditional narrative language appears to hold out certain advantages for evangelical women. As in the nineteenth century, its formulaic quality makes the telling easier for timid, retiring females, and also seems to take the selfish motives (self-realization, self-development) out of the narrative. Women use *God's* language, not their own. To the degree that the traditional rhetoric is somehow uniquely "feminine" in its orientation—in its frequent allusion to submission, surrender, yielding, service, self-sacrifice, and to converts as brides of Christ—it protects evangelical women narrators from the inroads of male sports and business language. It even buffers them to some extent from advertising language. Conversion rhetoric—for all its problematic aspects—helps women insofar as it retains a beauty, a rhythm, and perhaps most important, a safe distance from humdrum reality.

SEVEN

The Meanings of the
Twentieth-Century Narratives

During the twentieth century American women won more opportunities and rights than hitherto; they got the vote; they went into the work force in greater numbers; and they claimed or were granted more sexual freedom and greater leeway in the choice of personal style. True, the progress of women in the twentieth century was far from steady, but the general direction was toward greater freedom and opportunity.

By and large twentieth-century conservative evangelicals have set their faces against this gradual liberation and have turned conversion narratives to decidedly conservative social uses. They have employed the genre to affirm the conventional notion of marriage and the subordinate role of women within marriage. Troubled by an increasingly pluralistic view of marriage and besieged by divorce and employment statistics that belie the dominance of any one model of family life, they have persisted in designating the husband as economic provider and head of the household and the wife as keeper of the home and full-time mother of the children. They have taught women's submission, invoking Pauline directives such as "wives submit yourselves unto your own husbands" (Eph. 5:22; Col. 3:18). In citing such precepts they have been supported by an insistent biblical literalism that ignores considerations of historical context. When Paul tells wives to submit to their husbands, say the literalists, he is promulgating God's unchanging law for women for all time. Against calls for equality and enhanced career opportunities for women, evangelicals have argued, sometimes quite explicitly, through conversion narratives and other vehicles, for a clearly restricted role for women. Thus Shirley Boone's narrative is named *One Woman's Liberation*; her meaning of liberation is contrasted explicitly with the feminist meaning of the word.

Given such circumstances, one might expect to find fewer submerged plots than in the nineteenth-century conversion narratives. Why would women *bother* to express their ambitions and discontents subterraneously, we might ask, when they can much more freely construct their stories outside the evangelical orbit? Dissenters can easily resort to secular culture for a vastly enlarged view of women's abilities and opportunities. Yet those who remain within the evangelical fold can derive comfort from the presence of a group of feminist evangelicals; there now exists a small collection of overtly "feminist" conversion narratives that blend the language of feminism and conventional Christian conversion, link traditional conversion with the discovery of autonomy and self-worth, and attempt a reinterpretation of biblical pronouncements about women.[1]

And even the least "liberated" conversion narratives by the most determinedly unfeminist of narrators still contain subplots that contradict the conservative message at their surface. In fact, the rhetoric of female self-assertion has become so entrenched and "natural" in American culture recently that Ruth Bell Graham echoed it in her autobiography; she refused to remain entirely in her husband Billy's shadow, insisting in her title, *It's My Turn* (1982). This chapter will begin with an examination of the obvious plots of such narratives and then go on to investigate the more hidden ones.

SUBMISSION

In the typical version of later twentieth-century narratives, a converted woman learns to love "her man" better, including sexually, because she has learned surrender and submission to God. She no longer needs to doubt or prove her lovableness; she *feels* she is lovable. She better tolerates any failings or weaknesses of her husband. She submits with a lighter heart and more patience to the demands of her children. She becomes more self-confident about raising them because, as she might say, God is showing her the way. Her release from anxiety may give her energy to be better at the things women are supposed to do well: to be more loving and giving and nurturing and uncomplaining.

Converted women voluntarily—and sometimes gladly—forgo potential avenues of adventure and opportunity. But the typical narrator shows she is well aware of their existence. She knows there are more avenues open to women, both constructive and destructive, than in the nineteenth century. Even in conservative evangelical circles it has become less unthinkable for young women to express their sexuality, experiment with drugs, drink, marry and divorce several times, and make obvious their anger, hostilities, and rebellions. In other words, the number of possible female "sins" has expanded since the days when they rued their quick tempers and their novel reading. It has also been more acceptable for evangelical women to find outlets for their talents and ambitions. Often economic necessity—if not boredom and frustration—will drive evangelical wives and mothers into employment outside their homes.

Once a woman narrator is genuinely converted, however, a strict morality reasserts itself and she gives up many of these twentieth-century "freedoms." She reasserts her true femininity; she praises her authentic liberation from fear, insecurity, and guilt, which replaces the specious liberation vaunted by feminists. A "wayward" girl, once converted, learns to "sit, walk and stand like a lady."[2] Converted women may turn to careers outside their homes, but they tend to prefer the ones sanctioned for women—as secretaries, clerks, teachers, nurses, and missionaries. Generally they shun roles that suggest intentional competition with men.

A prominent adviser to evangelical women, Beverly LaHaye, dismisses the notion of women's rights, declaring flatly that when a woman's

> strongest desire is to be absolutely yielded to the Holy Spirit and totally obedient to God's will, submission becomes a natural part of her life. In the final analysis, this life is just a passing moment, in light of eternity, and female equality and personal rights seem trivial and insignificant.

LaHaye concedes that women may (indeed, *should*) enjoy married sex, but for the proper reasons: "The gift of sex was intended to be used unselfishly. It was not given for selfish fulfillment, but for surrendering oneself completely to another." A woman should cultivate a "meekness," a "gentle and quiet spirit." "This attitude is more than just a cultural condition of Paul's day. It is another of the differences God created between the male and female." Again she bows to twentieth-century reality: "a woman can develop interests outside of the home," but quickly qualifies her concession, adding firmly, "her top priority should and must be her home and family."[3]

Even pentecostal writers, who traditionally have allowed some spiritual authority to women, caution that though women may "prophesy," they must be submitted to male leadership—they must remain "under headship," in the words of the Bible.[4] And even an evangelical woman writer who subscribes partially to the thinking of the women's movement worries, "What are we doing to our men, oh God? . . . Are we robbing them of their maleness? Are we turning them into eunuchs? Are we confusing them in their role as leaders, lovers, providers?"[5]

The ideology of female submission to men is self-consciously honored in the conversion narratives of women. Virginia Mollenkott recalled doing most of the household work early in her marriage, even though she, like her husband, held a job; it didn't occur to her to complain because "we were Christians and were supposed to live by biblical standards. The Bible said that women were to submit to their husbands."[6] Olivia Plummer's marriage had been foundering before her conversion; afterward it became happy and harmonious. The chief threat to a satisfactory marriage had come from her hot temper; once converted, she learned to control it:

> When roused to anger I had been known to put sailors to shame. God began to convict me of these faults. He wanted me to assume the rightful role of being a gentlewoman, subject to her husband's desires, and in all manner loving and kind.

Once she succeeded in curbing her tongue, she said, "I know that the swallowed pride, or ugly thoughts not spoken were worth the price I had to pay."[7] At the outset of Ruth Graham's marriage to Billy, he informed her "firmly," "God will lead me and you will do the following." She assented, as expected: "I have been following ever since."[8]

Even the ablest and most talented women subscribe to these "biblical standards." The heroine of a 1930 novel had been converted well before the beginning of the narrative and remained much steadier in her spiritual direction than the man she loved. A strong personality, she was also a superb pianist. The hero was likewise a musician, but only gradually managed to become a better trumpeter as he learned to be a Christian. Yet, as the hero and heroine discussed their projected marriage at the end of the novel, she assured him of her subordinate status, referring both to music and marriage, "You'll always lead me, Ranny. I'm much better at accompaniment. Really."[9]

One might expect Ann Kiemel Anderson, a sort of yuppie evangelical Christian, to resist the notions of submission and a matrimonial hierarchy. At age thirty-five she was a marathon runner, had traveled for years as a popular religious speaker, described herself as a "professional woman," and owned a fashionable apartment on the Boston waterfront. When she met the man she was to marry, a "potato farmer" from Idaho, she wrote to him, "thanks . . . for accepting that i am a public person. for not denying it . . . but for working at not letting it intimidate you." Yet after her marriage, she strived to conquer her headstrong, independent propensities and become a submissive wife, because she believed obedience to one's husband was analogous to submission to God. "Submission. yes, Lord, as unto You." Such an attitude did not come easily to a woman used to making her own decisions:

> i was wanting so much to be a perfect wife for will anderson. say all the right things. cook everything he loved. keep a perfect house. smile sweetly. be totally submissive. "to submit" was a part of my marriage vow, and i had put that in because i really believed that to be God's will for our home. it was a lot easier to say it at the marriage altar than to live it out, day after day, in my marriage.

Time after time she rebelled, for instance when her husband asked her to reduce the amount of running she did:

> again . . . submission. trusting my huband. listening to him. letting him be God's voice to me. following the chain of command. submission to someone else is quite a challenge when one is used to being independent and traveling all over the world for years and years, a self-starter and a self-thinker. some people don't agree about this philosophy . . . and that is okay . . . but for me, i know this is right. there cannot be two presidents of the same corporation. just one . . . and a vice-president. (Punctuation is Anderson's.)[10]

Those spirited evangelical women who have looked for alternatives to submission have found a closed door; one reported that, as she approached marriage, "I looked through every book I could find on Christian marriage to discover whether they all held to the submission of wives. They did."[11] The logical if extreme outcome of this attitude was the timid wife who submitted again and again to the beatings of her drunken husband because she was a Christian.[12]

The experience of conversion is supposed to make accepting the headship of one's husband relatively easy. But as Ann Anderson's story testifies, this is not necessarily so. Surrender to God and to husband can still come hard, especially to a strong personality and especially in a culture at least rhetorically committed to expanded women's rights; the effort to obey may require constant struggle. Women endeavoring to submit both to God and to the men in their lives may receive help—as well as additional pressure—from holiness teaching. This teaching has emphasized and reinforced the idea of total dependence on God; it has endorsed the idea of the cessation of struggle and of self-effort even more thoroughly and insistently than conversion teachings by themselves. It has also accentuated the kinds of character traits that if embraced would keep women docile and yielding. The sanctified person—like the converted person, only more so—is supposed to be unassertive, selfless, serene, and slow to complain.

Theoretically at least, pentecostalism likewise prescribes a total yielding to God—including surrender even of one's language and of one's tongue. It too teaches the lessons of submission and passivity embraced by many evangelical women. To the degree that pentecostalism has been understood as an emotional experience, it has also reinforced the traditional stereotype of women as guided more by their emotions than by their reason or intellect and therefore in need of male oversight and wisdom. But both holiness and pentecostalism have had their more surprising consequences, as we shall see shortly.

SUBPLOTS TO POWER

As in the nineteenth century, conversion narratives, including their new components of holiness and pentecostalism, seem to conceal a subtext that suggests a real if circumscribed freedom and power for female narrators. As earlier, the ability to testify to conversion gives women a new authority; indeed, claiming the experiences of holiness and pentecostalism expands that authority. Obviously, such authority is not conferred by the twentieth-century women's movement, nor does it come from an enhanced political or economic status in life. (These sources may contribute indirectly, but only indirectly.) Rather, it stems from the convert's close connection with the source of all "true" authority: God. A converted Shirley Boone, until her conversion quite timid, surprised herself by "ordering" her father's widow, whose grief she thought was deteriorating into self-pity, to "get her head up." Boone reflected on her own behavior: "I could hardly believe I was taking such authority, because I wasn't naturally authoritarian. I'd always turned to Pat [her husband] for my strength."[13] A terrified Olivia Plummer, asked to speak on a panel of religious "experts," pulled it off, explaining, "I can only say that God spoke through me; he answered questions submitted to me with a wisdom I do not possess."[14]

Inevitably there are times when God's will appears to conflict with the will of worldly authorities. Strengthened by her sense of closeness to God, Jennifer Vanderford was empowered to go against the advice of male doctors in decisions about the care of her hydrocephalic son: "Several times God's direction was not the physician's advice." Needless to say, God's advice proved to be correct.[15] Mildred Meythaler, experiencing contradictions within her fundamentalist church, was able to separate the teachings of God from the teachings of the church: "I was freed to face the differences between church authority and God's authority over my life." The authors of *The Holy Spirit and You* unwittingly left a significant loophole when they directed that the wife should obey her husband, then conceded that "Obviously she does not obey him in things that would be against the Lord, but she obeys him in everything she can."[16]

With God so crucial a part of a female convert's universe, the usual objects of her concern recede just a bit from the center. A standard part of many stories is the realization that it is wrong for women to place husband and family "ahead of all" in their lives. In fact, it is worse than "wrong"; it is, in biblical terms, "idolatrous." Boone, quoted above, came to the realization that she had delayed turning to God for as long as she had because "*I'd subconsciously made Pat my God*. That was my overwhelming sin."[17] Joyce Stutt recalled that "I began to understand that I didn't need Earl [her husband] in the same way anymore. I'd found my center in Christ, I'd become my own person and no longer saw myself as an extension of my husband." She heartily agreed with a woman friend, who asserted, "I am first of all a child of God, and second a wife and mother."[18]

Ruth Bell Graham went even further. Brought up a Southern Presbyterian, she refused to join her husband's Baptist denomination despite considerable pressure from others. Explaining her stand, she commented, "it is a good thing to know how to disagree [with one's husband] and when." In fact, unless he is contradicted occasionally, the husband may become "insufferably conceited." She concluded with startling candor, "A Christian wife's responsibility balances delicately between knowing when to submit and when to outwit. Adapting to our husband never implies the annihilation of our creativity, rather the blossoming of it."[19]

This refusal to idolize one's husband (or children) implies a sort of covert (and at times subversive) liberation of a type not dreamed of by secular-minded feminists. To nudge a demanding family (child or spouse or parent) ever so slightly to the side of center stage in one's life and to replace it with a divine father (or friend, in the case of Jesus Christ) who loves unconditionally suggests the creation of at least a small space of one's own . . . if not a room of one's own.

In fact, it is even a possibility of the plot—though not a standard one—for the woman entirely to discard male love, married or otherwise. The narrator simply needs to turn to the hallowed Christian and biblical images of Jesus as lover and bridegroom. One convert, the veteran of several failed marriages, spoke of watching a young couple obviously in love. She, without a human

lover, felt she had the better bargain: "My love loved me unconditionally re-
gardless of what I was, what I did. And this love, unlike the human kind, cast
out fear."[20] Barbara Grizzuti Harrison, a Jehovah's Witness in her childhood,
observed "that it was not extraordinary for women who became Jehovah's
Witnesses to remove themselves from their husbands' bedrooms as a first step
to getting closer to God. Many unhappily married and sexually embittered
women fell in love with Jehovah."[21]

Other subplots suggest themselves. As in the nineteenth century, women
who have become God's servants can engage in activities normally closed to
unconverted woman. They can, in effect, protect themselves against possible
criticism by claiming that they do not use their own abilities or any authority
of their own but rather that God acts through them; not only is this good
theology but good sexual politics as well. With the twentieth-century introduction of pentecostal "power," achieved through the inflowing of the Holy
Spirit, the subplot thickens. Women can and do talk not only of following his
will and deriving strength from that, but also of gaining *power*. Take the following description from early in the century of Kathleen Scott, a teenager who
held forth in the "Upper Room" at Azusa Street, Los Angeles, where the pentecostal movement is said to have begun. According to the story, a man came
into the Upper Room while Scott was there: "The moment he entered, Kathleen, moved by the Spirit, arose and pointed to the man as he stood at the head
of the stairway, and spoke in a language other than her own for several min-
utes." At the beginning of the service immediately following Scott's outburst,
the man testified to Scott's marvelous powers,

> I am a Jew, and I came to this city to investigate this speaking in tongues. No person
> in this city knows my first or my last name, as I am here under an assumed name.
> No one in this city knows my occupation, or anything about me. I go to hear
> preachers for the purpose of taking their sermons apart, and using them in lecturing
> against the Christian religion.
>   This girl, as I entered the room, started speaking in the Hebrew language. She
> told me my first name and my last name, and she told me why I was in the city
> and what my occupation was in life, and then she called upon me to repent. She
> told me things about my life which it would be impossible for any person in this
> city to know.

Then, the story concluded, "the man dropped to his knees and cried and prayed
as though his heart would break." We read nothing further about Scott; we do
not know whether she ever became a pentecostal leader, but we are tempted to
suppose that at the very least the kind of power she displayed in this incident
altered her view of herself and others' view of her.[22]

With divine support, then, twentieth-century converts have embarked on
public ministries; sometimes they have been ordained, sometimes not. Pentecostal Aimee Semple McPherson came into extraordinary prominence in the
twenties as founder and leader of the Foursquare Gospel Tabernacle. A biog-

rapher suggests that by virtue of this role she also gained considerable sexual freedom and ample scope for her dramatic abilities.[23] More recently, another pentecostal, Kathryn Kuhlman, traveled all over the United States preaching and conducting divine healings; she also carried on a radio and television ministry.[24] A narrator recalled from her childhood the presence of numerous women ministers in the holiness Church of God—Anderson, Indiana. One of them, she added, was "responsible for bringing many of my relatives to Christ."[25]

Converted women who have shunned preaching nevertheless have become moral prophets. Phyllis Schlafly and Anita Bryant have occupied podiums all over the United States; champions of the family, they could not themselves spend a lot of time at home. Many less famous women have achieved busy speaking and organizing ministries. Millie Dienert, for instance, worked for the Billy Graham crusades, preparing for future campaigns and traveling all over the world in that role. Later she became National Consultant to the National Christian Women's Clubs.[26] Conversion launched Joyce Landorf into a singing and composing career, which propelled her "into contact with thousands of individuals with whom she shares her life-changing experience."[27] Jean Stone experienced a baptism in the Spirit in a Van Nuys, California, Episcopal Church and, though her husband told her she was attempting the impossible, she launched a successful "slick" and "sophisticated" charismatic magazine, *Trinity*, and lectured all over the United States.[28] Many evangelical women have conducted their "ministries" as volunteers rather than as professionals, yet have found these activities drawing them away from the domestic scene and into the public arena. After Ethel Renwick's conversion, in fact, she got drawn into so many absorbing and worthwhile Christian endeavors that her husband "took second place," until she recognized the problem and attempted to restore some balance by scaling down her agenda.[29]

At the very least, converted women have obeyed the command to go outside their homes and tell their stories. To do so they have had to conquer the shyness that frequently troubles women unused to speaking in public. Shirley Boone, asked to relate her experiences before a huge audience at UCLA, could not refuse despite her terror of addressing crowds. "I thought of the opportunity I was being given to share my Lord with young people." The talk went well. To put it in evangelical terms, the Lord gave her courage and strength of utterance. He also gave her the boldness to produce a book which "I felt terribly inadequate to write . . . I wondered who would care about what I had to say. . . . However, because of what the Father, Son and Holy Spirit have done for me, I have a story I can't contain."[30] Similarly, Dale Evans Rogers, about to testify at a "big religious meeting," "silently asked the Lord to reveal His will for my testimony, and to tell me what He wanted me to 'emphasize.' . . . It was as though I heard Christ say, '*I'll* do the talking. You just get up there and tell them the truth about what I did for you.' " She panicked briefly when she saw the size of the crowd, but God, she said, "unloosed my tongue" and she lost her fear.[31] Barbara Grizzuti Harrison noticed this same sort of verbal empowerment among the women Jehovah's Witnesses she had known. "As female Witnesses preach from door to door, instructing people in their homes, they experience a multiplication of their personalities. People *listen* to them; they are valuable, bearers of a life-giving message."[32] Hannah Hurnard offers the most dramatic example of all of verbal empowerment. Handicapped as a child by a terrible stammer, she resolved during her conversion to "yield my stammering mouth" to God and after great trepidation went on to speak in public. The stammer, she testified, was completely cured when she preached, and much improved in ordinary conversation.[33]

The sense of God's closeness and support released other strengths (or, as many of the women would put it, God gave *his* strength to them; frequently they quoted Phil. 4:13: "I can do all things through Christ which strengtheneth me"). All through her marriage, Virginia Womach had been dogged by a sense of inferiority and had completely depended on her husband. Then he was badly burned in a plane crash and required months of slow recovery and years of harrowing plastic surgery. She had long ago become a "Christian," but in response to the disaster her faith grew much stronger and enabled her to take on staggering responsibilities. In the process she became a "grown-up," she said: "It was hard to believe that the fainting housewife who wondered before the accident if she was really needed, could pull scabs, change messy sheets and make important decisions about air ambulances, burn wards, and plastic surgeons."[34]

In a category of their own are those converted women who have gone to the foreign mission fields, often accompanying husbands. These women are apparently as "submissive" as any; in order to do what they perceive to be the will of God, they must submit to the dangers and privations of lives as missionaries. And they usually adhere to conventional views of the place of wife and mother. Yet once in the field they find themselves fulfilling a multitude of additional roles. Elisabeth Elliot, for instance, categorically rejected feminism, describing her two marriages in thoroughly traditional evangelical terms: "Both of my husbands loved me, gave themselves to me and for me, and to both of them I willingly and gladly submitted." She ridiculed the idea of feminists that "it was a bunch of chauvinists, who decided that the one who has the baby feeds it and changes its diapers." Sensing the universality of the maternal role, she recalled caring for her own baby when she was in the mission field, just as did the mothers of the indigenous culture: those mothers, she said, "had the same weird idea I had about what women were supposed to do." But then she went on to admit that her life involved more than changing diapers:

Of course, I was breaking rules, too, that I didn't know about. I was managing a crew of thirty or forty workmen. I was learning an unwritten language and trying to translate the Bible into it. I was handling the money in our family (at my husband's request) and generally mixing things up, it seems—

The violation of gender roles became even more explicit after the sudden violent death of her husband, for she was forced to take over his missionary functions: "It didn't look like a woman's job but God's categories are not always ours. I had to shuffle my categories many times during my last eight years of missionary work."[35]

Perhaps the realities of the mission field shattered gender categories most radically, but the same categories sometimes became problematic even when women stayed safely at home in the United States. The most retiring converted women customarily became the spiritual leaders of their households, even if sometimes reluctantly. Shirley Boone experienced the baptism of the Spirit before her husband. She recalled feeling anxious and guilty about being in the vanguard: "Because Pat had been for so long the spiritual leader in our home, it was uncomfortable at first to find our situation reversed." She prayed about the problem and God responded that if she was willing to wash her husband's socks and care for his children, "why won't you be his spiritual helpmeet? Why are you reluctant to accept that role?"[36] The husbands may be the temporal heads of the household; they make the decisions about money, where to live, even what their wives should wear to a social function. Certainly they possess most of the political and economic power. But spiritually they are mere children; at best they follow the lead of their women. Or so runs the narrative stereotype. As in the nineteenth century the narratives rarely tell of a converted husband who leads his wife to grace. It is almost invariably the wife who shows the way for her sometimes reluctant and hesitant spouse. Or a mother who prays over a son until he finally surrenders. Spiritual authority may seem a poor substitute for temporal, but in a subculture that still greatly values the "religion once delivered to the saints," spiritual and moral leadership can carry profound political and social implications.

NO SISSIES: TWENTIETH-CENTURY MALE NARRATIVES

In the conversion narratives one of the ways a husband or father can reassert his spiritual authority is of course to convert (and perhaps also enter into holiness or experience a baptism of the Spirit). But for a man to testify to conversion is not that simple: a central worry reflected in the narratives of twentieth-century male converts has been the persistent question: can men accept Christ and still remain manly? As Billy Graham reportedly asked in his first revival, "Was it sissified to embrace Christ?"—obviously a rhetorical question to be answered in the negative.[37] Certainly there was a danger that converting would be seen as primarily a women's project. Male converts of the twentieth century have consistently acceded to behavioral changes; they have been described as gentler, less competitive. One male alcoholic who turned to Christ early in the century was described in explicitly feminine terms: "From being cruel, he became tender as a woman."[38] In the same series of male narratives the love of souls manifested by converts was thought of as almost a feminine trait. In

Charles Colson's *Born Again* a male who was describing his conversion was characterized as taking on a glistening eye and a gentle tone.[39] Male converts still report shedding tears, although they are often ashamed of them. On the night of his initial encounter with Christ, Colson wept: "Tears welled up in my eyes . . . Angrily I brushed them away and started the engine. 'What kind of weakness is this?' I said to nobody."[40] He was to weep even harder before the night was done, albeit still in private. Perhaps most damaging to their image of themselves, in converting men had to renounce the activities that tended to identify them as manly men—lusty drinking, gambling, smoking, womanizing. In the world of business they had to abandon their obsession with power and success. They forswore their evenings with "the boys" and rejoined their families, becoming companions to their wives and friends to their children. In short, they underwent domestication as well as salvation.

If this were the whole story it would be easy to see why few American males would have accepted Christ in this century. But to counter their worries about the feminizing tendencies in conversion narratives, men consistently emphasized narratives that feature a man's man. The most favored male narrators of the twentieth century were typically athletes, entrepreneurs, heads of companies, politicians in high places. One of the chief evangelists early in this century was Billy Sunday, a former professional baseball player, who continued to use sports rhetoric on the religious platform. Even criminals were made popular types for narratives—Jim Vaus, an electronic engineer who arranged illegal wiretaps; Jimmy Karam, a burly thug who for years led a bunch of "goons" whose main function was to break up the meetings of Orval Faubus's enemies; Starr Dailey, a hardened criminal who underwent a dramatic jailhouse conversion.[41] Typically, prospective male converts were rebellious, hostile toward authority, bored with routine, restless, lawless, and rambling. While these traits led them into terrible trouble, they also made them in some sense admirable. (Often, paradoxically, they attract the virtuous women they marry, who then suffer miserable married lives until their husbands' conversions.) The narratives are at pains to make it clear: these men were anything but soft and feminine before their conversions.

Having strenuously earned their masculine credentials, the narrators by no means relinquished them after conversion. Protested one former hot-headed high liver (with dubious orthodoxy), "I'm not a turn-the-cheek kind of Christian. I don't understand that business of putting up with everything. I like a Christian who stands up for what he believes in—in and out of religion."[42] A restless rebel was shielded from suggestions of femininity with the following demurral: "Bill's laugh was still hearty, and his new Christianity hadn't changed his adventuring soul at all."[43]

Ministers have run the biggest danger of seeming feminine and unmanned when they embrace Jesus. Probably for this reason the minister in Clyde Kirby's *Then Came Jesus* described himself as liking to fish and hunt, and before choosing the ministry he had battled God's will on the matter, and finally tried to dictate to God "the terms of his surrender"; further, the subjects of his solicitude

were often rough, foul-mouthed male scoffers. No pansy he, nor his male converts either.[44] In 1951 Catherine Marshall told the story of her late husband
Peter, who had served as Senate chaplain. She heard Peter's spirit approving
her writing of the book—"if it will prove that a man can love the Lord and not
be a sissy."[45]

Not only have male converts retained their manliness after conversion; they
have also attempted to "masculinize" Christianity itself. A schoolboy read the
Bible story of Joseph: "from it he caught his first vision of God. Here was a
way of life he could accept. It robbed him of none of his fire and spirit. It made
him neither a weakling or a sissy. Instead it would translate his talents worthy
to become 'father unto Pharaoh.' "[46] When Charles Colson spoke of "submitting" himself to God, he immediately connected the idea of submission not to
femininity but rather to the "founding fathers" of the United States, who knew
that "fallible men are nothing unless they learn to depend upon God."[47] Jesus
and God become persons men can relate to. Peter Marshall referred to God as
"the Chief," speaking as if he were taking orders from a corporation executive.
The image of Jesus as soft, gentle, effeminate received revamping: in 1924 Dean
Sellers of the Chicago Art Institute asked artist Warner Sallman to come up
with a "virile, manly Christ."[48] Jesus became an athlete in one male narrative—
he was the "champion," the "greatest who ever lived."[49]

Dependence on God has consistently led to business (and other) success,
and not only in the pages of Norman Vincent Peale. Charles Colson observed
of his friend Thomas Phillips, at age forty the chairman of the board of Raytheon, that "With any other man the notion of relying on God would have
seemed to me pure Pollyana. Yet I had to be impressed with the way this man
ran his company in the equally competitive world of business: ignoring his
enemies, trying to follow God's ways. Since his conversion Raytheon had never
done better. Sales and profits soaring. Maybe there was something to it; any
way it's tough to argue with success."[50] If it's not success precisely, then it's the
practicality of Christianity that men have latched onto. A husband who went
reluctantly to New York City's Calvary Church for his wife's sake was won
over; he was convinced that "religion is a practical thing."[51]

Although in the twentieth century women continued to lead the way to
deeper and richer spiritual experiences, men in the same century have forged
their own male organizations to promote the religious lives of their brothers.
The Men and Religion Forward Movement, founded in 1911, was one of the
first in this century. Youth for Christ originated in the activities of Jack Wyrtzen
who in the thirties began with an exclusively male organization, modeled on a
fraternity and called Chi Beta Alpha.[52] Not only was Charles Colson converted
by a male friend—Tom Phillips—but once a "Christian" he was welcomed into
the all-male prayer breakfasts in the White House.

In their attempts to "masculinize" evangelical Protestantism, men may have
found feminine allies. With varying degrees of self-consciousness, evangelical
women have pressed their men forward to take up leadership in churches and
fellowships in order to get them into religious activity. Observing one charismatic fellowship in upstate New York, sociologist Susan Rose explained the

intentional submission of wives to their husbands: "since women, historically, had been the ones in the church with the men staying at home on Sundays, the fellowship needed to bring men into the church 'for they are the natural head.' " Explained one of these women, a former feminist, "a lot of us had to step down in order for our husbands to rise to their God-given responsibilities and positions." Rose speculates that these women "see themselves as knowingly and willingly relinquishing authority and power in order to attract their men into the fellowship . . . By defining themselves as soft, they believe they have allowed their men to appear as strong and in control. In the process, many men, in fact, have come to feel more competent, capable, and responsible."[53]

Over the past two centuries the narratives have consistently served many of the same purposes in women's lives. On the one hand, they tell of—and assist—the socialization of women into a patriarchal culture. On the other hand, they allow for another, divine patriarch whose will does not always concur with the human patriarch's. In fact, they do more than "allow" for the divine patriarch; the most intense conversion narrators place him emphatically at the very center of their lives. In some narratives, when his will is ignored—often because it contradicts social norms—he makes life dreadfully uncomfortable. Thus, there is always the chance that God's commands will force radical changes upon a woman, as often they did in the narratives of nineteenth-century black women.

There is also the possibility that the main text—that which describes the woman's submission to men—will become increasingly "rhetorical." The twentieth century—and to a lesser extent the late nineteenth century—has offered women a great many competing texts—women's rights, equality of the sexes, the alteration in family configurations, the statistics showing mothers in the job force and heading households; the "mess" that men have made of things. Conservative evangelicals of course attempt to protect their daughters (and sons) from those contravening stories. They enroll them in "Christian" schools and colleges, ban or discourage television, movies, the things of "the world." But as long as they take seriously their evangelical imperative—to bring the good news to others—and also as long as they have their economic and political reasons to participate in the culture, they cannot afford to remain completely ignorant of or oblivious to other texts. Yet the larger culture supports the subtext of the conversion narratives insofar as they advance the empowerment of women—more than it endorses the main evangelical text of male headship. It seems likely the "subversive" aspects of the subtext will continue to be potent. Of course, we could perhaps discern a subtext in the rhetoric of the dominant culture—a nostalgic yearning for the old, simpler day when "men were men and women were women" and the hierarchies were safely in place. It will be interesting to see how evangelical conversion stories develop from here. It's my guess that the female conversion narratives of whatever decade depend for their power on the interplay between—the tensions between—the text and subtext. If one or the other becomes "mere rhetoric," outmoded and hollow convention, then we will begin to hear a very different kind of story.

EIGHT

Twentieth-Century
Out-of-Church Narratives

In the twentieth century the classical Christian conversion narrative has had to compete with a multitude of other narrative accounts of personal transformation. Americans have been converted to other religions—Buddhism, Judaism, the Church of Scientology. And they have experienced radical transformations as a result of encounters with powerful secular ideas and movements—psychotherapy and other forms of emotional healing, new attitudes toward the body, and compelling intellectual and political ideas.

It may seem arbitrary to draw distinctions between secular and religious conversion narratives, because many a radical personal transformation is remembered as miraculous and inherently religious, whether or not it takes the classical form. To further complicate matters, many converts tell stories that are difficult to categorize as either wholly religious or secular, for example, those from the Church of Scientology.[1] Yet this chapter will assume the existence of a rough category of secular narrative; it will look at conversion narratives that begin in personal transformation but do not result in adherence to an identifiable religious group; rather, there follows a fervent adoption of a political or cultural movement or idea. The conversion may be spurred by discovery of a new academic discipline, of feminism, or of a life free of drugs; typically young women have been "converted" by a saving knowledge of an innovative pedagogy or feminist studies. Early in the twentieth century Sophia Fahs taught an experimental Sunday school at New York's Teachers College:

> Altogether this experience was more thrilling than any previous teaching experience I had known. When combined with the further *awakening* that came to my mind as a result of the dynamic courses I was taking under Dr. McMurry and others at Teachers College, the visiting I could do in the Teachers College experimental and practice week-day school, I felt myself being *born again*.[2]

Under the impact of a new pedagogy, Fahs's life changed dramatically; she became a much more effective teacher; as a result her pupils, she herself, and even the world all looked radically different to her.

A secular conversion can result in "deconversion" from Christianity; as a young girl Elizabeth Cady Stanton broke with Protestant theological teaching and was "converted" to a rational, scientific view of the world; she used traditional language to describe her new sense of freedom: "I found my way out of the darkness into the clear sunlight of Truth. My religious superstitions gave place to rational ideas based on scientific facts, and in proportion, as I looked at everything from a new standpoint, I grew more and more happy, day by day."[3]

As these two examples show, the essential movement of many twentieth-century conversion narratives is no longer from sinfulness to salvation, but rather from an undesirable condition—confusion, depression, fear, despair, boredom, ignorance, aimlessness—to a desirable one—freedom, unity, joy, serenity, knowledge, wholeness, purposefulness. The transformation may well carry strong moral overtones: the narrator engages in movement from "bad" to "good," from destructive to constructive, from negative to positive. As this allusion to polarities suggests, there is a more than casual relationship between the traditional religious and secular narratives, although the nature of the relationship varies and is not always easy to identify or make claims about. In some cases an actual, demonstrable link connects evangelical Protestantism and out-of-church narrators, for example, in the case of Alcoholics Anonymous, whose roots clearly lie in the evangelical Protestant Oxford Group. Sometimes the connection is more presumptive: the "secular" convert is the son or daughter of a minister and employs the familiar religious language learned in childhood in a new context. In the case of American feminism, the women's movement has until recently evolved in close connection with Protestant evangelicalism: leading feminists such as Elizabeth Cady Stanton and Frances Willard have grown up in evangelical families, and some of them have remained closely tied to the evangelical tradition.

At the very least one can claim that the pattern of a radical religious conversion has remained a powerful metaphor in our culture. And well it might. Conversion language pervades the ordinary rhetoric available to most Americans; it remains a pervasive presence in the hymns and literature of twentieth-century America. The most secular-minded Americans sing "Amazing Grace," and speak routinely of "Paul on the road to Damascus," or Bunyan's pilgrim's "slough of despond." And with a push of radio or TV buttons, the unchurched tune into millions of evangelical Protestants who still use the language not as metaphor but as a description of their deepest spiritual reality.

Perhaps most telling of all, advertisers have developed an addiction to the conversion pattern. The use of the right mouthwash rescues Americans from halitosis and wallflower status; a switch in shampoo yields shining hair and brilliant social standing in place of ignominy and lifeless strands; iron pills turn the party pooper into the life of the party; with the correct floor wax, dirty floors gleam. Over and over Americans presumably worried about their low sex and personal appeal, their lack of savor for life, and their filthy surroundings are reborn to happiness, popularity, cleanliness, health, and perfection—

in short, a state of heavenly bliss. Not infrequently, women, still inclined to accuse themselves of falling short, are the intended recipients of these appeals.

Whether in its secular or sacred form, then, the conversion narrative remains an understandably powerful genre. It is inherently dramatic, setting up a dialogue between opposing views of the world. It insists upon surprise: the saint emerges from the sinner, or in more secular versions, the swan issues from the ugly duckling, the success from the failure. The genre enshrines the impossible, the miraculous event. It promises radical personal improvement, and peace and happiness. It makes use of rhetoric that can stir at a deep level: rhythmic, repetitive language (some claim that our language is rhythmic, alliterative, and repetitive when it is expressing our most intense feelings). It imposes meaning and pattern on experiences that may otherwise appear chaotic, idiosyncratic, random, inexplicable, and even frightening.

Interestingly, the pattern of radical conversion has not been the only one available to the twentieth century. In the concept of evolution—that is, of gradual and progressive change and growth—we possess a potent metaphor. We might expect that a society proud of its thoroughly scientific orientation would readily embrace such a "scientific" model of change. Indeed, the evolutionary viewpoint has attracted its able exponents: John Dewey preeminently, or earlier, Horace Bushnell. In the field of medicine there may be "miracle" cures and vaccines; on the other hand, we've learned a single "cure" for cancer is unlikely; cancer, it seems, will yield only to slow incremental developments, and many other medical advances proceed in the same way. Reform in American politics involves mostly slow and uncertain compromise and negotiation; our last violent revolution took place over two hundred years ago. Psychoanalysis and many psychotherapies are evolutionary; their healing takes effect over time, often over years. Sigmund Freud did not think of psychoanalysis as a process of conversion. Rather, it was a painstaking exercise in understanding oneself, gaining a critical distance on one's culture, and learning to tolerate ambiguity and complexity. Most people, if pressed, will admit that our periods of sudden illumination, of epiphany—our apparent conversions—are actually a long time in the making: they evolve. And once we've had our illuminations, we may struggle a long while before they thoroughly transform our outlook and behavior.

And yet the eagerness to pattern experience as a sudden, instantaneous, and dramatic metamorphosis keeps reasserting itself. If Freud did not regard therapy as a conversion vehicle, many of the psychotherapies with their roots in Freudian understanding have insisted on accelerating, dramatizing, and sometimes even sacralizing the process. Freud's one-time disciple, Carl Jung, moved much closer to conceiving of analysis as a religious transaction. EST and other popular psychological techniques rely on the notion of sudden, forced transformation. And patients of even the most conservative psychotherapies half expect moments of sudden life-transforming insight.

It is tempting to claim that the penchant for the conversion pattern—whether religious or secular—is peculiarly American. Yet the idea of conversion is obviously far from unique to American Protestantism or even to Christianity. Many of our model narratives have come not from the United States at all, but from Great Britain or the ancient Middle East. Dwight L. Moody's first conversions on a massive scale took place not in his native America but rather in England and Scotland. And students of non-Western cultures have helped us see that those societies abound in narratives that include many of the same "conversion" elements.

But if the American affinity for telling conversion stories is not unique, the theme of radical change is still deeply embedded in American consciousness. Some of the most fundamental historical narratives of American life are about far-reaching transformation: the immigrant experience of leaving the Old World for the New, the American Revolution that brought the colonies from tyranny to liberty, the deliverance of the black slaves from bondage to freedom, the nineteenth-century journey from Eastern civilization to Western wilderness, the change from an agrarian identity to an urban industrial one, the Horatio Alger myth of meteoric rise from rags to riches. Often the past is left so far back as to be almost unrecognizable. Fixity, tradition, immobility, unchangingness often seem foreign to the American psyche. One 1950s observer captured the sense of infinite possibility gained by turning one's back on the limitations of the past and looking to the future: "Whether it's plants or people, starting from scratch is an old custom in America. I thank God for a country where the 'nobody' can become 'somebody,' the handicapped rises above any obstacle, and the impossible, is, through God's help, accomplished with regularity."[4]

And certainly American women have experienced transformations as far-reaching as those of any group in this century. They have achieved the vote, have embarked on careers outside their homes, and have discovered feminism and liberation, their own sexuality, lesbianism, and women's studies. It would be surprising if women had not felt a need to understand and legitimate radical changes that so often fly in the face of social and cultural norms and of their own socialization. Nor is it startling that often they have needed to borrow language to describe such experiences, for they have had few female literary traditions (other than fiction) of their own. As Carolyn Heilbrun observes, "there still exists little organized sense of what a woman's biography or autobiography should look like."[5] Feminist literary critics have noted the existence of "the woman's quest for her own story," a quest that still goes on a couple of decades after the beginning of the most recent phase of the women's movement.

As we will see when we discuss the narratives of lesbians later in the chapter, this group of women has possessed the fewest usable literary traditions. Again and again lesbians who have "come out" say that until a certain point in their lives they could not make sense of their feelings and inclinations, in part because they could not name them. They either did not know the word "lesbian" or attached such negative connotations to it as to find it virtually unusable. In the words of one lesbian writer, "even our most personal herstories are denied us, because we do not have the information to identify them for what they are."[6] Adrienne Rich described the problem:

> A woman can say. . . . "Yesterday I slept with men and called myself heterosexual; today I am interested only in women; tomorrow I will be a lesbian." But much depends on how she names her own past, how she remembers it, how she has been permitted to name it and remember it given the limitations of language.[7]

Another writer explained the necessity for lesbians to tell their stories: "In our society, the becoming of a Lesbian is a leap into the void of the inconceivable, that which is unutterable, that which has no name. . . . Our stories must be told, and they must be heard."[8] The need to name is of course not limited to lesbians. Robin Morgan, discussing her embrace of feminism, remarked, "It is as if women were realizing that, to paraphrase Mary Daly, the ultimate degradation foisted on any oppressed people is a thievery of the right 'to name'— to name ourselves and our relation to the universe."[9]

But women have possessed one "right to name" for a long time, albeit one conferred by the patriarchy—the right to name themselves sinners converted into heirs of God. They have not held a monopoly on the Protestant conversion narrative, of course—men needed to name their spiritual experiences too—but they have used it with particular zeal and fervor. It would be remarkable, then, if twentieth-century women did not draw upon the conversion narrative—consciously or unconsciously—as a source in their quest to "name" their most intense emotional transformations.

CONVERSION TO FEMINISM

Since the late 1960s thousands of women have told stories of the radical change wrought in their lives by the discovery of feminism. The editors of *Ms.* magazine reported in late 1973 that they were receiving two hundred letters a day, the majority of which were "intensely personal accounts of how one's individual life is changing."[10] Like the traditional conversion narrative, the feminist narrative has followed a predictable story line. The narrator has been raised to play the role of conventional mother and wife. Often she has spurned college education (why does she need it?) or, if she goes to college, she pays little attention to the question of career. (Certainly she shuns the "male" subjects of math and science.) She fulfills the role expectations; she becomes a good wife, mother, and housekeeper. Then she reaches a crisis. Ostensibly a woman who has "everything," she may find herself unaccountably bored, restless, depressed, and angry with her husband. She may stumble into an activity outside the home that unexpectedly reveals skills, enthusiasm, and competence for something besides her household roles. More radical crises may occur when her husband abruptly demands a divorce or takes up with another woman. Another radical turning point sometimes develops when a middle-aged woman must face the fact that her grown children need her less. A victim of the "empty nest" syndrome, she is suddenly unemployed. Usually in these situations the woman blames herself for her misery and inability to adjust. What typically resolves the crisis is the discovery of the women's movement, often through the reading of feminist literature. Betty Friedan's *Feminine Mystique* is usually the first book a prospective feminist encounters, but she goes on to Kate Millett, Susan Brownmiller, Robin Morgan, and others, sometimes devouring all the feminist literature she can get her hands on (in the manner of a Christian convert looking for devotional guides). She may form or join a consciousness-raising group, tell her story, listen to the stories of others, and realize that many women are undergoing similar turmoil in their lives. The outcome of this reading and sharing of experiences is the emergence of a new self, sometimes signaled by declaring oneself a "feminist," and by location in a supportive community of women. The narrator may return to school, go on to develop or resume a career, leave behind her marriage and find a new lover or, if her husband is willing, adapt her marriage to new understandings of her worth and role. There are variations of course. Women who have grown up after the current resurgence of the women's movement may take its teachings too lightly, only to reach a crisis later and discover how meaningful they really are.

A feminist "convert," Jane O'Reilly, tells us she had married and divorced twice; from one of her marriages she had a son. Though she was writing about women as part of her professional life, she had difficulty connecting the lessons of women's liberation to her own circumstances. She was wary of "the selfish whining of spoiled crybabies who place self-fulfillment above responsibility." Typically, she blamed herself and her choices for the "oddities of my life." Between 1972 and 1975 she underwent an extended crisis:

> I stopped speaking to old friends, provoked scenes in editorial offices, became irrationally attached to inexplicable love affairs. I could barely write, and finally I could barely speak. Yet not once did it ever occur to me that my terror, my outraged sense of betrayal, my insistence on romance as a solution, had anything to do with the phrases I was reading and even writing. "The courage to change," "fear of success," "the risk of autonomy," did not seem to describe my feeling, . . .

She "thrashed bitterly against the discovery that the only way out was forward. There was no going back." She insisted that she was bored writing about women until she happened to review Susan Brownmiller's *Against Our Will*. She was finally able to go forward, scared but no longer bored or depressed.[11] Like other conversion narrators, O'Reilly contrasts her life before liberation, when she seldom ventured to go anyplace, even the movies, by herself and feared speaking in public, to her life after liberation, when she had learned self-confidence and self-reliance. "I could probably walk through brick walls now if I had to."[12]

O'Reilly's narrative, while written according to familiar expectations, is individualized, the work of a professional writer. Other narratives follow the formula for feminist conversion narrative more closely, especially if they must conform to space or time limitations. Suzanne Rodriguez wrote the *Ms.* editors in 1973,

> I am a woman who, almost all my life, believed without question what I was told—women aren't as smart as men, women aren't happy being successful, to get ahead you should be pretty, witty, and secretly wise. I consequently floundered around in secretarial jobs for years, involving myself in work that was never challenging to me intellectually, work that never lit a spark in me. I tried to find meaning through the men in my life—fortunately for me I *was* pretty and witty. But I never wanted to marry, and whenever I looked forward to the rest of my life, I felt lost, because the thought of being autonomous by doing work I hate far, far into the future, made me panic. Then I discovered the movement, both through a con-sciousness-raising group and through a heavy amount of reading. I realized that I wasn't the only woman who felt inferior, stupid, restless, underutilized, unused, intellectually underfed. That realization turned to anger, anger turned slowly to action, and action, eventually, forced me to change my life around. At the age of twenty-five I started college on a full-time basis and finished my first semester with a four-point average and a small scholarship.[13]

Like other narratives of rapid transformation, the feminist version has de-veloped its own language—its characteristic phrases and its own labels. Nar-rators will often recall a moment when they realized they didn't know who they really were and must start anew to carve out an identity. Some narrators, especially *Ms.* readers, have adopted the "click! of recognition" introduced by Jane O'Reilly in a 1973 *Ms.* article entitled "Click! The Housewife's Moment of Truth." The "click" described by O'Reilly was "that parenthesis of truth around a little thing that completes the puzzle of reality in women's minds— the moment that brings a gleam to our eyes and means the revolution has begun."[14] Usually the click is occasioned by some seemingly minor but outra-geous male remark or action.

Most feminist writers recognize that the matter of transformation is a com-plex phenomenon, rarely accomplished without struggle over time. "Personal change is at best painstaking and incremental," acknowledged Mary Thom, in introducing the collection of letters to *Ms.*[15] O'Reilly's own liberation was more complicated than the before-click-after pattern would suggest. In fact, she ad-mits she still has not solved the "hopeless entangled problems of love and sex." She needs both simultaneously, she says, the love of a man and the stimulation of her work, but they rarely seem to work well together.[16] Yet narratives con-tinue to get built around a structure of radical change—a needful fiction be-cause it is an effective way to interpret the meaning of one's experiences to oneself and others. Indeed, so needful is it that I suspect that feminists, like more traditional converts, *remember* a transformation experience as sudden and sweeping, even when it was actually more gradual.

By and large the connection between many feminist narratives and the tra-ditional Protestant conversion narrative lies in the common structure of radical personal change rather than in shared language and allusions. But while feminist conversion language is often peculiar to the feminist experience, in some cases the tie between the two narrative genres extends even to the language, as when one woman asks herself, "Where is the Promised Land?" and another describes the women's community as like a "church group." New feminists are "taken in—in the same way a church takes in a new member. I see feminism as very much like a religious thing."[17] Religious language is especially pervasive in Rosemary Daniell's story of her discovery of feminism. Growing up as a "Southern woman," Daniell mastered even more thoroughly than her northern peers the financial and emotional dependence on men deemed approriate to women; she also learned she should suppress her anger and sexuality. At sexual suppression she was unsuccessful, but the Baptist rhetoric she had imbibed as a child stayed with her. When she gave in to sexual passion she thought of herself as "defiled," a "vessel of evil," a "wretch." She lamented, "I did wrong, sinned—what's worse, wanted to. Everything Mother, Grandmother Lee, and my Baptist Sunday school teacher said was true: if you let boys have their way, you'll be ruined."[18] Lying awake in bed after a petting session, she described herself "writhing in the eternal hellfire I was so sure would be my only fate."[19] She also faulted herself for being "stubborn," "rebellious," much in the manner of sinners under conviction. When she was able to curb her sexuality, on the other hand, or sanctify it with marriage vows, she felt "held in the arms of Jesus."[20] This comfort never lasted long, however, nor did her marriages.

At length Daniell read *The Feminine Mystique*: it "affected me like successful surgery on a person who has been blind."[21] Not all of her narrative echoed the language of conversion ("I was blind and now can see"); other images competed. At one point she reflected, "I . . . felt like a kamikaze pilot of Southern feminine experience, shooting forward in the grips of a vision from which there was no return."[22] But, launched on a career as a poet, she goes on the road alone conducting poetry workshops and again borrows the language of conversion. At first the experience frightened her, she recalled, but at last she adjusted: "It was as though a new self had been born, the self I was when I was alone."[23] Clearly, in becoming a liberated woman Daniell had to reject the Protestant teachings of her girlhood. But she had not abandoned its language and rhetorical patterns; rather she had adapted them to her new experiences, and with their assistance she had been "born again" into a new identity.[24]

NARRATIVES OF FEMALE DELIVERANCE FROM ADDICTION

In their greater twentieth-century freedom, women have become more vulnerable than previously to drug addiction; among other problems, they have had to grapple with the ravages of excessive and habitual drinking. They have also managed to recover from this affliction—often with the help of Alcoholics Anonymous—and like their male counterparts have told the stories of their

deliverance. Many of their narratives have closely followed the evangelical Protestant pattern. The typical female alcoholic starts by finding the world empty
and pointless and herself unloved. She begins drinking but remains confident
that she can stop any time she really wants to. Like the prospective religious
convert, she is convinced she can save herself—but she does not wish to just
yet. Before she can be freed from drink, she must come to realize the wrong-
headedness of her assumption; she must admit that she does not have the
strength to stop drinking on her own; like the sinner, she must be driven by
misery and helplessness to throw herself onto divine mercy. Once this is accomplished, she experiences the redeemed sinner's sense of peace, serenity, and
love. She goes on to help others suffering the same miseries, in part through
the telling and retelling of her story. She may backslide—that is, she may resume
drinking—but as soon as she returns to the right relationship with the "higher
power," she can successfully put away drink again.

The connections between Protestant female narratives and the narratives of
women in Alcoholics Anonymous are far from accidental. Billy Wilson, the
reformed alcoholic who started AA in 1935, had managed to break free of
drink with the help of a friend who had himself been assisted to sobriety
through the ministrations of the Oxford Group. This Protestant evangelical
organization was the creation of Frank Buchman (1878–1961), a Lutheran
minister and one-time lecturer in personal evangelism at Hartford Seminary.
Buchman, believing he had "received from God a commission to convert the
world,"[25] began the organization that became known by various names: "Moral
Re-Armament," the "First-Century Fellowship," and the Oxford Group. It was
especially active in the United States and England, though it extended elsewhere
around the world; it peaked in the twenties and thirties and waned after World
War II. Its aim was to evangelize individuals through the vehicle of house parties
held in the homes of the wealthy. The Oxford Group largely avoided taking
particular theological positions in favor of its primary goal of "changing"—
that is, converting—individuals. Those who had been "changed" were charged
to go out and help change others. For Oxford Group members change involved,
among other ingredients, "conviction"—the realization of one's sinfulness;
"confession," that is, the public or private narration of one's sins; and of course
conversion. The Group also taught a set of moral precepts referred to as the
"Four Absolutes"—perfect honesty, purity (in a mostly sexual sense), unself-
ishness, and love. Buchman, who had been converted at an English Keswick
meeting, taught holiness attitudes. Adherents spoke often of "surrendering"
themselves to God, not only at the time of conversion but also repeatedly ever
afterward, and they spoke constantly of abandoning "self-will" to follow the
divine will.

The impact of the Oxford Group upon Wilson, AA's founder, is clear from
the AA literature. Though Wilson

> could not accept all the tenets of the Oxford Group, he was convinced of the need
> for moral inventory, confession of personality defects, and restitution to those

harmed, helpfulness to others, and the necessity of belief in and dependence upon God.[26]

These Oxford Group emphases made their appearance in many of the "Twelve Steps" prescribed by AA for recovering alcoholics.

"Confession" was considered central to the Oxford Group goals of convincing oneself and others of the need for a change of life. As Oxford Group adherents described the misery of their lives in sin, so alcoholics were expected to tell the story of their degradation and helplessness under the influence of alcohol. Just as potential converts could not recognize their need for grace until they acknowledged that they were in the bonds of sin, so alcoholics could not break free of the domination of alcohol until they realized how truly they were under its power. Oxford converts had to undergo the painful confession that they were sinners; AA participants had to confess that they were alcoholics. (Even after they stopped drinking, they remained alcoholics, albeit "recovering alcoholics"; similarly, Oxford Group members remained "sinners," albeit redeemed ones.) Members of both groups had to admit their utter helplessness and hence their total dependence on God. For both, an important "fruit" of conversion was the impulse to tell others what had happened, in the hope that they could be helped also. Both groups talked of a definite program, a set of steps to salvation, whether from sin or drink.

Not surprisingly, given the ties to the Oxford Group, then, AA language has echoed the rhetoric as well as the structural patterns of classical conversion narratives. In both forms the narrator comes to realize the emptiness of what the world has to offer. One female AA narrator recalled that "I rushed from pleasure to pleasure, and found the returns diminishing to the vanishing point." Another related, "I lived mostly for pleasure." As in evangelical narratives, alcoholic narrators recall a descent into misery, which they relate to feeling unloved, unlovable, inferior, rejected, and abandoned. One AA narrator recalled, "I spent most of my life worrying about myself, thinking that I was unwanted, that I was unloved." And there are the familiar motifs of defiance, self-will, and rebellion: "I rebelled against everything I'd ever heard as a child, and I lived to suit myself." Another narrator recalled, "I hated myself worse and worse, and as I hated myself I became more defiant toward everything and everybody." Often alcoholics hit bottom—or a series of bottoms. Bottom often takes the form of a drinking spree that outlasts previous ones and that threatens to destroy the alcoholic's physical and mental being. Often the alcoholic welcomes the threat to her life, for she feels so full of self-loathing—as do "convicted" sinners—that she longs to die. Prospective converts and alcoholics reach similar turning points. Converts come to the recognition that they are far too sinful to save themselves. Alcoholics reach the realization that, contrary to what they have been telling themselves, they cannot control their drinking—or, as the first of the "Twelve Steps" puts it, "We admitted we were powerless over alcohol—that our lives had become unmanageable." While traditional converts often arrive at this point of no return through the aid of the Bible and converted friends, alcoholics come to this juncture through the literature of the AA—especially the "Big Book," the AA "Bible"—and the friendship of recovering alcoholics. In their helplessness both groups of converts turn to God. As the AA steps two and three read, "2. [We] Came to believe that a Power greater than ourselves could restore us to sanity. 3. [We] Made a decision to turn our will and our lives over to God."[27]

Once converted, narrators—both evangelical and alcoholic—strive for a closer and more complete relationship with God. As AA's eleventh step directs, "[We] Sought through prayer and meditation to improve our conscious contact with God . . . , praying only for knowledge of His will for us and the power to carry that out." This is the holiness experience, perhaps at one remove, and as mediated through the Oxford Group.[28] One recovering alcoholic echoed the language of the "deeper life" when she said, "In the spiritual strength I had found—because of AA, I felt that I had made a complete surrender, that I really had turned my life over [to God] that summer." Then her husband became terminally ill, and in the manner of many Christian converts she found that she was not completely "yielded" after all; she could not accept his death: "I knew then that I hadn't made a total surrender, because I tried to bargain with the God I had found, 'Anything but that! Don't do that to me!' " At length she came to accept even her husband's death—she "made the surrender" after all. Another "surrendered" female AA narrator turned to Matthew 26:42: "my once over-weening will has finally found its proper place, for I can say many times daily, 'Thy will be done, not mine.' "[29]

In addition to this closer communion with God, another "fruit" of conversion AA-style has proved similar to the outcome of more traditional twentieth-century conversions. The sobered and transformed alcoholic experiences love, acceptance (including self-acceptance), security, serenity, and emotional healing. One female AA member was enabled to forgive the mother who had deserted her when she was seven. Another reported that "great floods of enlightenment showed me as I really was and I was like them [other recovering alcoholics, her friends] . . . Suddenly I could accept myself, faults and all, as I was for weren't we all like that? And, accepting, I felt a new inner comfort, and the willingness and strength to do something about traits I couldn't live with." She went on, "the light streamed in. I wasn't trapped. I wasn't helpless. I was free and I didn't have to 'show them.' This wasn't 'religion'—this was freedom! Freedom from anger and fear, freedom to know happiness." Though she downplayed the religious dimension of her experience (could religious experience involve freedom for women, she may have wondered), it was clearly religious at its core.[30]

As in traditional conversions, backsliding was always a peril for alcoholics and came of forgetting the need for dependence on God and for the renunciation of self-will. One narrator had briefly returned to drinking because, she said, she insisted on "sitting in the driver's seat," on "running the show." As soon as she restored control of her life to God, she could once again stop drinking:

I feel that I have been restored to health and sanity these past years, not through my own efforts nor as a result of anything I may have done, but because I've come to believe—to really believe—that alone I can do nothing, that my own innate selfishness and stubbornness are the evils which if left unguarded, can drive me to alcohol . . . I know that for help in the spiritual sphere I have to turn to a Higher Power.[31]

Finally, of course, a sign that an alcoholic had experienced conversion was for her to tell her story, to witness, to provide an example and encouragement for others. The "Big Book" of AA starts by outlining the "how" of the recovery process, but then devotes the remaining three quarters of its 575 pages to the "Personal Stories" of male and female alcoholics. As the preface explains, "to show other alcoholics *precisely how we have recovered* is the main purpose of this book . . . We think this account of our experiences will help everyone to better understand the alcoholic . . . " And the passage ends with the typical evangelical faith that witnessing will encourage others (including even nonalcoholics) to change their lives: "we are sure our way of living has advantages for all."[32]

Recovered female drug addicts tend to recount similar narratives. As a child, one such narrator, Susan Lydon, was convinced her father did not love her; she felt "unloved and unlovable." Starting with marijuana, she moved on to more and more serious drugs. Like many addicts she clung to the illusion that she could control her habit, that she could stop anytime she really wished. But life grew more and more bleak; dealing drugs on the Lower East Side of Manhattan, she recalled, using Christian imagery, that "with its abandoned buildings and hollow-eyed people, the Lower East Side looked like a circle of hell." She experienced several low points: she lost the ability to hold writing jobs (a source of pride during the earlier phases of her addiction), came to wish for death as the only release, and—worst of all—discovered that the drugs had ultimately lost their power to blot out her pain. Then came the moment of conversion, with its typical surrender: "I gave up. And at that moment of hopelessness and despair, the grace of God entered my life." Lydon's recovery, though a difficult struggle, steadily advanced from this point. "Like Lazarus, I was coming back from the dead, and it hurt." Slowly she began to love herself, to feel serene and content, and even joyful. Lydon, who had been raised a Jew, did not say much about the precise nature of her religious faith. But, though she did not speak much about God or her relationship to the divine, clearly the narrative of spiritual transformation had furnished the model for her story. After a deeper and deeper descent into misery she had finally realized her utter dependence on drugs and like Christians had been driven to accept grace. Like religious converts also, she had been born again (raised from the dead), experienced the rich fruits of rebirth, and now was telling her story, obviously in the hope of helping other addicts like herself.[33]

Overindulgence in food has represented another addiction, especially for women, who, according to popular lore, overeat because they are depressed, or dislike themselves, or feel unloved. Certainly they are assumed to worry more than men about the consequences for their bodies of overeating. Interestingly, the early participants in Weight Watchers were all women; men joined only later. Jean Nidetch, who founded the group in the early sixties, outlined the typical women's conversion tale. Like sinners, alcoholics, and drug addicts, overweight people fooled themselves: they were only "chubby" or "plump," certainly not "fat"; there was "more of them to love." They claimed gland problems. They bought candy or chips for their children, then ate the stuff themselves. They retained the illusion of control over their habit by a series of diets, some of them successful in the short run. As with others gripped by an injurious habit, salvation lay in the ability finally to level with oneself: "I am *fat*; I'm not able to control my eating." As in other cases of addiction, some of the necessary support came from telling one's story to others, including the confession of what traditional narrators would call their "sins." Nidetch confessed eating cookies in the bathroom in the middle of the night; a teacher told of surreptitiously digging out a doughnut discarded by a pupil in a school wastebasket.

When Weight Watchers had succeeded in losing weight they had not merely accomplished weight reduction and a change in eating habits, but, more significantly, they had also embarked on "a new way to live."[34] Like sinners and alcoholics, Weight Watchers told their conversion narratives. One wrote to Nidetch,

> If it weren't for you, I would still be sitting behind 422 pounds of wall. Now I'm within striking distance of a new life. I've thought about suicide more than once. I had tried every diet, psychiatry, hypnotism. I would have let a witch doctor do a rain dance on my chest if he would tell me that weight would come off. The combination of love, information, companionship and commiseration of fellow fat persons I found at the lectures did it for me.

Clearly Nidetch saw herself as evangelist: "I wish I could reach every obese person in existence, to help them learn to live the life of a thin person." She recalled the early days of Weight Watchers in a biblical image: "It was like walking into the wilderness. I didn't really know what was happening."[35]

Nidetch claimed that Weight Watchers (and by implication its language) was not modeled on any other organization, for example Alcoholics Anonymous (which it *sounds* most like); rather, she said, it grew directly out of the needs and experience of herself and her friends and of those who were later attracted to the group. Yet it is difficult to believe that Nidetch and her associates had not somewhere unconsciously imbibed the patterns and language of other conversion narrators.

Another similar group, Overeaters Anonymous, started in 1960, explicitly followed the AA formula. Its device was *psychomachia*, "that inward battle for the soul which could be resolved only by a human admission of weakness: 'It is weakness, not strength, that binds us to each other and to a higher power and somehow gives us an ability to do what we cannot do alone.' "[36] The similarities between dieters and traditional converts did not escape Elisabeth Elliot, the evangelical writer, when she compared the "testimonies" of those who were losing weight (as in Weight Watchers or Overeaters Anonymous) and those who embrace Christianity. Most strikingly, she had heard the newly-thin refer to themselves as "being born again."[37] And Joan Scobey, who lost forty pounds in a year, recalled the experience as "my rebirth, a new person in a new body," and referred more generally to the " 'born again' quality of a successful diet."[38]

LESBIAN COMING OUT STORIES

The connections between traditional conversion narratives and the testimonies of those who have conquered their addictions are quite clear. In contrast, lesbian coming out stories would be least likely to avail themselves of the "patriarchal" language of spiritual conversion narratives. Or so we would expect. In declaring themselves lesbians, women embark on the most radical life changes possible: they turn their backs on the romantic love of males, the roles of wives and, sometimes, of mothers, and most of the usual forms of emotional and financial dependence on men. Their rejection of patriarchal language is so intense that some even eschew standard spellings: "woman" may become "womon"; "women" may change into "wimmin." One would expect them studiously to avoid a narrative pattern in which a woman submits to a male God. Gay men do not necessarily have this problem, at least not to the same degree, and indeed a collection of gay coming out stories is likely to have a coming out tale that doubles as spiritual narrative.[39]

Unlike their gay brothers, though, lesbians have faced a special difficulty: they have had very little language with which to describe their radical life-changing experiences, very few models to consult.[40] Few women before them have related lesbian life stories; and it is a rare mother who can or will tell her daughter of a lesbian experience of her own. Even the word "lesbian" has proven difficult: either it is unknown (one woman heard it for the first time at age forty-six) or inconceivable: "Me, who had gone to bed with all those men? Me, who hated that awful word 'lesbian'?"[41] One woman found the word so impossible to apply to herself that "I wrote in my journal over and over, 'I am a lesbian, I am a lesbian, I am a lesbian,' hoping it would sink in and become comprehensible."[42]

Even the social sciences of the twentieth century—a source of some feminist theory—have failed lesbians as a source for language and ideas, since by and large they have either ignored lesbianism or treated it as deviant. As a resource the language of heterosexual relationships has its obvious limitations too. While heterosexual feminists can modify this language to suit their politics and experience, lesbians tend to find it totally unsatisfactory when applied to their own relationships.[43]

Many lesbian narrators, in their search for language and patterns with which to understand their experiences, have drawn upon the bipolar structure of the classical conversion story. They trace the familiar journey from misery to wholeness, from darkness to light. Though the precise details of their stories differ from those of conventional conversion narratives, the general movement is the same: from potential damnation to unconditional love. Lesbian narrators begin by thinking they are abnormal and therefore deservedly lonely and despised, and end with the glad understanding and acceptance of themselves as women "who love other women." One lesbian summed up her experience in the traditional terms of dark and light: "I had emerged from the shadowy closet into the light of my own joyous existence as a lesbian."[44] Many of the individual events in lesbian stories are analogous to those in traditional conversion narratives. The narrator can recall a conversion *moment*—usually when she was forced to admit to herself and to at least one other person that she is a lesbian. The conversion involves birth (one coming out story is entitled "I Am Born . . . ") to a new, lesbian self. As in traditional narratives the coming out story instills meaning in a life that has until now seemed pointless, shapeless, and unhappy; the lesbian realizes that her life has followed a plan all along, even though she failed to perceive it at the time. Beverly J. Toll's girlhood was miserable because she could not respond to the sexual advances of males in the manner of her female friends; after her coming out she recognized that her life had been a series of "steps leading to my eventual discovery of the joy of loving wimmin."[45] Barbara Grier described a successful reexamination of her pre-coming out life (before age twelve) "in order to find instances of behavior that would indicate that I would grow up and be a Lesbian."[46]

As in conventional narratives, a consequence of conversion is a sense of satisfaction and completion: both converts and self-acknowledged lesbians feel they have come "home." Nona Caspers recalled that "as I became familiar with more lesbians and aware that a lesbian culture did exist, I began remembering and understanding my childhood and adolescence. And I began to relax. There was a place for me. . . . I was lesbian. I was home."[47] If Caspers was "home," another lesbian had reached heaven: "I had the fervor of a new convert. I threw myself into women's activities, meetings, women's groups, coming out groups, gay causes, gay bars, and lesbians! . . . I felt I had died and gone to lesbian heaven."[48]

I am not claiming that lesbians, lacking a language to describe their experiences, deliberately looked to spiritual narrative for either a rhetorical or experiential model. What I do mean to suggest is that the basic bipolar structure—from defeat to triumph, from blindness to sight, from darkness to light—is so embedded in their cultural inheritance that they could hardly overlook the metaphor of radical religious change when they sought to give coherence, drama, meaning, and political correctness to their life stories. Indeed, often the users of this bipolar conversion structure seem unconscious of its origins. Susan Leigh Star, though, clearly recognizes them; she parodies the conversion form, poking fun at the sorts of claims that lesbians (and other converts) sometimes make:

> "Yes before I was a Lesbian I had no natural rhythm, my acne was terrible, I was constipated. And now . . . "
> " . . . you see before you . . . "
> " . . . the natural beauty of the earth . . . "
> " . . . the bliss of being queer . . . "
> " . . . the glory of sisterhood fulfilled . . . "[49]

If we look more closely at the various stages in the coming out story we will see further parallels between it and the classical narrative. First, the period before transformation contains some of the same miseries and also some of the same efforts to cope with the misery. Like traditional narrators, lesbian storytellers recall feeling rebellious—"rebellion against the traditionally female activities I was encouraged to enjoy," as one woman put it.[50] Another recalled that "I was in trouble all the time—fighting with my parents, dealing drugs, drinking. I see now it was because I realized I was different and didn't know what to do about it." Yet another "sassed" her teacher and was ejected from class. Lesbian narrators do not normally talk about having felt sinful, but they recall something analogous when they report having thought of themselves as "queer," "deviant," "different," "strange," isolated, the only women in the whole world who feel as they do. Often they strive mightily to be "normal," just as more traditional narrators struggle to be virtuous. They take comfort in a mother's reassurances that their attraction to women is just a "stage" or a "phase" in their growing up; when they engage in sexual relationships with girlfriends they tell themselves they are merely practicing for grown up heterosexual relationships; they turn to psychiatry; against their deeper inclinations they marry and bear children. But no matter how hard they try to adjust to heterosexual expectations they find themselves violating their inner natures.

Often a crisis stems from the establishment of an intense friendship with a girl or woman, a friendship whose sexual components cannot be ignored or denied or rationalized. The lesbian narrator realizes the futility of struggling against her nature any longer, much as the would-be convert recognizes how helpless are her efforts to reform herself and thereby earn her own salvation. Usually the relationship is sexually consummated, and then confessed in public.

Of course, the coming out is possible only because the appropriate language finally exists to give it meaning; thanks to the naming done by the gay movement, the convert has available the words with which to describe and acknowledge her experience. She has found a supportive community of women whose stories help shape her own emerging narrative. Her ability to name herself "lesbian" is in fact one of the high points of her coming out, just as the twentieth-century evangelical's ability to come out as a real "Christian" is a crucial part of her conversion.

A new life follows for the woman who has come out, though she may need time to get all the pieces into place. The narrator locates a new community of women, much as the traditional convert finds a supportive community of Christians or the alcoholic a group of sympathetic AA members. Also like the twentieth-century convert, the lesbian comes to accept and love herself, as she experiences the love and acceptance of those (mostly lesbians and sometimes gay men) around her. She begins to feel pride in her new self. Pride is not traditionally a "Christian" quality, but if pride is translated into self-confidence, boldness, and courage, one can find some commonality in the new lives of both classes of convert, lesbian and Christian. And of course lesbians, like born-again Christians, tell their stories—their "testimonies," to invoke the title of a recent book of lesbian coming out stories—to hearten, encourage, and instruct those they hope will come after them, as well as to affirm once again the choices they themselves have made.

To be sure, classic conversion narratives and coming out stories diverge in important and interesting ways. Coming out stories are not as formulaic (the formulas have yet to be created), and many of the formulaic phrases differ from those of the conversion narrative. (One formula, for instance, is to refer to oneself as a "woman-identified woman"; another is to label those hostile to homosexuals "homophobic.") Still, coming out stories contain verbal echoes of conversion narratives. One narrator calls her coming out story an "awakening"; another speaks of the "vile" associations of the word lesbian; yet another worries that she will be "hopelessly empty or lost" if she cannot manage to accept her identity as a lesbian.

There are other striking contrasts besides verbal ones. The converted narrator realizes how bad—how sinful—was her life before conversion; the lesbian learns to see at least some of her pre-awakening feelings and activities as healthy and *good* (though she had thought at the time that they were bad). The lesbian, once "out," learns to respect and even take pride in her woman's body and her once-aberrant sexuality. Obviously this is not an ingredient in the conversion narrative, though a converted narrator in the Beverly LaHaye and Marabel Morgan mold might claim to feel more comfortable with her body and her sexuality, understanding them as divine gifts (as long as they are exercised only within marriage). The lesbian tells of rejecting social and cultural norms and expectations about the role of women. Many coming out stories feature a narrator who starts out by keeping up heterosexual appearances, that is, staying in the closet, and ends up advertising and celebrating her homosexuality despite the possible disapproval of friends and family. The nineteenth-century conversion narrative traced the opposite movement: when one claimed to have abandoned sin and turned to God one was, on the contrary, accepting and affirming the norms of a dominant Protestant culture. One quit being aberrant and became exemplary.

In the twentieth century the contrast between coming out stories and spiritual narratives is not quite so stark as it would have been in the nineteenth century. In "accepting Christ as her Savior," the narrator acquiesces in the expectations of her subculture and wins its approval, but often finds herself violating what conservatives call the "secular humanist" values of the larger social establishment, which tends to respond with embarrassment or consternation to her avowal. In some contexts declaring herself a "Christian" can require as much courage as for a woman to name herself a lesbian.

Not all the coming out stories can locate one point in time, one event that marked the narrator's "coming out" (any more than all converted narrators can designate a precise moment of conversion). Occasionally lesbian narrators admit that life is a continuous process of coming out, more an evolutionary development than a sudden transformation. Susan Leigh Star expressed skepticism about how true to life the conversion pattern is. She says, "Coming out. And going back in. And peeking through the keyhole. Different parts bubble up from time to time. There's no such thing as a linear Lesbian." Ruth Baetz, in introducing a collection of lesbian stories, expressed surprise that not all the women she interviewed had experienced the same abrupt change in their lives she had: "I assumed the women had come to a sudden realization and that it had changed their lives drastically as it had mine."[51] Nevertheless, even "gradualist" narrators sometimes honor the narrative norm by looking for a turning point or points or at least remarking the absence of such a turning point. The lesbian who can state matter-of-factly that she has always been aware of her sexual identity and never uncomfortable with it—who claims to have experienced slow rather than abrupt change, or very little change at all—is the exception and not the rule.[52]

It is understandable that some feminists have deplored the imposition of formula and already existing pattern on women's experiences, arguing that such a practice ignores the real differences among women. Though they admit that the pattern is sometimes valuable because it affirms female commonalities and helps create a women's community, they claim that it denies the richness and variety in women's lives. For instance, Mab Segrest comments, "The assertion of the decolonized [i.e., liberated] self . . . can trap the fugitive into a new repression, into another death-dealing denial of our complex selves. And if the decolonized self slips into the born-again self, we are really in trouble."[53]

To feminists like Segrest, traditional conversion narratives, entangled in patriarchal and distinctly unfeminist assumptions, would seem problematical at the very least. One of the core ideas of the traditional narrative is surrender, a theme which runs counter to the notion of "getting control of one's life," to use the phrase frequently heard these days. Rather, the narratives tell of *giving up* control, yielding, abandoning one's will. Thus, evangelical women surrender utterly to God. Even out-of-church narratives echo this surrender motif: alcoholics in AA give in to a "higher power"; lesbians, often after a struggle to be "normal," yield to their sense of who they really are and have always been intended to be. It is obvious that the pattern of surrender in traditional and modern conversion narratives is not without its dangers.

But in one sense the problematical nature of conversion narratives is beside the point. They have been an important part of women's literary heritage for three centuries at least, and continue to speak to many women. For that reason alone they demand our attention. If we are to understand how women have written of their experiences, we must read their narratives. But there are also reasons, I think, to celebrate those narratives. They have led in surprising ways to an expanded role for women in the world, and to healing for troubled minds. And as I hope I have shown, often the surrender of control has resulted in a sense of greater control—or at least in an alleviation of anxiety over control and its possible loss.

The narratives encourage us to ask whether in the late twentieth century a pragmatic and measured yielding to reality—an acceptance of the way things are and the way one is—may sometimes prove a mark of maturity, adulthood, even the beginning of wisdom. "Converts" to environmentalism, for instance, repudiate the dream that "men," as "masters" of nature, can control their environment. Rather, they argue that the arrogant effort to control knocks nature out of balance, threatens the environment, and may even result in disaster. It is time, they counsel, to accept human limitations. Women, too, may need realistically to assess their limitations, now that they have begun to realize their possibilities.

In converting, women narrators reject—or at least loosen their hold on— the quest for perfection, that is, perfection as defined by the culture. Lesbians give up the goal of heterosexual romance and domesticity usually urged upon women. Feminists—theoretically, at least—leave behind the notion of becoming peerless wives and mothers and daughters—"total women," in Marabel Morgan's phrase. Potentially they give up the goal of being "superwomen," to invoke another, somewhat discredited phrase. Protestant evangelical women forego the hope of sinlessness and perhaps are freed in the process from the worst rigors of the nineteenth-century-style concept of "true womanhood."

What makes it possible for women to get out from under some of the sense of frustration and guilt involved in the (always fruitless) quest for perfection? One answer lies in the assurance in the conversion plotline that they have been accepted "just as they are," with all their weaknesses and failings, their angers and jealousies, their omissions and indiscretions. Traditional Protestant converts celebrate their acceptance by God despite all their sins and "vileness" and also experience acceptance and approval by a community of like-minded converts. Converts of other kinds may not speak of acceptance by God (they *may* feel "right" with the universe, or experience a sense of what they recognize as "grace"), but virtually all converts find a community of other sympathetic converts to love and support them "for themselves." There, in a community that is defined among other elements by its discourse, they can compose a narrative—naming themselves and their experiences and receiving understanding and approval from the tellers of similar stories.

The account of conversion—whether it occurs in or out of church, whether it is part fiction or mostly reality—can confer psychic wholeness, happiness, serenity, and freedom and liberation. The sense of liberation is obvious in the case of feminists and former addicts. It is usually less explicit in the writings of evangelical narrators, but it is there nonetheless, when they tell of release from the burden of sin, of fear, of loneliness, and of a sense of unworthiness and inadequacy.

Finally, conversion gives women a genuine calling—a "mission," to use the Protestant phrasing. The work may be paid or not. But it is almost always rewarding.

Conclusion

Though it is almost impossible to say exactly when certain changes in conversion narratives had become normative and conventional, it is possible to discern several trends over the past couple of centuries. First, the experiences of holiness, healing, and speaking in tongues becomes crucial in more and more narratives, sometimes eclipsing the significance of the initial conversion itself. Second, the stage of conviction receives less and less emphasis. It is a period less well demarcated by elements such as *original* sin, deep pollution in one's very nature, and direct struggle with God. To be sure, misery continues to afflict even the most recent narrators before their conversions, and normally it is still understood as tied to ineradicable human sinfulness. However, the blame for evil is shared more than in the past; it also arises from outside, in Satan's activity, and sometimes in environmental factors. Third, hell as a physical place, as a fiery lake, has receded, despite Satan's still considerable role in introducing and sustaining troubling doubts and temptations. Fourth, the narrator has within herself more power to determine her destiny. She merely has to make a decision, exert an effort of will. That done, she is no longer expected to express tentativeness about her salvific status. She doesn't even necessarily need to *feel* the "correct" way. Self-confidence, assurance, positive-mindedness tend to be the order of the day. God's response to a properly surrendered will is absolutely reliable. The holiness experience complicates the picture, to be sure, and makes the narrator's spiritual status seem less self-determined. Holiness requires the narrator to place herself entirely in God's hands, and yield her heart and life and will utterly to him. At the extreme she must rely on him for health, economic livelihood, even at times (if she is a pentecostal) speech. Yet the initial effort of will, the prior decision, is hers.

We might expect the issue of authenticity in narratives to have shifted ground in the twentieth century—from questions such as "Am I really converted? Is my conversion authentic?" to ones like "Can *anyone* be converted? *Is* there a God? Is conversion an authentic experience? Could my 'conversion' be all in my mind?" Yet this does not seem to be the case, at any rate no more so than in the nineteenth century. Perhaps this is because so many narrators grow up in a subculture that assumes God's existence and authority. Twentieth-century narrators may flirt briefly with atheism (as nineteenth-century narrators may briefly have entertained the idea that they were "damned forever"). The forbidden thought has its peculiar, if temporary, attractions. Much to her mother's shock and dismay, Aimee Semple McPherson announced at a Salvation Army service that "there was no God, nothing in the Bible." But her apostasy was shortlived; her conversion came that very night.[1] The usual issue for later converts is not God's existence—they tend to accept it as a given—but rather whether one can muster sufficient trust in the reality of his concern for all his children.

The literature of conversion over the past two centuries is enormous in its scope. This book only touches the surface. It is *everywhere*, though it often doesn't advertise itself as conversion literature. In the end, the task of identifying changes in conversion narratives over these two centuries remains unfinished. The continuities in the narratives are relatively easy to delineate—the enduring words, phrases, and attitudes. But the changes—both dating them and describing them precisely—are extremely troublesome.

Much remains to be done. Looking at twentieth-century conversion literature makes us realize how much more we need to know. First, we are lacking a full interpretive scheme for religion in the twentieth-century United States—one that takes into account significant developments outside the white liberal male Protestant establishment. We require a more complete understanding of particular stories—those of holiness and pentecostal adherents, for instance, and of distinct grouping within holiness and pentecostal traditions.[2] We need to know more about gender differences, especially in the twentieth century, in particular the ways in which women have "received Christ" compared to men. How has conversion altered the relationship between men and women? Has it changed the distribution of authority? Has it gotten harder or easier for men to experience and talk about conversion as the century has gone on? A prior requirement in getting at the answers to these questions is a more refined notion of masculinity (as well as femininity) in the twentieth century. We have some studies of masculinity in the late nineteenth and early twentieth centuries, but still need exploration that takes us further into this century.[3]

We require more investigation into the relation of conversion language to other rhetorics: above all we would benefit from more study of the interplay between advertising and conversion narratives. Our thinking about narratives and about religious language in general needs greater integration with recent analyses of the influence of advertising on American culture: how it has shaped our ideas of gender roles, of the language appropriate to each gender, and in fact how it has changed *all* language in the twentieth century. Closer study of the connections between conversion and popular literature—and television programing—intended for women would be instructive.[4] So also would attention to the ties between conversion language and the rhetorics of sports and business, though these would presumably have more to do with male narratives than with female ones.

Another direction for study would be an exploration of black women's conversion narratives in light of what we know about the conventions used by white female narrators. Joanne Braxton has suggested that in hewing to standard biblical language—the same used by white converts—black women narrators ended up slighting issues of race and gender.[5] This thinking is worth further exploration. More generally, though, we need more familiarity with the ways black and white female narratives differed. Did—as I think—black women use more explicit language about how the will of God conflicted with social and cultural norms, both white and black? Were black female narratives more likely to include a call to preach? (I suspect this was the case.) Did the experience of holiness become normative for them earlier? What else did conversion bring black women in addition to spiritual development? A quest for literacy? For emotional or physical freedom? How did conversion intersect with the particularities of black life—in slavery, after emancipation, in the twentieth century? In the nineteenth century the spiritual narratives of black women chronicle a willingness to flout social norms; this may or may not be the case for the twentieth century.

It would also be worth thinking more about the effect of conversion language upon the rest of the culture. (Chapter 8 is infinitely expandable.) Comparative studies might be useful: how deeply has conversion language influenced the rhetoric of the British Isles, for example, or of Germany? In regions where the conversion narrative has not been as central to religious experience, is the conversion pattern less prominent in the general culture?

In our study of conversion narratives we, like the converts, are slowly moving from what they might have called the darkness of confusion and puzzlement to the light of knowledge and recognition. Ours may be a less spiritual journey than those taken by Protestant women, but nevertheless it seems an important intellectual pilgrimage.

Notes

INTRODUCTION

1. Several scholars have made use of nineteenth-century conversion narratives, to be sure, e.g., Barbara Leslie Epstein, *The Politics of Domesticity: Women, Evangelism and Temperance in Nineteenth-Century America* (Middletown, Connecticut: Wesleyan University Press, 1981); Joseph F. Kett, *Rites of Passage: Adolescence in America, 1790 to the Present* (New York: Basic Books, 1977); Richard Rabinowitz, *The Spiritual Self in Everyday Life: The Transformation of Personal Religious Experience in Nineteenth-Century New England* (Boston: Northeastern University Press, 1989). These authors have not dealt with the narratives *as* narratives, however. On the twentieth century we have a few new sources. Kathleen C. Boone, *The Bible Tells Them So: The Discourse of Protestant Fundamentalism* (Albany: State University of New York Press, 1989), is a valuable study of evangelical sermonic rhetoric. Two studies make use of conversion narratives: Elaine J. Lawless, *Handmaidens of the Lord: Pentecostal Women Preachers and Traditional Religion* (Philadelphia: University of Pennsylvania Press, 1988), and Susan F. Harding, "Convicted by the Holy Spirit: The Rhetoric of Fundamental Baptist Conversion," *American Ethnologist* 14, 1 (Feb., 1987): 167–81.

2. To judge from oral narratives collected and transcribed by Fisk University scholars, they were quite different from the "literary" ones, though they employed some of the same phrasing. See Clifton H. Johnson, ed. *God Struck Me Dead: Religious Conversion Experiences and Autobiographies of Ex-Slaves* (Philadelphia: Pilgrim Press, 1969).

3. Christine M. Bochen, *The Journey to Rome: Conversion Literature by Nineteenth-Century American Catholics* (New York: Garland, 1988); Jay P. Dolan, *Catholic Revivalism: The American Experience, 1830–1900* (Notre Dame: University of Notre Dame Press, 1978); Debra Renee Kaufman, "Patriarchal Women: A Case Study of Newly Orthodox Jewish Women," *Symbolic Interaction* 12, 2 (1989): 299–315.

1. THE PATTERN AND TRADITION

1. William W. Woodward, *Increase of Piety, or the Revival of Religion in the United States of America* (Newburyport, Mass.: Angier, 1802), p. 24. For "belly of hell" see Jonah 2:2. Also cf. Psalm 40:2, 3: "He brought me up out of an horrible pit, out of the miry clay, and set my feet upon a rock, and established my goings. And he hath put a new song into my mouth, even praise unto our God."

2. Jonathan Edwards, "A Narrative of Surprising Conversions," in *Select Works of Jonathan Edwards*, vol. I (London: The Banner of Truth Trust, 1965), pp. 39–40.

3. Elijah Waterman, "The Noble Convert," sermon preached at Bridgeport, Connecticut, May 28, 1809, p. 9.

4. Barbara Welter, "The Feminization of American Religion, 1800–1860," in Mary Hartman and Lois Banner, eds., *Clio's Consciousness Raised* (New York: Harper Torchbooks, 1973), pp. 137–55; Nancy F. Cott, "Young Women in the Second Great Awakening," *Feminist Studies* 3 (Fall 1975): 15–16; Richard D. Shiels, "The Feminization of American Congregationalism, 1730–1835," *American Quarterly* 33 (Spring 1981): 46–62.

5. Sarah Hamilton, *A Narrative of the Life of Mrs. Hamilton* (Boston, 1803), p. 4.

6. William James in *Varieties of Religious Experience* (New York: Collier Books, 1961) suggested an explanation for the timing of conversion:

When you find a man living on the ragged edge of his consciousness, pent in to his sin and want and incompleteness, and consequently inconsolable, and then simply tell him that all is well with him, that he must stop his worry, break with his discontent, and give up his anxiety, you seem to him to come with pure absurdities. The only positive consciousness he has tells him that all is *not* well, . . . There are only two ways in which it is possible to get rid of anger, worry, fear, despair, or other undesirable affections. One is that an opposite affection should overpoweringly break over us, and the other is by getting so exhausted with the struggle that we have to stop—so we drop down, give up, and *don't care* any longer. Our emotional brain centers strike work, and we lapse into a temporary apathy. Now there is documentary proof that this state of temporary exhaustion not unfrequently forms part of the conversion crisis. So long as the egotistic worry of the sick soul guards the door, the expansive confidence of the soul of faith gains no entrance. But let the former faint away, even but for a moment, and the latter can profit by the opportunity, and, having once acquired possession, may retain it. (pp. 176–77)

7. Hamilton, *Narrative*, p. 12.

8. This study deals mostly with the "literary" narratives from the Northeast. It would be instructive to look at the narratives of "frontier" Baptists and Methodists as a group. It is my hunch that they might furnish some links to the colloquialism and informality of later "shirt sleeves" evangelists, among them fundamentalists such as Billy Sunday.

9. E.g., Hosea 14:1; Jer. 31:18; Job 11:13, 15; 1 Sam. 7:3; Acts 3:19; Phil. 2:12, 13; Luke 11:13. Few nineteenth-century converts mentioned that classic conversion narrative, Augustine's *Confessions*.

10. Philip Doddridge, *On the Rise and Progress of Religion in the Soul* (New York: American Tract Society, n.d.).

11. Benjamin Franklin, who knew a good seller when he saw one, published the Alleine work in 1741.

12. For Puritan autobiography see Daniel B. Shea, Jr., *Spiritual Autobiography in Early America* (Princeton: Princeton University Press, 1968); Carol Edkins, "Quest for Community: Spiritual Autobiographies of Eighteenth-Century Quaker and Puritan Women in America," in Estelle C. Jelinek, ed., *Women's Autobiography: Essays in Criticism* (Bloomington: Indiana University Press, 1980), pp. 39–52; Edmund S. Morgan, *Visible Saints: The History of a Puritan Idea* (New York: New York University Press, 1963), esp. pp. 66–73; Patricia Caldwell, *The Puritan Conversion Narrative* (New York: Cambridge University Press, 1983); Norman Pettit, *The Heart Prepared: Grace and Conversion in Puritan Spiritual Life* (New Haven: Yale University Press, 1966).

13. E.g., *New-York Evangelist* 15 (February 1, 1844): 20.

14. Hester Ann Rogers, *Account of the Experience of Hester Ann Rogers and Her Funeral Sermon, by Rev. T. Coke* (New York: T. Mason and G. Lane, 1837); Jeanne Marie Bouvier de la Motte Guyon, *Autobiography of Madame Guyon* (Philadelphia: Words of Faith, n.d.). The Rogers account was printed numerous times during the early nineteenth century. Many of the printings were done for the Methodist Episcopal Church. The Guyon autobiography appeared less frequently, but was published in New Bedford, Mass., in 1805, New York City in 1820, and Baltimore in 1821. (The last translation of Guyon listed in the *National Union Catalogue*, an abridged version, came out in 1911, under the imprint of The Evangel Publishing House, Chicago.)

15. Elizabeth Hanson, "God's Mercy Surmounting Man's Cruelty," in Alden T. Vaughan and Edward W. Clark, eds., *Puritans among the Indians* (Cambridge: The Belknap Press of Harvard University Press, 1981), p. 243.

16. For captivity narratives see Roy Harvey Pearce, "The Significance of the Captivity Narrative," *American Literature* 19 (1947): 1–20; Richard Slotkin, *Regeneration*

through Violence: The Mythology of the American Frontier, 1600–1860 (Middletown, Conn.: Wesleyan University Press, 1973), chapters 4–5; and Annette Kolodny, "Captives in Paradise: Women on the Early American Frontier," in Leonore Hoffmann and Margo Culley, eds., *Women's Personal Narratives* (New York: Modern Language Association, 1985), 93–111.

17. When a phrase such as "howling wilderness" was introduced by nineteenth-century Easterners, it was almost ipso facto a literary affectation. See, e.g., "Fugitive Pieces," in F. M. McAllister, *A Memorial of Louisa C. McAllister* (New York, 1869), privately printed.

18. The Geneva Bible was also in use among American Puritans—a copy arrived on the *Mayflower*—but during the seventeenth century it gradually yielded hegemony to the King James.

2. THE LANGUAGE OF THE CONVERT

1. John A. Clark, *The Young Disciple; or, a Memoir of Anzonetta R. Peters* (Philadelphia: William Marshall & Co., 1837), p. 36.

2. Clark, *Disciple*, pp. 42, 47–48.

3. Clark, *Disciple*, p. 51.

4. Clark, *Disciple*, pp. 70–71.

5. Clark, *Disciple*, pp. 70–71.

6. Geoffrey Tillotson, *Eighteenth Century English Literature: Modern Essays in Criticism* (New York: Oxford University Press, 1959), pp. 212–32. Black women narrators quote from the Bible—both directly and indirectly, and constantly ("I have borrowed much of my language from the holy Bible," said Maria W. Stewart). But even more striking, they also adopt some of the eighteenth-century poetic language typical of early nineteenth-century narratives: e.g., Zilphaw Elaw uses "abode," both as a noun and verb (54, 60, 103), "vapourish bubble of worldly gaiety and pleasure" (60), and "the clear circle of the sun's disc" (66). She speaks of a married couple "whose heads were blanched by the frost of time" (67). Her "mental hemisphere" becomes "obscured and cloudy" (107) (Zilphaw Elaw, *Memoirs of the Life, Religious Experience, Ministerial Travels, and Labours of Mrs. Elaw*, in William L. Andrews, ed., *Sisters of the Spirit: Three Black Women's Autobiographies of the Nineteenth Century* [Bloomington: Indiana University Press, 1986]). Maria W. Stewart's poetic language is even more abundant. She too speaks of "abodes" (26), "fierce billows" that "roll beneath" the unconverted (34), "realms of endless bliss" (44), the world as a "vale of tears" (45), and "Afric's daughters" (54). Of herself she writes, "shortly this frail tenement of mine will . . . lie mouldering in ruins" (81). An old person is "whited with the frosts of seventy winters" (55). See her "Productions" and "Farewell Address," in *Spiritual Narratives* (New York: Oxford, 1988). Stewart's statement about quoting from the Bible is from p. 24. Julia A. J. Foote wrote, "when I drop anchor again it will be in heaven's broad bay" (*A Brand Plucked From the Fire: An Autobiographical Sketch*, in *Spiritual Narratives*).

7. Daniel B. Shea, *Spiritual Autobiography in Early America* (Princeton: Princeton University Press), p. 106.

8. Jonathan Edwards had written in his "Treatise on Religious Affections,"

A rule received and established by common consent has a very great, though to many persons an insensible influence in forming their notions of the process of their own experience. I know very well how they proceed as to this matter, for I have had frequent opportunities of observing their conduct. Very often their experience at first appears like a confused chaos, but then those parts are selected which bear the nearest resemblance to such particular steps as are insisted upon; and these are dwelt upon in their thoughts, and spoken of from time to time, till they grow more and more conspicuous in their view, and other parts which are neglected grow more and more obscure. Thus what they have experienced is insensibly strained, so as to bring it into exact conformity to the scheme already established in their minds. And it becomes natural also for ministers, who have to deal with those who insist upon distinctness and clearness of method, to do so too. (Quoted in William James, *Varieties of Religious Experience* [New York: Collier Books, 1961], p. 168)

9. In recent decades much has been written on the function and utility of formula in the composition and transmission of oral poetry, particularly in the Homeric epics. See, e.g., Milman Parry, *The Making of Homer's Verse* (New York: Oxford University Press, 1971); Albert Lord, *The Singer of Tales* (Cambridge: Harvard University Press, 1960).

10. Perhaps the preoccupation with guilt had temperamental sources as well as traditional and pedagogical ones. Lewis Saum has remarked on the "abiding moroseness" of ordinary Americans during the pre-Civil War period—more like the moods of Melville and Hawthorne than of Emerson. See his *The Popular Mind of Pre-Civil War America* (Westport, Conn.: Greenwood Press, 1980.)

11. Persons under conviction were also said to be "engaged," "anxiously inquiring," "under serious impressions," "awakened," "alarmed," "wrought upon by the Spirit of God," and "under great concern."

12. Cf. Gen. 6:3: "My spirit shall not always strive with man." For "trembling" see Phil. 2:12: "Work out your own salvation with fear and trembling."

13. For "enmity against God" see, e.g., Rom. 8:7 and James 4:4. "Rebellion" against God is a common theme throughout the Old and New Testaments.

14. Cf. Job. 30:29: "I am a brother to dragons, and a companion to owls" (Harriet Livermore, *A Narration of Religious Experience* [Concord, Mass., 1826], p. 42). This loathing and self-disgust fit squarely into a long narrative tradition. Jonathan Edwards had described himself returning "like a dog to his vomit" (Prov. 26:11; 2 Pet. 2:22), and the Puritan Elizabeth White had compared herself to spiders and wolves.

15. John Bunyan, *Grace Abounding to the Chief of Sinners*, p. 27; Jonathan Edwards, "Personal Narrative," in Clarence H. Faust and Thomas H. Johnson, ed., *Jonathan Edwards* (New York: Hill and Wang, 1962), pp. 70, 71.

16. Many of the standard phrases and images for hell had been well established by the nineteenth century. Doddridge, for instance, had described the "thousands and ten thousands of despairing wretches, trembling and confounded," and had warned his reader, "There shall I hear thy cries among the rest, rending the very heavens in vain." Philip Doddridge, *On the Rise and Progress of Religion in the Soul* (New York: American Tract Society, n.d.), p. 164. The phrase, the "bottomless pit," came from Revelation, where it appears seven times, and was taken up by Bunyan, among others. Edwards reported that during an illness, God "shook me over the pit of hell" (Edwards, "Personal Narrative," p. 58). Thomas Shepard had written, "I did see God like a consuming fire & an everlasting burning, & myselfe like a poor prisoner, leading to that fire, & the thoughts of eternall reprobation & torment did amaze my spirits" (Thomas Shepard, *Autobiography* [Boston: Pierce and Baker, 1832], p. 25). For the source of the lake of fire and brimstone see especially Rev. 19:20 and Rev. 21:8. The elements "fire" and "brimstone" appear elsewhere in the Bible as well. For "horrible pit" see Psalm 40:2; for "pit of destruction" see Psalm 55:23.

17. Sarah Hamilton, *A Narrative of the Life of Mrs. Hamilton* (Boston, 1803), p. 6.

18. Livermore, *Narration*, pp. 46–51.

19. For "pluck sinners as brands . . ." see Amos 4:11; "watchmen on the wall"

comes from Isa. 62.6. "Laborers" in the "vineyard" is a familiar biblical image (e.g., Matt. 20:1).

20. Hamilton, *Narrative*, p. 8.

21. *A Brand Plucked*, pp. 112–13.

22. For "clothed in righteousness" see, e.g., Job 29:14 and Isa. 61:10. For "white robes" see Rev. 6:11; 7:9; 7:13; 7:14. For peace "like a river" see Is. 66:12; and for peace which "passeth understanding" see Phil. 4:7.

23. Emily Dickinson parodied this rhetoric: "Papa above! / Regard a Mouse / O'erpowered by the Cat! / Reserve within thy kingdom / A "Mansion" for the Rat! / Sung in seraphic cupboards / to nibble all the day, / While unsuspecting Cycles / Wheel solemnly away!"

24. Bernard Weisberger notes that Charles G. Finney dropped the qualification "hope" (*They Gathered at the River* [Boston: Little, Brown, 1958], pp. 93–94).

25. "The Unanswerable Argument," *New-York Evangelist* 15 (April 11, 1844): 57.

26. George Duffield, "Pastor and Inquirer; or, what is it to repent and believe in the gospel? An authentic narrative . . . " (Philadelphia: William S. and Alfred Martien, n.d.), p. 2 (ca. 1848).

27. Norman Pettit, *The Heart Prepared: Grace and Conversion in Puritan Spiritual Life* (New Haven: Yale University Press, 1966).

28. Joseph Alleine, *An Alarm to Unconverted Sinners* (Philadelphia: American Sunday-School Union, n.d.), p. 10.

29. Clark, *Disciple*, p. 43.

30. Phoebe Hinsdale Brown, "Twilight Hymn," quoted in Edward S. Ninde, *The Story of the American Hymn* (New York, Cincinnati: Abingdon Press, 1921), p. 180.

31. Walter Jackson Bate has noted the increasing preeminence of feeling as the eighteenth century went on, because, he said, it seemed that empiricism had "disposed of the mind as a rational instrument" (*From Classic to Romantic: Premises of Taste in Eighteenth-Century England* [New York: Harper Torchbooks, 1961], p. 129). Some observers, of course, intensely distrusted the emotional display. One spoke of the "animal feeling" (W. Emerson Wilson, ed., *Diaries of Phoebe George Bradford* [Wilmington, Del.: The Historical Society of Delaware, 1976], p. 4). See also Menzies Rayner, "A dissertation upon extraordinary awakenings, or religious stirs; Conversion, regeneration, renovation, and a change of heart; etc" (New Haven, 1816). Said Rayner, when young people "see one of their acquaintances or friends, or even a stranger, whose mind is agitated by fear and terror, the same emotions are irresistibly produced in themselves; and, ere they are aware of it, they find themselves trembling and in tears, they know not why. Now such emotions are not the effect of a rational conviction, or of genuine penitence" (p. 12). Phoebe Palmer was an evangelical who questioned the intense emphasis on feeling. She recalled of herself, "Not unfrequently she felt like weeping because she could not weep, imagining if she could plunge herself into overwhelming sorrows, and despairing views of relationship to God, spoken of by some, she could then come and throw herself upon his mercy with greater probability of success" (*The Way of Holiness, with Notes by the Way: Being a Narrative of Religious Experience Resulting from a Determination to Be a Bible Christian* [New York: Printed for the Author, 1854], p. 73).

32. A male convert described his conversion to his fellow workers: "That was hard. I did it with the tears running down my cheeks. A man does not like to cry before other men" (D. L. Moody, *Prevailing Prayer* [Chicago: Revell, 1885], p. 123).

33. Hannah More, "Strictures on the Modern System of Female Education," in *Complete Works of Hannah More*, vol. I (New York: Harper Bros., 1844), p. 379. On the subject of sensibility see Northrop Frye, "Towards Defining an Age of Sensibility," in James Clifford, ed., *Eighteenth Century Literature*, pp. 311–18.

34. For the sentimental novel see Herbert Ross Brown, *The Sentimental Novel in*

America (New York: Pageant Books, 1959), and Helen Papishvily, *All the Happy End-ings* (New York: Harper and Bros., 1956).

35. See, e.g., Charles Brockden Brown's *Jane Talbot*, whose skeptical hero returned home from a harrowing sea voyage to testify to the truth of Christianity, thereby ren-dering himself worthy to marry the devout and feeling Jane.

36. Harriet Beecher Stowe, *The Minister's Wooing* (Ridgewood, N.J.: Gregg Press, 1968), pp. 16–17.

37. Brown, *The Sentimental Novel*, p. 343. Catharine Beecher's advice to her students sounds novelistic: "You can not now realize and I pray you may never experience how bereft, how lonely, how desolate is a heart that has no portion in heaven, when the hopes of the world pass away, when the bright visions of life are shrouded in darkness, when the midnight pillow is bathed in tears of bitter loneliness, and the dawn of day brings no light to the soul" (quoted in Kathryn Kish Sklar, *Catharine Beecher: A Study in American Domesticity* [New York: Norton, 1976], p. 65).

38. Livermore, *Narration*.

3. THE NINETEENTH-CENTURY NARRATIVE
AND THE LIVES OF WOMEN

1. The notion of a "surface plot," "which affirms social conventions," and a "sub-merged plot," "which encodes rebellion," is developed, e.g., in Elizabeth Abel, Marianne Hirsch, and Elizabeth Langland, eds., *The Voyage In: Fictions of Female Development* (Hanover, N. H.: University Press of New England, 1983), p. 12.

2. Maggie Van Cott, *The Harvest and the Reaper: Reminiscences of Revival Work of Mrs. Maggie N. Van Cott* (New York: N. Tibbals & Sons, 1876), p. 67.

3. Jarena Lee, "Religious Experiences of Mrs. Jarena Lee," in *Spiritual Narratives* (New York: Oxford, 1988), p. 5.

4. John A. Clark, *The Young Disciple; or, a Memoir of Anzonetta R. Peters* (Phila-delphia: William Marshall & Company, 1837), p. 80.

5. Charles Hyde, *Memoir of Caroline Hyde* (New York: American Tract Society, n.d.).

6. Harriet Livermore, *A Narration of Religious Experience* (Concord, Mass.: 1826), pp. 12, 13.

7. Harriet B. Cooke, *Autobiography of Harriet B. Cooke* (New York: Robert Carter & Bros., 1861), p. v.

8. Mrs. Julia A. J. Foote, "A Brand Plucked from the Burning," in *Spiritual Nar-ratives*, pp. 3–4.

9. Phebe B. Slocum, *Witnessing: A Concise Account of a Marvelous Event with Its Happy Results in the Life of Phebe B. Slocum* (Brattleboro, Vt., 1899), p. 61. Barbara Leslie Epstein notes that "Some women found themselves converted, and in the midst of a crowded assembly, and in a loud voice, began to pray for their husbands" (*The Politics of Domesticity: Women, Evangelism and Temperance in Nineteenth-Century America* [Middletown, Conn.: Wesleyan University Press, 1981], p. 59).

10. Hester Ann Rogers, *Account of the Experience of Hester Ann Rogers and Her Funeral Sermon, by Rev. T. Coke* (New York: T. Mason and G. Lane, 1837), p. 25.

11. Sarah Hamilton, *A Narrative of the Life of Mrs. Hamilton* (Boston, 1803), p. 9.

12. Foote, "A Brand Plucked," p. 78.

13. Epstein, *Politics of Domesticity*, pp. 59–60.

14. William C. Conant, *Narratives of Remarkable Conversions and Revival Incidents* (New York: Derby & Jackson, 1858), pp. 101–102, 106.

15. Conant, *Narratives of Remarkable Conversions*, pp. 102–103.

16. Quoted in Epstein, *Politics of Domesticity*, p. 56.

17. Elizabeth Prentiss, *Stepping Heavenward* (New York: Anson D. F. Randolph, 1869), pp. 12, 24.

18. Prentiss, *Stepping Heavenward*, p. 189.

19. Diary of Mary Boit, August 30, 1891. Schlesinger Library. I am grateful to Jane Hunter for bringing this passage to my attention.

20. The Rev. Charles Hyde, writing about Caroline Hyde (no relation), turned aside from his narrative to address readers (most of them presumably female), who may have been too ready to belittle their abilities (and too lax about exercising them):

Instead of excusing ourselves from active labors in promoting the kingdom of Christ and the welfare of our fellow men, because we have not the gifts that qualify us at once for the widest sphere of influence, how much more becoming and wise it would be to improve the *little* that we have and something may be done by all. If we cannot be ministers of the Gospel, or missionaries to the heathen, we can perhaps teach a class in a Sabbath School, or we can persuade children to attend; we can converse with a friend or neighbor upon the concerns of his soul; by economy and industry we can save something to give to benevolent objects. (*Memoir of Caroline Hyde*, p. 19)

21. *Memorials of a Young Christian* (Philadelphia: Merrihew and Gunn, Printers, 1837), p. 14. A young woman, the daughter of a wealthy West Indian planter, is said to have given up "gay society" upon reading More's "Practical Piety" (Mrs. John Farrar, *Recollections of Seventy Years* [Boston: Ticknor and Fields, 1866], pp. 219–20).

22. Prentiss, *Stepping Heavenward*, pp. 265, 237–42.

23. At the same time, some women demonstrated a peculiar reticence in confiding in their mothers; they seem to have been especially loath to confess their anxieties, rebelliousness, and sense of self-condemnation. Perhaps the paragon status of many mothers was inhibiting; would-be converts were convinced those mothers were too saintly ever to have experienced similar feelings.

24. Minerva Brace Norton, *A True Teacher: Mary Mortimer* (New York, Chicago, Toronto: Fleming H. Revell, 1894), p. 19.

25. Cooke, *Autobiography*, pp. 20–22.

26. *Memorials of a Young Christian*, p. 24.

27. *Memorials of a Young Christian*, p. 23.

28. *The Literary Remains of Martha Day; with Rev. Fitch's Address at Her Funeral; and Sketches of Her Character* (New Haven: Printed by Hezekiah Howe & Co., 1834), pp. 109–110.

29. The author of *The Closet Companion*, a popular guide, seems to try to strike a balance between warning of the danger that sinners will not recognize how bad they are on the one hand and that they will condemn themselves too much on the other hand (*The Closet Companion; or a Help to Self-Examination*, in *The Publications of the American Tract Society*, vol. I [New York: American Tract Society, n.d.], p. 234).

30. Phebe Slocum, whose progress from utter unconcern with religion through conviction to conversion took only three days and could be dated exactly, prefaced her account with the hope for her readers that "this simple testimony . . . of His manner of dealing with me, will not confound you by causing you to expect that He will deal with you in the same way" (Phebe B. Slocum, *Witnessing: An Exact Account of a Marvelous Event with Its Happy Results in the Life of Phebe B. Slocum* [Brattleboro, Vt., 1899], p. viii). Advised *The Closet Companion*: "Let not the issue of this trial depend at all upon your knowledge of the exact time in your conversion, or the particular minister or sermon first instrumental in it. Many are wrought upon by slow and insensible degrees" (p. 234).

31. See, e.g., "The Moral Man Tried. In Three Dialogues," in *Publications of the American Tract Society*, vol. I, pp. 213–28, especially the first dialogue. The popular

notion of the difference between male and female approaches to religion is captured in a jingle a churchwoman recalled in the early 1950s: "Woman weeps o'er sins she's done, and makes them seem like double; man straightaway forgives himself, and saves the Lord the trouble" (Mossie Allman Wycker, "The Church Women's Opportunities," in Elizabeth A. Hartsfield, et al., *Women in the Church: A Symposium on the Service and Status of Women among the Disciples of Christ* [Lexington, Ky.: The College of the Bible, 1953], p. 63). Wycker did not know the source of this jingle; it sounds as if it could have been circulating for some time. For another idea of the differences between male and female narratives, see Susan Juster, " 'In a Different Voice': Male and Female Narratives of Religious Conversion in Post-Revolutionary America," *American Quarterly* 41 (March 1989): 34–62.

32. Cooke, *Autobiography*, pp. 101, 105.

33. Prentiss, *Stepping Heavenward*, pp. 267–68.

34. Robert E. Speer, *Young Men Who Overcame* (New York, Chicago, Toronto: Fleming H. Revell, 1905), p. 14.

4. CHANGE AND CONTINUITY IN TWENTIETH-CENTURY NARRATIVES

1. Billy Graham, *How to Be Born Again* (Waco, Texas: Word Books, 1977), pp. 152–53.

2. In the nineteenth century, however, the scoffer would rarely have been a woman; he was almost always a man, one who might never convert or convert only on his deathbed, after a long period of rebellion against God. Though even in the twentieth century, relatively few women in narratives were outspoken unbelievers, it *had* become a possible role for a woman. The wife in Adela Rogers St. Johns's *Tell No Man* (Garden City, N.Y.: Doubleday, 1966) was a strong-minded atheist, not at all happy about her husband's conversion or decision to enter the ministry.

3. Elizabeth Burns, *The Late Liz: The Autobiography of an Ex-Pagan* (New York: Meredith Press, 1957).

4. Burns, *Late Liz*, pp. 17, 59, 64, 25.

5. Burns, *Late Liz*, pp. 174, 176, 177.

6. Burns, *Late Liz*, p. 193.

7. Burns, *Late Liz*, pp. 183, 252, 256, 253. The standard formulations included here are self-surrender and the idea of self-will in conflict with God's; "cleansed," "emptied," "service" are common conversion words. Burns undoubtedly leavened her rhetoric with more "respectable" sources; e.g., she read C. S. Lewis after her conversion.

8. See a hymn from a collection used by the Sunday campaigns. It is a comment about language as well as beliefs:

> I am somewhat old fashioned, I know,
> When it comes to religion and God;
> Many think I am painfully slow,
> Since I walk where my fathers have trod.
>
> I believe in repentance from sin,
> And that Jesus within us must dwell;
> I believe that if heaven we win,
> We must flee from the terrors of hell.

(N. A. McAulay, "The Old Fashioned Faith," in Homer Rodeheaver and Charles H. Gabriel, *Awakening Songs for the Church, Sunday School and Evangelistic Services* [Chicago, Philadelphia: Rodeheaver Co., n.d.] p. 70.)

9. Nancy T. Ammerman, *Bible Believers: Fundamentalists in the Modern World*

(New Brunswick: Rutgers University Press, 1987), p. 87; Susan Atkins (with Bob Slosser), *Child of Satan, Child of God* (Plainfield, N.J.: Logos, 1977), pp. 263–64.

10. Hannah Whitall Smith, *The Christian's Secret of a Happy Life* (Waco, Tex.: Word Books, 1985), pp. 33–34.

11. Dennis Bennett and Rita Bennett, *The Holy Spirit and You* (Plainfield, N.J.: Logos, 1971), pp. 62, 184.

12. David Watt, "Evangelicals and Modern Psychology," paper presented in New World Colloquium, Harvard Divinity School, fall 1985.

13. Marjorie Holmes, *Who Am I God? The Doubts, the Fears, the Joys of Being a Woman* (Garden City, N.Y.: Doubleday, 1971), p. 4.

14. Susan B. Anthony, *The Ghost in My Life* (Old Tappan, N.J.: Revell, 1971), p. 227.

15. Diana Bertholf, *Diana's Star* (Wheaton, Ill.: Tyndale House, 1983), p. 62.

16. A. Z. Conrad, ed., *Boston's Awakening* (Boston: The King's Business Publishing Co., 1909), pp. 32–33.

17. Laura Hobe, *Try God* (Garden City, N.Y.: Doubleday, 1977).

18. Virgina Ramey Hearn, *Our Struggle to Serve: The Stories of 15 Evangelical Women* (Waco, Tex.: Word Books, 1979), p. 143.

19. Bertholf, *Diana's Star*, p. 107.

20. Hearn, *Our Struggle*, p. 137.

21. Eugenia Price, *The Burden Is Light: The Autobiography of a Transformed Pagan Who Took God at His Word* (Old Tappan, N.J.: Spire Books, 1985; first published by Revell in 1955), p. 22.

22. Shirley Boone, *One Woman's Liberation* (Carol Stream, Ill.: Creation House, 1972), p. 93.

23. George Jackson, *The Fact of Conversion* (New York: Revell, 1908), pp. 127–28.

24. Hearn, *Our Struggle*, p. 155.

25. Eugenia Price, *Early Will I Seek Thee* (Westbrook, N.J.: Revell, 1956), p. 36.

26. Atkins, *Child of Satan*, p. 227.

27. Dale Evans Rogers, *My Spiritual Diary* (Revell, 1955), p. 14; see also Price, *Early*, p. 58: "the devil is having the time of his evil life. . . . Making use of my futile self-effort."

28. Rebecca Manley Pippert, "Ethel Renwick," in Ann Spangler, ed., *Bright Legacies: Portraits of Ten Outstanding Women of Faith* (Ann Arbor: Servant Books, 1983), p. 183.

29. David Wilkerson, *Jesus Person Maturity Manual* (Glendale, Calif.: G/L, 1971), p. 4.

30. Joni Eareckson (with Joe Musser), *Joni* (Grand Rapids, Mich.: Zondervan, 1976), p. 35.

31. Helen Kooiman, *Cameos: Women Fashioned by God* (Wheaton, Ill.: Tyndale House, 1968), p. 20.

32. Atkins, *Child of Satan*, p. 285.

33. Hearn, *Our Struggle*, p. 31.

34. Dennis Bennett and Rita Bennett, *The Holy Spirit and You* (Plainfield, N.J.: Logos, 1971) p. 185.

35. Plummer, *Cameos*, p. 21.

36. Eareckson, *Joni*, p. 127.

37. Kooiman, *Cameos*, p. 82.

38. Jamie Buckingham, *Kathryn Kuhlman . . . Her Story* (Plainfield, N.J.: Logos, 1976), p. 20.

39. Hobe, *Try God*, p. 155.

40. Clyde Kirby, *Then Came Jesus* (Grand Rapids, Mich.: Zondervan, 1967), pp. 7, 18, 16.

41. See, e.g., Curtis Mitchell, *Those Who Came Forward: Men and Women Who Responded to the Ministry of Billy Graham* (Philadelphia: Chilton, 1966), pp. 6, 9, 147.

42. Atkins, *Child of Satan*, p. 230.

43. J. Wesley Ingles, *The Silver Trumpet* (Philadelphia: The [American Sunday School] Union Press, 1930), p. 182.

44. Moody said, "During the last few years I was not occupied with the person of Christ; it was more about the doctrine and about the form. But lately Christ is more to me personally. And it would be a great help to you to cultivate his acquaintance personally, and come to Him as the personal Saviour, and be able to take Him and look up to Him and say, 'He is my Saviour' " (Quoted in James Findlay, *Dwight L. Moody: American Evangelist* [Chicago: University of Chicago Press, 1969], pp. 229–30); Conrad, *Boston's Awakening.*

45. Atkins, *Child of Satan*, p. 222.

46. Hobe, *Try God.*

47. Anthony, *Ghost*, p. xi.

48. Wilkerson, *Manual*, p. 19.

49. Rogers, *Diary*, p. 83.

50. Jennifer R. Vanderford, *Joy Cometh in the Morning* (Eugene, Oreg.: Harvest House, 1982), pp. 63, 152.

51. Kathryn Koob, "Catherine Marshall," in Spangler, *Bright Legacies*, p. 50.

52. Bertholf, *Diana's Star*, pp. 136, 142.

53. Price, *Early*, p. 30.

54. Rogers, *Diary*, p. 23.

55. Bertholf, *Diana's Star*, pp. 114, 121.

56. Kooiman, *Cameos*, p. 31.

5. FINDING WORDS FOR NEW EXPERIENCES

1. Methodists preferred the designation "holiness," while Calvinists (Baptists, Presbyterians, and Congregationalists, e.g.) tended to use "sanctification."

2. Reprinted in *Spiritual Narratives* (New York: Oxford, 1988).

3. David Edwin Harrell, Jr., *All Things Are Possible: The Healing and Charismatic Revivals in Modern America* (Bloomington: Indiana University Press, 1975).

4. Elizabeth V. Baker, *Chronicles of a Faith Life* (New York: Garland, 1984), p. 11.

5. Albert Hughes, *Renamed: Saul Becomes Paul* (Philadelphia: American Bible Conference Association, 1935), p. 78.

6. The quest for criteria to set off the truly holy from merely nominal Christians seems a continuing motif of American Protestant life. David D. Hall argues that when New England ministers introduced the Halfway Covenant in 1662, allowing children of church members to receive baptism and become sort of junior church members themselves, they reserved the Lord's Supper for those who had truly searched their consciences and achieved the new birth (*Days of Wonder, Days of Judgment* [New York: Knopf, 1989]).

7. Joni Eareckson (with Joe Musser), *Joni* (Grand Rapids, Mich.: Eerdmans, 1976), p. 155.

8. Eugenia Price, *Early Will I Seek Thee* (Westwood, N.J.: Revell, 1956), p. 58.

9. Exactly what total reliance on God meant was of course not always clear. Believers were not expected to stop using their own powers to reason, observe, and decide. For example, if they crossed a busy street they were expected to employ ordinary caution and common sense. But beyond that, they were not to worry, not to feel anxiety, even if, unbeknownst to them, a drunken driver might loom on the horizon or they should sprain an ankle on the way across. These contingencies lay outside their control and hence were in the plan of God, and they were not to feel distressed about them.

10. Price, *Early*, p. 52.

11. Helen Kooiman, *Cameos: Women Fashioned by God* (Wheaton, Ill.: Tyndale House, 1968), p. 154.

12. Price, *Early*, pp. 129–30.

13. Kooiman, *Cameos*, p. 114.

14. Glenn Clark, *A Man's Reach: The Autobiography of Glenn Clark* (New York: Harper and Row, 1949), pp. 203–204.

15. Kooiman, *Cameos*, pp. 140–41.

16. Hughes, *Renamed*, p. 63.

17. Quoted in John L. Sherrill, *They Speak with Other Tongues* (Old Tappan, N.J.: Revell, 1964), p. 124.

18. Holmes, *Who Am I God? The Doubts, the Fears, the Joys of Being a Woman* (Garden City, N.Y.: Doubleday, 1971), p. 172.

19. D. Wesley Myland, *The Latter Rain Covenant and Pentecostal Power: With Testimony of Healings and Baptism* (Chicago: The Evangel Publishing House, 1910), p. 63.

20. David Wilkerson, *The Cross and the Switchblade* (Westwood, N.J.: Revell), 1962, p. 160.

21. Agnes Sanford, *The Healing Gifts of the Spirit* (New York: Lippincott Co., 1966), p. 28.

22. Shirley Boone, *One Woman's Liberation* (Carol Stream, Ill.: Creation House, 1972), p. 120; Dennis and Rita Bennett, *The Holy Spirit and You* (Plainfield, N.J.: Logos, 1971), p. 75.

23. Sherrill, *Other Tongues*, p. 89.

6. ESTABLISHING THE TWENTIETH-CENTURY TEXT

1. "Decay of Evangelism," *Moody Bible Institute Monthly* (February 1928): 259.

2. Diana Bertholf, *Diana's Star* (Wheaton, Ill.: Tyndale Books, 1983), pp. 122–23.

3. Dennis Bennett and Rita Bennett, *The Holy Spirit and You* (Plainfield, N.J.: Logos, 1971), pp. 10, 113.

4. A. Z. Conrad, ed., *Boston's Awakening* (Boston: The King's Business, 1909), p. 180.

5. Susan Atkins (with Bob Slosser), *Child of Satan, Child of God* (Plainfield, N.J.: Logos, 1977), p. 225. A chronicler of the Billy Graham crusades spoke of "the difficulty presented by the obscure phraseology of King James's scholars." See Curtis Mitchell, *Those Who Came Forward: Men and Women Who Responded to the Ministry of Billy Graham* (Philadelphia: Chilton Books, 1966), p. 48.

6. Harold Begbie, *Twice-Born Men: A Clinic in Regeneration* (New York: Fleming H. Revell, 1909), p. 60. Begbie also felt the need to explain the phrase "love for souls": "This is a phrase which means the intense and concentrated compassion for the unhappiness of others which visits a man who has discovered the only means of obtaining happiness," p. 56.

7. Shirley Boone, *One Woman's Liberation* (Carol Stream, Ill.: Creation House, 1972), p. 98.

8. Eugenia Price, *Early Will I Seek Thee* (Westwood, N.J.: Revell, 1956), p. 45.

9. Tom Skinner, *Black and Free* (Grand Rapids, Mich.: Zondervan, 1968), pp. 29, 48.

10. George Jackson, *The Fact of Conversion* (New York: Fleming H. Revell, 1908), p. 122).

11. Philip Yancey and Tim Stafford, *Unhappy Secrets of the Christian Life* (Grand Rapids, Mich.: Zondervan, 1979), p. 11. We should note that Yancey, who told this story, was eventually convinced by his own rhetoric and genuinely converted.

12. Lewis W. Gillenson, *Billy Graham and 7 Who Were Saved* (New York: Trident Press, 1967), p. 150.

13. Bennett and Bennett, *The Holy Spirit*, p. 216.

14. Virginia Ramey Hearn, *Our Struggle to Serve: The Stories of 15 Evangelical Women* (Waco: Tex.: Word Books, 1979), p. 37.

15. David Wilkerson, *The Cross and the Switchblade* (Westwood, N.J.: Revell, 1962), p. 125.

16. Hannah Hurnard, *Hearing Heart* (Wheaton, Ill.: Tyndale House, 1988), p. 30.

17. David Wilkerson, *Jesus Person Maturity Manual* (Glendale, Calif.: G/L Publications, 1971), p. 24. Wilkerson's emphasis.

18. For a history of advertising see Stephen Fox, *The Mirror Makers: A History of American Advertising and Its Creators* (New York: Random House, 1984).

19. Jackson, *The Fact of Conversion*, p. 208.

20. Bennett and Bennett, *The Holy Spirit*, p. 69; Nancy Tatum Ammerman, *Bible Believers: Fundamentalists in the Modern World* (New Brunswick: Rutgers University Press, 1987), p. 90.

21. Price, *Early*, p. 140.

22. Vicki Huffman, *Plus Living: Looking for Joy in All the Right Places* (Wheaton, Ill.: Harold Shaw, 1989), p. xvii.

23. Ann Kiemel Anderson, *I Gave God Time* (Wheaton, Ill: Tyndale House, 1982), p. 26.

24. Huffman, *Plus Living*, p. 7.

25. These sources for the phrase appear in the 1980 edition of *Bartlett's Familiar Quotations*, but the phrase is absent from a 1955 edition of Bartlett's.

26. Elisabeth Elliot, *Twelve Baskets of Crumbs* (Chappaqua, N.Y.: Christian Herald House, 1976), p. 92.

27. Elliot, *Twelve Baskets*, p. 164.

28. V. Raymond Edman, *They Found the Secret* (Grand Rapids, Mich.: Zondervan, 1984).

29. But, e.g., William Law's *A Serious Call to a Devout and Holy Life* has recently become available in several editions, including that of the Roman Catholic Paulist Press in the scholarly series "Classics of Western Spirituality." Perhaps Doddridge and others will reappear. Generous selections from the writings of Phoebe Palmer, who helped bring about the revival of holiness among Methodists, issued from Paulist Press in 1988.

30. Hannah Whitall Smith, *The Christian's Secret of a Happy Life* (Waco, Tex.: Word Books, 1985), p. vii.

31. Andrew Murray, *With Christ in the School of Prayer* (titled *The Believer's School of Prayer* [Minneapolis: Bethany House, 1982]).

32. Atkins, *Child of Satan*, p. 248; Joni Eareckson, *Joni* (Grand Rapids, Mich.: Zondervan, 1976), p. 147.

33. Other British religious writers recently discovered by evangelicals are Charles Williams and George MacDonald. Interestingly, *American* Catholics also found themselves attracted to English Catholics, especially in the 1920–1940 period. Like some Protestant evangelicals today, those Catholics aspired to transcend their religious and cultural ghettos in search of intellectual substance to counter modernist thought.

34. Francis Thompson, "Hound of Heaven," in Francis Thompson, *Works of Francis Thompson* (New York: Charles Scribners, 1913), vol. 1, pp. 107–13.

35. The important revisions of the past century or so have included the English Revised Version (1881–88), the American Standard Version (1901), the Revised Standard Version (1946, 1952, 1955), and the New American Standard Version (1971). Conservative evangelicals have regarded these translations from varied viewpoints; many initially refused to accept any but the King James but have gradually softened their attitudes. In 1978 the New International Version came out; its "dignified but readable style" and its assumptions about the harmony of the Old and New Testaments have made it popular

among conservative Protestants (Keith R. Crim, "Bible Translations by Committees," in Ernest S. Frerichs, *The Bible and Bibles in America* [Atlanta, Georgia: Scholars Press, 1988], p. 38).

36. Hearn, *Our Struggle*, p. 155.

37. Laura Hobe, *Try God* (Garden City, New York: Doubleday, 1977), p. 129.

38. E.g., Price, *Early*, p. 29, and J. Wesley Ingles, *The Silver Trumpet* (Philadelphia: [American Sunday School] Union Press, 1930), p. 181.

39. Price, p. 141, e.g.

40. For obvious reasons I concentrate on the *words* of hymns, although of course their melodies must receive at least part of the credit for their success.

41. Curtis Mitchell, *Those Who Came Forward: Men and Women Who Responded to the Ministry of Billy Graham* (Philadelphia: Chilton, 1966), pp. 69, 179, 252.

42. Wilkerson, *Cross and Switchblade*, p. 166.

7. THE MEANINGS OF THE TWENTIETH-CENTURY NARRATIVES

1. See especially Virginia Ramey Hearn, *Our Struggle to Serve: The Stories of 15 Evangelical Women* (Waco, Tex.: Word Books, 1979); see also Nancy A. Hardesty, *Women Called to Witness: Evangelical Feminism in the 19th Century* (Nashville, Tenn.: Abingdon, 1984).

2. Laura Hobe, *Try God* (Garden City, N.Y.: Doubleday, 1977), p. 129.

3. Beverly LaHaye, *I Am a Woman by God's Design* (Old Tappan, N.J.: Revell, 1980), pp. 55, 61–62, 77, 87.

4. Dennis Bennett and Rita Bennett, *The Holy Spirit and You* (Plainfield, N.J.: Logos, 1971), p. 104.

5. Marjorie Holmes, *Who Am I, God?* (Garden City, N.Y.: Doubleday, 1971), p. 71.

6. Hearn, *Our Struggle*, p. 157.

7. Helen Kooiman, *Cameos: Women Fashioned by God* (Wheaton, Ill.: Tyndale House, 1968), p. 21.

8. Ruth Bell Graham, *It's My Turn* (Old Tappan, N.J.: Revell—Spire Books, 1982), p. 52.

9. J. Wesley Ingles, *The Silver Trumpet* (Philadelphia: The [American Sunday School] Union Press, 1930), p. 359.

10. Ann Kiemel Anderson, *I Gave God Time* (Wheaton, Ill.: Tyndale House, 1982), pp. 135, 133, 137.

11. Hearn, *Our Struggle*, p. 115.

12. Harold Begbie, *Twice Born Men: a Clinic in Regeneration* (New York: Fleming H. Revell, 1909), p. 84.

13. Shirley Boone, *One Woman's Liberation* (Carol Stream, Ill.: Creation House, 1972), p. 123.

14. Kooiman, *Cameos*, p. 18.

15. Jennifer R. Vanderford, *Joy Cometh in the Morning* (Eugene, Oreg.: Harvest House, 1982), p. 10.

16. Hearn, *Our Struggle*, p. 58; Bennett and Bennett, *Holy Spirit*, pp. 204–205.

17. Boone, *Liberation*, p. 106.

18. Hearn, *Our Struggle*, pp. 150, 151.

19. Graham, *My Turn*, p. 54. James Davison Hunter in *Evangelicalism: The Coming Generation* (Chicago: University of Chicago Press, 1987) points to another source of evangelical women's relative independence of their spouses. He argues that though the husband is supposed to rule his family, he is also expected to be affectionate, a friend to his children, and a companion to his wife. Those roles, Hunter insists, conflict with

his patriarchal position. He is nearly as subject to the needs and desires of his family as his wife. Hunter says, "his authority becomes theoretical and abstract" (97). As we would expect, evangelicals agreed that a woman should put her husband and children "ahead of her career," but surprisingly they make the same point about the husband (99). It seems that possibly evangelical women enjoy more practical than rhetorical equality.

20. Susan B. Anthony, *The Ghost in My Life* (Old Tappan, N.J.: Fleming H. Revell, 1971), p. 232.

21. Barbara Grizzuti Harrison, *Visions of Glory* (New York: Simon and Schuster, 1978), p. 28.

22. John Sherrill, *They Speak with Other Tongues* (Old Tappan, N.J.: Revell, 1964), pp. 40–41.

23. Thomas Lately, *Storming Heaven: The Lives and Turmoils of Minnie Kennedy and Aimee Semple McPherson* (New York: Morrow, 1970).

24. Interestingly, Kuhlman denied her role as preacher: "I never think of myself as a woman preacher. I tell you the truth. I am a woman; I was born a woman, and I try to keep my place as a woman. . . . I never try to usurp the place of authority of a man— never! That's the reason I have no church. I leave that to the men. I am a woman. I know my place . . . I do not believe that those who know me best think of me as being a woman preacher. I never do. Never!" (Quoted in James Morris, *The Preachers* [New York: St. Martin's Press, 1973], p. 246). She also insisted that "Without the Holy Spirit, I haven't a crutch, I haven't anything to lean on. I don't have a thing. I don't have a thing. You see, if I had been born with talent, I might have been able to lean on that. Had I had education, I might have used that as a crutch. But I don't have a thing. I don't have a thing" (quoted on p. 239).

25. Hearn, *Our Struggle*, p. 64.

26. Kooiman, *Cameos*.

27. Kooiman, *Cameos*, p. 47.

28. Sherrill, *They Speak with Other Tongues*, pp. 125–27.

29. Rebecca Manley Pippert, "Ethel Renwick," in Ann Spangler, ed., *Bright Legacy: Portraits of Ten Outstanding Women of Faith* (Ann Arbor, Mich.: Servant Books, 1983), p. 185.

30. Boone, *Liberation*, pp. 137, 140–41.

31. Dale Evans Rogers, *My Spiritual Diary* (Westwood, N.J.: Fleming H. Revell, 1955), pp. 26, 27.

32. Harrison, *Visions*, p. 83.

33. Hannah Hurnard, *Hearing Heart* (Wheaton, Ill.: Tyndale House, 1986).

34. Merrill and Virginia Womach, *Tested by Fire* (Old Tappan, N.J.: Fleming H. Revell, 1976), p. 112.

35. Elisabeth Elliot, *Twelve Baskets of Crumbs* (Chappaqua, N.Y.: Christian Herald House, 1976), pp. 59, 167.

36. Boone, *Liberation*, p. 136.

37. Norman Vincent Peale, ed., *Guideposts Anthology* (New York: Prentice-Hall, 1953), p. 153.

38. Begbie, *Twice-Born Men*, pp. 167, 61.

39. Charles Colson, *Born Again* (Old Tappan, N.J.: Revell-Chosen Books, 1976), p. 110.

40. Colson, *Born Again*, p. 116.

41. For Vaus and Karam see Lewis W. Gillenson, *Billy Graham and Seven Who Were Saved* (New York: Trident Press, 1967); for Starr see Peale, *Guideposts Anthology*.

42. Gillenson, *Seven Who Were Saved*, p. 180.

43. Gillenson, *Seven Who Were Saved*, p. 40.

44. Kirby, Clyde, *Then Came Jesus* (Grand Rapids, Mich.: Zondervan, 1967).

45. Catherine Marshall, *A Man Called Peter* (New York: McGraw-Hill, 1951), n.p.

46. Peale, *Guideposts Anthology*, p. 181.

47. Colson, *Born Again*, p. 10.

48. Carol Flake, *Redemptorama: Culture, Politics and the New Evangelicalism* (Garden City, N.Y.: Doubleday-Anchor, 1984), p. 111.

49. Peale, *Guideposts Anthology*, p. 173.

50. Colson, *Born Again*, p. 112.

51. Peale, *Guideposts Anthology*, p. 148.

52. Forrest Forbes, *God Hath Chosen: The Story of Jack Wyrtzen and the Word of Life Hour*, in Joel A. Carpenter, ed., *The Youth for Christ Movement and Its Pioneers* (New York: Garland, 1988).

53. Flake, *Redemptorama*, pp. 67, 61.

8. TWENTIETH-CENTURY OUT-OF-CHURCH NARRATIVES

1. Harriet Whitehead, *Renunciation and Reformulation: A Study of Conversion in an American Sect* (Ithaca, N.Y.: Cornell University, 1987).

2. Quoted in Edith F. Hunter, *Sophia Lyon Fahs: A Biography* (Boston: Beacon Press, 1966), p. 62 (my emphases).

3. Jon Alexander, *American Personal Religious Accounts, 1600–1980* (New York: Edwin Mellen, 1983), p. 164.

4. Jane Froman, "Disaster Was No Calamity for Jane," in Norman Vincent Peale, ed., *Guideposts Anthology* (New York: Prentice-Hall, 1953), p. 6.

5. Carolyn G. Heilbrun, *Writing a Woman's Life* (New York: Norton, 1988), p. 27.

6. Julia Penelope Stanley and Susan J. Wolfe, *Coming Out Stories* (Watertown, Mass.: Persephone Press, 1980), p. xviii.

7. Quoted in Stanley and Wolfe, *Coming Out Stories*, pp. xviii-xvix.

8. Stanley and Wolfe, *Coming Out Stories*, p. xviii.

9. Quoted in Alexander, *Personal Religious Accounts*, p. 404.

10. Mary Thom, ed., *Letters to Ms., 1972–1987* (New York: Holt, 1987), p. 211.

11. Jane O'Reilly, *The Girl I Left Behind* (New York: Macmillan, 1980), p. xvi.

12. O'Reilly, *Girl I Left Behind*, p. 40.

13. Thom, *Letters to Ms.*, p. 209.

14. O'Reilly, *Girl I Left Behind*, p. 25.

15. Thom, *Letters to Ms.*, p. xviii.

16. O'Reilly, *Girl I Left Behind*, p. 40.

17. Linda Gray Sexton, *Between Two Worlds: Young Women in Crisis* (New York: Morrow, 1979), p. 28; Luree Miller, *Late Bloom: New Lives for Women* (New York and London: Paddington Press, 1979), p. 209.

18. Rosemary Daniell, *Fatal Flowers* (New York: Avon, 1980), pp. 126, 109, 118, 125, 114.

19. Daniell, *Fatal Flowers*, p. 120.

20. Daniell, *Fatal Flowers*, p. 135.

21. Daniell, *Fatal Flowers*, p. 170.

22. Daniell, *Fatal Flowers*, p. 171.

23. Daniell, *Fatal Flowers*, p. 179.

24. Daniell, *Fatal Flowers*, pp. 170, 171, 179.

25. Sidney E. Ahlstrom, *A Religious History of the American People* (New Haven: Yale University Press, 1972), p. 925.

26. *Alcoholics Anonymous: The Story of How Many Thousands of Men and Women Have Recovered from Alcoholism* (New York: AA World Services, 1955), p. xvi.

27. *AA*, pp. 226, 532, 538, 532, 265, 59.

28. AA leaders are aware that potential participants may be offended by the idea of calling on God or religion as an aid in their troubles, so although they clearly advance

the idea of the deity and of spiritual experience, they shy away from a particular concept of God. When they mention "God" in the "Twelve Steps," they hastily append the qualification, "as we understood Him," indicating that each person is free to create his or her own image of the divine—some "Power greater than ourselves."

29. *AA*, pp. 59, 271–72, 229.

30. *AA*, pp. 561, 228.

31. *AA*, pp. 493, 494.

32. *AA*, p. xiii.

33. Susan Lydon, "Getting Free: An Addict's Story," *The Boston Globe Magazine* (July 31, 1988): 22, 26–34.

34. Jean Nidetch (as told to Joan Rattner Heilman), *The Story of Weight Watchers* (New American Library, 1972), p. 9.

35. Nidetch, *Story of Weight Watchers*, pp. 9, 131, 117, 125.

36. Hillel Schwartz, *Never Satisfied: A Cultural History of Diets, Fantasies, and Fat* (New York: Free Press, 1986), p. 207.

37. Elisabeth Elliot, *Twelve Baskets of Crumbs* (Chappaqua, N.Y.: Christian Herald House, 1976), p. 109.

38. Joan M. Scobey, *Short Rations: Confessions of a Cranky Calorie-Counter* (New York: Holt, Rinehart and Winston, 1980), p. 205.

39. See, e.g., Dan Restid, "Ending the Charade," in Wayne Curtis, ed., *Revelations: A Collection of Gay Male Coming Out Stories* (Boston: Alyson Publications, 1988). A Jehovah's Witness unable to accept his homosexuality, Restid recounts sliding into "an unequaled depression." About to be hospitalized, he suddenly has a conversion experience that is traditional but with a difference:

> Turning my face to the wall, I laid everything on God's shoulders, telling Him that I could not honestly serve Him as a Jehovah's Witness or as one of a moral majority who denounced homosexuals, but just as me—just as I am.
> The depression evaporated; my improvement was gradual and steady. God fortified me for the significant changes that were to take place in my life. . . . I discovered that gays have a place in God's heart, and many have been saved and experienced the baptism of the Holy Spirit. They have, like me, reclaimed their sense of self-worth. (Pp. 22–23)

40. See the particular problem of lesbian nuns: "We had no language with which to think about our feelings and actions. We had no name" (Nancy Manahan in Rosemary Curb and Nancy Manahan, *Lesbian Nuns: Breaking Silence* [Tallahassee, Fla.: The Naiad Press, 1985], p. xxxviii).

41. Sarah Holmes, ed., *Testimonies: A Collection of Lesbian Coming Out Stories* (Boston: Alyson Publications, 1988), p. 56.

42. Holmes, *Testimonies*, p. 143. One woman spoke of the joy of finding a name for her proclivities—"bulldagger." "I was so happy at thirteen to have a word for what I knew myself to be. The word was mysterious and curious, as if from a new language that used some alphabet which left nothing to cling to when touching its curves and crevices. But still a word existed and my grandmother was not flinching in using it. In fact she'd smiled at the good heart and good looks of the bulldagger who'd liked her" (Holmes, p. 49). However, not many grandmothers have used such a word, let alone used it in a positive way, and so most lesbian granddaughters have been left wordless and speechless.

43. The pattern of a butch-femme relationship, in which the butch acts the part of the man to the femme's passivity, has come increasingly under criticism from lesbians as simply reproducing the worst of heterosexual hierarchy.

44. Stanley and Wolfe, *Coming Out Stories*, p. 186.

45. Stanley and Wolfe, *Coming Out Stories*, p. 23.

46. Stanley and Wolfe, *Coming Out Stories*, p. 235.
47. Holmes, *Testimonies*, p. 23.
48. Holmes, *Testimonies*, p. 58.
49. Stanley and Wolfe, *Coming Out Stories*, p. 232.
50. Stanley and Wolfe, *Coming Out Stories*, p. 23.
51. Ruth Baetz, *Lesbian Crossroads: Personal Stories of Lesbian Struggles and Triumphs* (New York: William Morrow and Co., 1980), p. 19. Baetz also says, "The process of 'coming out' is a continual one, and although we may already have made it safely through some of these passages, moving to a new town or job will raise these issues again and require new strategies" (p. 21).
52. See the story of Barbara Grier in Stanley and Wolfe, *Coming Out Stories*. Interestingly, women from other ethnic groups do not seem to adopt the conversion motif as readily as native white middle class women. For instance, a lesbian named Rose, who had grown up in Italy, claimed always to have loved women without any shame: "it just seemed to be live and let live at the time I was there." And while naming or accepting a name is very important to many lesbians, a black woman said of her love for women: "It wasn't like I ever labeled it, it was just that I preferred women. In those days, for Black people, you didn't put a label on it. If you label it, then you gotta think, 'What is my dad gonna say?' " (Baetz, *Lesbian Crossroads*, pp. 49, 36).
53. Quoted in Biddy Martin, "Lesbian Identity and Autobiographical Difference[s]," in Bella Brodzki and Celeste Schenck, ed., *Life/Lines* (Ithaca: Cornell University Press, 1988), p. 101.

CONCLUSION

1. Aimee Semple McPherson, *This Is That* (New York: Garland, 1985), p. 34.
2. Susan D. Rose, in *Keeping Them Out of the Hands of Satan: Evangelical Schooling in America* (New York: Routledge, 1988), makes clear some of the striking and considerable differences (in the present) between a middle-class charismatic fellowship and a working-class independent Baptist congregation, both of them in upstate New York.
3. See John Higham, "The Reorientation of American Culture in the 1890s," in John Higham, ed., *Writing American History* (Bloomington: Indiana University Press, 1970); Margaret Marsh, "Suburban Men and Masculine Domesticity, 1870–1915," *American Quarterly* 40 (June 1988): 165–86.
4. Janice A. Radway, *Reading the Romance* (Chapel Hill: University of North Carolina Press, 1984).
5. Joanne M. Braxton, *Black Women Writing Autobiography: A Tradition within a Tradition* (Philadelphia: Temple University Press, 1989), pp. 62–63.

Selected Bibliography

NINETEENTH-CENTURY NARRATIVES

Bonar, A. A. *Robert Murray McCheyne*. Grand Rapids: Zondervan, 1983. Originally appeared 1844.

Bradley, Stephen H. *A Sketch of the Life of Stephen H. Bradley from the age of five to twenty-four years including his remarkable experience of the holy spirit, on the second evening of Nov. 1829*. Madison, Conn., 1830.

Brown, Clark. *Funeral Sermon for Mrs. Maria Lane, Aet. 25*. Keene, N. H.: Prentiss, 1815.

Clark, John D. *The Young Disciple: Or, a Memoir of Anzonetta R. Peters*. Philadelphia: Marshall, 1837.

Cooke, Harriet B. *Autobiography of Harriet B. Cooke*. New York: Robert Carter, 1861.

[Day, Martha.] *The Literary Remains of Martha Day; with Rev. Fitch's Address at Her Funeral; and Sketches of Her Character*. New Haven, Conn., 1834.

[Douglas, Mrs. Catherine Waldo.] *Memorial of Mrs. Catherine Waldo Douglas*. New York: Board of Publications of the Reformed Church in America, 1879.

[Graham, Mrs. Isabella.] *The Power of Faith, Exemplified in the Life and Writing of the Late Mrs. Isabella Graham*. Boston: American Tract Society, 1843.

[Grew, Harriet Catherine.] *Memorials of a Young Christian*. Philadelphia: Merrihew and Gunn, 1837.

Hallock, William A. *Memoir of Justin Edwards*. 1855.

———. *Memoir of Harland Page or the Power of Prayer and Personal Effort for the Souls of Individuals*. New York: American Tract Society, 1835.

Hamilton, Sarah. *A Narrative of the Life of Mrs. Hamilton*. Boston, 1803.

Hyde, Charles. *Memoir of Caroline Hyde*. New York: American Tract Society, n.d.

[Jackson, Rebecca.] *Gifts of Power: The Writings of Rebecca Jackson, Black Visionary, Shaker Eldress*. Ed. Jean McMahon Humez. University of Massachusetts Press, 1981.

Lathrop, Joseph. *Two Sermons, Delivered at Southwick, July 23, 1809. On the Occasion of the Death of Four Young Women, Who Were Drowned in a Pond in That Town*. Springfield, Mass., 1809.

Livermore, Harriet. *A Narration of Religious Experience*. Concord, Mass., 1826.

McAllister, F. M.. *A Memorial of Louisa C. McAllister*. New York, 1869.

Müller, George. *The Autobiography of George Müller*. Springdale, Pa.: Whitaker, 1984.

North, Elizabeth Mason. *Consecrated Talents: Or, the Life of Mary W. Mason*. New York: Garland, 1987. Originally published 1870.

Norton, Minerva Brace. *A True Teacher: Mary Mortimer*. New York: Revell, 1894.

Palmer, Phoebe. *The Way of Holiness with Notes by the Way; Being a narrative of religious experience resulting from a determination to be a Bible Christian*. New York, 1854.

Prentiss, Elizabeth. *Stepping Heavenward*. New York: Anson D. F. Randolph, 1869.

Memorials of Anna P. Sill, First Principal of Rockford Female Academy, 1849–1889. Rockford, Ill., 1889.

Slocum, Phebe B. *Witnessing: A Concise Account of a Marvelous Event with Its Happy Results in the Life of Phebe B. Slocum*. Brattleboro, Vt., 1899.

Smith, Amanda. *An Autobiography: The Story of the Lord's Dealings with Mrs. Amanda Smith*. New York: Garland, 1987. Originally published 1893.

Stearns, Norris. *The Religious Experience of Norris Stearns, written by divine command, shewing the marvellous dealings of God to his soul, and the miraculous manner*. Greenfield, Mass., 1815.

The Missionary's Daughter, or Memoir of Lucy Goodale Thurnston of the Sandwich Islands. New York: Dayton and Newman, 1842.

Van Cott, Maggie. *The Harvest and the Reaper: Reminiscence of Revival Work of Mrs. Maggie N. Van Cott.* New York: N. Tibbals, 1876.

White, E. G. *Testimonies for the Church with a Biographical Sketch of the Author.* Mountain View, Calif.: Pacific Press, n.d.

Winslow, Octavius. *Life in Jesus: A Memoir of Mrs. Mary Winslow.* New York: Robert Carter, 1862.

TWENTIETH-CENTURY NARRATIVES

Anderson, Ann Kiemel. *I Gave God Time.* Wheaton, Ill.: Tyndale House, 1982.

Anthony, Susan B. *The Ghost in My Life.* Old Tappan, N.J.: Revell, 1971.

Atkins, Susan (with Bob Slosser). *Child of Satan, Child of God.* Plainfield, N.J.: Logos, 1977.

Baker, Elizabeth V. *Chronicles of a Faith Life.* New York: Garland, 1984. Originally published ca. 1916.

Barnhouse, Margaret N. *That Man Barnhouse.* Wheaton, Ill.: Tyndale House, 1983.

Bertholf, Diana. *Diana's Star.* Wheaton, Ill.: Tyndale House, 1983.

Boone, Shirley. *One Woman's Liberation.* Carol Stream, Ill: Creation House, 1972.

Bowie, Mary Ella. *Alabaster and Spikenard: The Life of Iva Durham Vennard.* Chicago: Chicago Evangelistic Institute, 1947.

Buckingham, Jamie. *Kathryn Kuhlman . . . Her Story.* Plainfield, N.J.: Logos, 1976.

Burns, Elizabeth. *The Late Liz: The Autobiography of an Ex-Pagan.* New York: Meredith Press, 1957.

Bryant, Anita. *The Anita Bryant Story: The Survival of Our Nation's Families and the Threat of Militant Homosexuality.* Old Tappan, N.J.: Revell, 1977.

Clark, Glenn. *A Man's Reach: The Autobiography of Glenn Clark.* New York: Harper and Row, 1949.

Colson, Charles. *Born Again.* Old Tappan, N.J.: Revell-Chosen Books, 1976.

Cruz, Nicky. *Run Baby Run.* Plainfield, N.J.: Revell, 1968.

Dorsett, Lyle W. *And God Came In: The Extraordinary Story of Joy Davidman.* New York: Macmillan, 1983.

Dyer, Donita. *Bright Promise: The Phenomenal Story of the Korean "Helen Keller."* Grand Rapids, Mich.: Zondervan, 1983.

Eareckson, Joni (with Joe Musser). *Joni.* Grand Rapids, Mich.: Zondervan, 1976.

Eddy, Sherwood. *Eighty Adventurous Years: An Autobiography.* New York: Harper and Brothers, 1955.

Elliott, Elisabeth. *Twelve Baskets of Crumbs.* Chappaqua, N.Y.: Christian Herald House, 1976.

Graham, Ruth Bell. *It's My Turn.* Old Tappan, N.J.: Revell-Spire, 1982.

Hadley, Samuel H. *Down in Water Street.* New York: Revell, 1902.

Harrison, Barbara Grizzuti. *Visions of Glory.* New York: Simon and Schuster, 1978.

Holmes, Marjorie. *Who Am I God? The Doubts, the Fears, the Joys of Being a Woman.* Garden City, N.Y.: Doubleday, 1971.

Grubb, Norman. *Rees Howells, Intercessor; The Welsh Coalminer: A Prince with God.* Ft. Washington, Pa.: Christian Literature Crusade, 1983.

Hughes, Albert. *Renamed: Saul Becomes Paul.* Philadelphia: American Bible Conference Association, 1935.

Hurnard, Hannah. *Hearing Heart.* Wheaton, Ill.: Tyndale House, 1988.

LeTourneau, R. G. *Mover of Men and Mountains: An Autobiography of R. G. LeTourneau.* Chicago: Moody Press, 1960.

McPherson, Aimee Semple. *This Is That: Personal Experiences, Sermons and Writings.* New York: Garland, 1985. Autobiography originally published 1919.

Marshall, Catherine. *To Live Again*. New York: McGraw-Hill, 1957.

Martin, Dorothy. *The Story of Billy McCarrell*. Chicago: Moody Press, 1983.

"Henrietta Mears." In Nathaniel Olson, ed., *Women to Remember: Portraits of Women Who Helped Shape America*. Westchester, Ill: Good News Publishers, 1976.

Montgomery, Carrie Judd. *The Life and Teachings of Carrie Judd Montgomery*. New York: Garland, 1985. Originally published 1936.

Price, Eugenia. *The Burden is Light: The Autobiography of a Transformed Pagan Who Took God at His Word*. Old Tappan, N.J.: Revell-Spire, 1985. Originally published 1955.

Ray, Emma J., and L. P. Ray. *Twice Sold, Twice Ransomed: Autobiography of Mr. and Mrs. L. P. Ray*. Freeport, N.Y.: Books for Libraries Press, 1971. Originally published 1926.

Rogers, Dale Evans. *My Spiritual Diary*. Revell, 1955.

Rohrer, Norman. *Leighton Ford: A Life Surprised*. Wheaton, Ill.: Tyndale House, 1981.

St. Johns, Adela Rogers. *Tell No Man*. Garden City, N.Y.: Doubleday, 1966.

Sanford, Agnes. *The Healing Gifts of the Spirit*. New York: Lippincott, 1966.

Schaeffer, Edith. *The Tapestry: The Life and Times of Francis and Edith Schaeffer*. Waco, Tex.: Word Books, 1981.

Skinner, Tom. *Black and Free*. Grand Rapids: Zondervan, 1968.

Smith, Logan Pearsall. *Unforgotten Years*. Boston: Little, Brown and Co., 1939.

Smith, Susy. *The Conversion of a Psychic*. Garden City, N.Y.: Doubleday, 1978.

ten Boom, Corrie. *In My Father's House*. Old Tappan, N.J.: Revell, 1976.

Tozer, A. W. *Wingspread: A. B. Simpson: A Study in Spiritual Attitude*. Harrisburg, Pa.: Christian Publications, 1943.

Vanderford, Jennifer R. *Joy Cometh in the Morning*. Eugene, Oreg.: Harvest House, 1982.

Womach, Merrill and Virginia. *Tested by Fire*. Old Tappan, N.J.: Revell, 1976.

COLLECTIONS OF NARRATIVES

Alexander, Jon. *American Personal Religious Accounts, 1600–1980*. New York: Mellen, 1983.

Andrews, William L., ed. *Sisters of the Spirit: Three Black Women's Autobiographies of the Nineteenth Century*. Bloomington: Indiana University Press, 1986.

Bailey, Faith Coxe. *These, Too, Were Unshackled*. Grand Rapids, Mich.: Zondervan, 1962.

Begbie, Harold. *Twice Born Men: A Clinic in Regeneration*. New York: Revell, 1909.

Carpenter, Joel, ed. *The Youth for Christ Movement and Its Pioneers*. New York: Garland, 1988.

Conant, William C. *Narratives of Remarkable Conversions and Revival Incidents*. New York: Derby and Jackson, 1858.

Conrad, A. Z., ed. *Boston's Awakening*. Boston: The King's Business, 1909.

Edman, V. Raymond. *They Found the Secret*. Grand Rapids, Mich.: Zondervan, 1984.

Finkelstein, Louis, ed. *American Spiritual Autobiographies: 15 Self-Portraits*. New York: Harper and Row, 1948.

Gillenson, Lewis W. *Billy Graham and Seven Who Were Saved*. New York: Trident Press, 1967.

Graham, Billy. *How to Be Born Again*. Waco, Tex.: Word Books, 1977.

Hearn, Virgina. *Our Struggle to Serve: The Stories of 15 Evangelical Women*. Waco, Tex.: Word Books, 1979.

Jackson, George. *The Fact of Conversion*. New York: Revell, 1908.

Johnson, Clifton H., ed. *God Struck Me Dead: Religious Conversions and Autobiographies of Ex-Slaves*. Philadelphia: Pilgrim Press, 1969.

Kerr, Hugh T., and John M. Mulder. *Conversions: The Christian Experience*. Grand Rapids, Mich.: Eerdmans, 1983.

Kirby, Clyde. *Then Came Jesus.* Grand Rapids, Mi.: Zondervan, 1967.
Kooiman, Helen. *Cameos: Women Fashioned by God.* Wheaton, Ill.: Tyndale House, 1968.
Mitchell, Curtis. *Those Who Came Forward: Men and Women Who Responded to the Ministry of Billy Graham.* Philadelphia: Chilton, 1966.
Peale, Norman Vincent, ed. *Guideposts Anthology.* New York: Prentice-Hall, 1953.
Spangler, Ann, ed. *Bright Legacies: Portraits of 10 Outstanding Women of Faith.* Ann Arbor, Mich.: Servant Books, 1983.
Speer, Robert E. *Young Men Who Overcame.* New York: Revell, 1905.
Spiritual Narratives. New York: Oxford, 1988.
Wise, Daniel. *Some Remarkable Women.* 1887.
Woodward, William W. *Increase of Piety, or the Revival of Religion in the United States of America.* Newburyport, Mass.: Angier, 1802.

SECONDARY SOURCES

Abel, Elizabeth, Marianne Hirsch, and Elizabeth Langland, eds. *The Voyage In: Fictions of Female Development.* Hanover, N. H.: University Press of New England, 1983.
Ammerman, Nancy Tatom. *Bible Believers: Fundamentalists in the Modern World.* New Brunswick: Rutgers University Press, 1987.
Bochen, Christine M. *The Journey to Rome: Conversion Literature by Nineteenth-Century American Catholics.* New York: Garland, 1988.
Boone, Kathleen C. *The Bible Tells Them So.* Albany: State University of New York, 1989.
Braxton, Joanne M. *Black Women Writing Autobiography: A Tradition Within a Tradition.* Philadelphia: Temple University Press, 1989.
Brodzki, Bella, and Celeste Schenck, eds. *Life/Lines.* Ithaca: Cornell University Press, 1988.
Brown, Herbert Ross. *The Sentimental Novel in America.* New York: Pageant Press, 1959.
Bruce, Dickson D., Jr. *And They All Sang Hallelujah: Plain-Folk Camp-Meeting Religion, 1800–1845.* Knoxville: University of Tennessee Press, 1974.
Bynum, Caroline Walker, Steven Harrell, and Paula Richman. *Gender and Religion: On the Complexity of Symbols.* Boston: Beacon Press, 1986.
Caldwell, Patricia. *The Puritan Conversion Narrative.* New York: Cambridge University Press, 1983.
Cott, Nancy F. "Young Women in the Second Great Awakening." *Feminist Studies* 3 (Fall 1975).
Douglas, Ann. *The Feminization of American Culture.* New York: Knopf, 1977.
Epstein, Barbara Leslie. *The Politics of Domesticity: Women, Evangelism and Temperance in Nineteenth-Century America.* Middletown, Conn.: Wesleyan University Press, 1981.
Flake, Carol. *Redemptorama: Culture, Poltics and the New Evangelicalism.* Garden City, N.Y.: Doubleday-Anchor, 1984.
Gillespie, Joanna Bowen, "Gasping for Larger Measures: Joanna Turner, Eighteenth Century Activist," *Journal of Feminist Studies in Religion* 3, 2 (Fall 1987): 31–55.
Harding, Susan F. "Convicted by the Holy Spirit: the Rhetoric of Fundamentalist Baptist Conversion." *American Ethnologist* 14 (February 1987): 167–81.
Harrell, David Edwin, Jr. *All Things Are Possible: The Healing and Charismatic Revivals in Modern America.* Bloomington: Indiana University Press, 1975.
Hoffmann, Leonore, and Margo Culley, eds. *Women's Personal Narratives.* New York: Modern Language Association, 1985.
Jelinek, Estelle, ed. *Women's Autobiography: Essays in Criticism.* Bloomington: Indiana University Press, 1980.

Juster, Susan. " 'In a Different Voice': Male and Female Narratives of Religious Conversion in Post-Revolutionary America." *American Quarterly* 41 (March 1989):
34–62.

Kaufman, Debra Renee. "Patriarchal Women: A Case Study of Newly Orthodox Jewish
Women." *Symbolic Interaction* 12, 2 (1989): 299–314.

Kelley, Mary. *Private Woman, Public Stage: Literary Domesticity in Nineteenth-Century
America.* New York: Oxford, 1984.

King, John Owen, III. *The Iron of Melancholy: Structures of Spiritual Conversion in
America from the Puritan Conscience to Victorian Neurosis.* Middletown, Conn.:
Wesleyan University Press, 1983.

Lawless, Elaine J. *Handmaidens of the Lord: Pentecostal Women Preachers and Traditional Religion.* Philadelphia: University of Pennsylvania Press, 1988.

Marsh, Margaret. "Suburban Men and Masculine Domesticity, 1870–1915." *American
Quarterly* 40 (1988): 165–86.

Mason, Mary Grimley, and Carol Hurd Green. *Journeys: Autobiographical Writings
by Women.* Boston: G. R. Hall, 1979.

Morgan, Edmund S. *Visible Saints: The History of a Puritan Idea.* New York: New
York University Press, 1963.

Papishvily, Helen. *All the Happy Endings.* New York: Harper, 1956.

Peshkin, Alan. *God's Choice: The Total World of a Fundamentalist Christian School*
Chicago: University of Chicago Press, 1986.

Pettit, Norman. *The Heart Prepared: Grace and Conversion in Puritan Spiritual Life.*
New Haven: Yale University Press, 1966.

Porterfield, Amanda. *Feminine Spirituality from Sarah Edwards to Martha Graham.*
Philadelphia: Temple University Press, 1980.

Rabinowitz, Richard. *The Spiritual Self in Everyday Life: The Transformation of Personal Religious Experience in Nineteenth-Century New England* (Boston: Northeastern University Press, 1989).

Radway, Janice A. *Reading the Romance: Women, Patriarchy, and Popular Literature.*
Chapel Hill: University of North Carolina Press, 1984.

Reynolds, David S. *Faith in Fiction: The Emergence of Religious Literature in America.*
Cambridge, Mass.: Harvard University Press, 1981.

Rose, Susan D. *Keeping Them Out of the Hands of Satan: Evangelical Schooling in
America* New York: Routledge, 1988.

Rosenberg, Bruce. *The Art of the American Folk Preacher.* New York: Oxford, 1970.

Ryan, Mary P. *The Cradle of the Middle Class: The Family in Oneida County, New
York, 1790–1865.* New York: Cambridge University Press, 1981.

Sasson, Diane. *The Shaker Spiritual Narrative.* Knoxville: University of Tennessee Press,
1983.

Saum, Lewis. *The Popular Mind of Pre-Civil War America.* Westport, Conn.: Greenwood
Press, 1980.

Sharisranian, Janet, ed. *Gender, Ideology, and Action: Historical Perspectives on Wom-
en's Public Lives.* Westport, Conn.: Greenwood Press, 1986.

Shea, Daniel B., Jr. *Spiritual Autobiography in Early America.* Princeton: Princeton
University Press, 1968.

Shiels, Richard D. "The Feminization of American Congregationalism." *American
Quarterly* 33 (Spring 1981): 46–62.

Smith-Rosenberg, Carroll. *Disorderly Conduct: Visions of Gender in Victorian America.*
New York: Oxford, 1985.

Staples, Clifford L., and Armand L. Mauss. "Conversion or Commitment? A Reassess-
ment of the Snow and Machalek Approach to the Study of Conversion." *Journal
for the Scientific Study of Religion* 26 (1987): 133–47.

Weisberger, Bernard. *They Gathered at the River.* Boston: Little Brown, 1958.

Welter, Barbara. "The Feminization of American Religion, 1800–1860." In Mary Hart-

man and Lois Banner, eds., *Clio's Consciousness Raised*. New York: Harper Torchbooks, 1973, pp. 137–55.
White, Charles Edward. *The Beauty of Holiness: Phoebe Palmer as Theologian, Reviv-
alist, Feminist, and Humanitarian*. Grand Rapids, Mich.: Francis Asbury Press,
1986.

Index

VIRGINIA LIESON BRERETON has taught at the University of Michigan and Long Island University. She currently teaches history and writing at Harvard University. She has published widely in the fields of women's religious history and conservative Protestant evangelicalism, including *Training God's Army: The Formation of the Fundamentalist Bible Schools, 1880–1940*, recently published by Indiana University Press, and an essay, "Women as Insiders and Outsiders," in *The Protestant Establishment in the Twentieth Century*, edited by William Hutchison.